The Female Dominant

The Art of Sensual Female Dominance: A Guide for Women

From the review by Lisa Sherman in *Skin Two* magazine:

> "Full of solid practical advice that no one ever tells you . . . and plenty of ideas to keep you inspired and interested. Varrin proves that the skills of domination are easily within the reach of any adventurous woman."

Erotic Surrender: The Sensual Joys of Female Submission

From the review by Lisa Sherman in *Skin Two* magazine:

> "Like her previous book (*The Art of Sensual Female Dominance*), this is a useful discussion aid . . . and Miss Varrin vividly communicates the delight that can be found in the delicious depravity of sensual submission."

A Guide to New York's Fetish Underground

From the review by Tony Mitchell in *Skin Two* magazine:

> "In a handy pocket-size form, it is clearly designed for the perv on the move. Equally clearly, it has been a labor of love. Claudia has visited every one of the listed establishments and events, and it shows. . . . For well-researched listings and well-informed, entertaining writing about the kink culture in one of the world's most exciting cities, it's the bee's knees."

From the review by Helen Lane in *Skin Two* magazine:

> "Pro dom Claudia Varrin imparts knowledge, wisdom, and deep insight in a sensitive and often touching way. . . . [The book] is so well written. . . . Throughout the book, Claudia invokes the mysterious symbiosis between dominant and submissive."

⤜⧉⤛

The
FEMALE
DOMINANT
Games She Plays

Claudia Varrin

CITADEL PRESS
Kensington Publishing Corp.
www.kensingtonbooks.com

CITADEL PRESS BOOKS are published by

Kensington Publishing Corp.
850 Third Avenue
New York, NY 10022

All Kensington titles, imprints, and distributed lines are available at special quantity discounts for bulk purchases for sales promotions, premiums, fund-raising, educational, or institutional use. Special book excerpts or customized printings can also be created to fit specific needs. For details, write or phone the office of the Kensington special sales manager: Kensington Publishing Corp., 850 Third Avenue, New York, NY 10022, attn: Special Sales Department; phone 1-800-221-2647.

This book is a work of fiction. Names, characters, businesses, organizations, places, events, and incidents either are the product of the author's imagination or are used fictitiously. Any resemblance to actual persons, living or dead, events, or locales is entirely coincidental.

Illustrations courtesy of Laurent Le Beau

First printing: July 2005

10 9 8 7 6 5 4 3 2 1

Printed in the United States of America

Library of Congress Control Number: 2005922703

ISBN 0-8065-2669-6

To Meris, Josephine, Anna and Frank, and Nancy

Contents

Disclaimer

(READ THIS . . .)

This book relates stories of controversial, risky, and sometimes dangerous sexual activities and is *for entertainment purposes only*. Neither the author nor her publisher assumes *any responsibility whatsoever* if the reader attempts any practices described in this book. Any person putting this information into practice does so at his or her own risk. In other words, proceed at your own peril, and do not come crying to the author or her publisher if you screw up. The onus is entirely on you, and you should not shed your common sense when you shed your clothes. In addition, the author is not a lawyer and cannot say whether anything written in this book is legal or not. In all probability, the stories related in this book are illegal where you live, even if you are consenting adults. Being a law-abiding citizen, the author used her creative mind in imagining and relating these tales to you.

Of course, all safe and safer sex practices should be used if engaging in any and all applicable situations, especially if *not* playing with one's regular/monogamous partner. Male or female condoms, surgical gloves, dental dams, et al., have been found beneficial in halting the spread of sexually transmitted disases.

In addition, practitioners of romantic consensual Bondage/Discipline, Sadism/Masochism (BDSM) make a real and explicit distinction between what are consensual acts between adults for mutual pleasure and what are all acts of violence against unwilling or underage nonconsenting partners or both. Imposing any sexual activity on any reluctant partner is immoral, morally reprehensible, and offensive and in many places constitutes rape.

Preface

Greetings, Sisters in Dominance and male creatures, and welcome back to my magical, wonderful, midnight-purple world behind the veil of BDSM! As you know from my previous works, it is my goal to share with you the knowledge and experience I have accumulated over the years so that you, too, can release the dominant tigress, or seductive domina, inside of you. One reason I enjoyed writing this book so much is that it is so very different from my other works. Unlike my other books, this one is not a how-to guide filled with psychological and practical instruction but rather a collection of consensual romantic BDSM stories and tales from my real-life playtimes. If you wish to seek instructive material, of course the most appropriate books to read to learn about the techniques described here would be my previous works, *The Art of Sensual Female Dominance* and *Female Dominance: Rituals and Practices*. For more insight into the mind of a submissive, I suggest *Erotic Surrender* as a good starting point, but many other books could supplement my own.

This book is grouped into four parts. In the first, "Casual Toys," you will read about chance encounters with submissive men whom I met at clubs and at both private and house parties. I clicked with these men and liked them well enough to play with, something like that "old black magic had me in its spell." Some of them are mild, and for a casual toy, some of them are quite wild. The part entitled "Friends" relates planned playtimes with submissive men I already knew and enjoyed playing with in previous encounters. You will find that the playtimes in these stories are on a slightly higher level than those in "Casual Toys" because a relationship had already been established with these male creatures. Some are amusing and others are more serious, depending on whom I was playing with at the time and how much I liked him. There are all different levels of "friends," as we all know.

The "Lovers" part of the book tells of more intimate playtimes I have had with men who were my lovers as well as my playmates. In some tales, the grand finale is much more intimate than in others, depending on the depth and duration of the relationship. In this part, you will once again find that the playtimes escalate beyond those in the first two parts. The "Multiples" part is about playtimes in which more than two people—the submissive male creature and I—were involved in the action. These stories include fem dom/fem dom/sub male (a threesome) and fem dom/fem dom/male sub/male (a four-some), sub scenarios. I included these stories because they are entertaining. If the sensual female dominant wishes to bring a third party into the scenario, these scenarios can give her planning ideas. I also know that my male readers often have fantasies about being controlled and used by more than one fem dom or by another male, so these tales will be exciting for them as well.

I have divided this book into four parts so that my readers, especially the male ones, will realize that I play with the different submissives based on how well I know them and how much I like, or even love, them. To a woman it is obvious that what one does with a casual toy is very different from what one does with one's lover, but men sometimes are not capable of making that distinction; grouping the stories into these parts clarifies the distinction.

I've made every attempt to include a cross section of the different aspects of BDSM, but like you, I've a list of favorite activities and another list of activities that turn me off. Bondage, verbal and physical humiliation, face slapping, spitting, strap-on play, corporal, golden showers, foot worship, play piercing, forced feminization, and objectification are my personal favorites, but other types of encounters have been included because I found them extremely interesting, amusing, or unusual. In some stories you'll find that I demand foot massage. Well, if I have to walk around in killer shoes for *his* benefit, shouldn't I get a foot massage? Of course, I won't relate stories about things that turn me off. I apologize in advance if branding your submissive is a big turn-on for you, for instance—no such tale will be found here.

However, that does not mean that you will not enjoy the rest of these tales. I think some of them contain very humorous ingredients that I hope will make you smile, if not laugh. And maybe by reading them, you will become interested in an aspect that hasn't previously appealed to you. Sometimes all it takes is a different way of looking at the aspect to arouse your curiosity and encourage you to experiment further. Or you might not have indulged in a particular area simply because you didn't know how to! This book isn't meant only to amuse and entertain but also to suggest scenarios, aspects, and combinations of aspects that may not at first seem compatible.

Also, as I wrote the stories, I found that some worked better as third-person narratives, others in the first person, and yet others read better from the submissive's point of view. I decided that telling these stories from different points of view would make the book a more interesting read, and I hope that you will agree. Whenever possible, I have included descriptions of the playrooms, my wardrobe, the submissive's appearance, and other details to help you to visualize the setting: I like to smell the roses as I write. It is my sincere hope that sensual female dominants will pick up new ideas to add to their repertoire of "games," and I do not mind at all if my male readers use this book to arouse themselves. Without you, the male creatures, I would not have been able to write this book. So go ahead and enjoy yourselves—you have my permission!

Acknowledgments

To Anna, my dearest grandmother who has passed on; the gorgeous Mistress Antoinette for her giving, nurturing nature; Bert Wibo of *DDI* and *Massad* magazines for being my "happy pill"; Betsy Rochette for her friendship and the frequent hospitality of her home; Bob and Gina for their great parties; Bruce Bender for his invaluable help and for all those lovely Wiccan books I raid his office for; Goddess Christina of The Temple.cc for giving freely of her computer expertise; Dolenta at Breathless; Mistress Elizabeth for a fantastic realization of an alter ego; Franco, hair stylist and colorist extraordinaire, for giving me something I always wanted and never had; Frank, my dearest grandfather who is now with Anna; and to Maitresse Françoise for her open heart, warm hospitality, loving nature, and infinite understanding.

To my beloved and much-missed Aunt Josephine who has passed on; Kevin, for reasons unknown even to me; Margaret Wolf, my editor, both the benign Margaret and the evil One, for her support and friendship above and beyond the call of duty; Master Keith and slave joy for their hospitality and his creativity as a dom; Nancy, my dear grandmother who has passed on; Pat B., for his respect, kindness, and generosity; Paul Dinas, for being my "angel"; Rosemary, for her unfailing friendship whether she is near or far; Lady Scorpion, for recognizing an olive branch when she sees one; Simon at Libidex; the inimitable Ted and Diane for their friendship and their unwavering support of me; to the beautiful Ms. Toni, for being the sweet Southern Belle that she is and one sharp cookie too; and Tim Woodard, Tony Mitchell, and all the staff at *Skin Two* magazine for their help and support over the years.

PART ONE

Casual Toys

Devin's Punishment

At his university, Miss Varrin was the dean of boys as well as a professor. She also was the professor most well known for not putting up with any infractions or inattentiveness in her class. She taught ancient history and was quite passionate about her chosen subject, using slides from sites of antiquity she had visited and bringing in objects of art and other items of interest to enliven the class. Although one might think that a woman with a Ph.D. in history would be a dried-up old stick, Miss Varrin was quite the opposite. She was medium tall and slender, with long, shining, straight auburn hair and blunt-cut bangs, full breasts, a beautiful round ass, long, lovely legs, and the most beautiful feet Devin had ever seen.

Most of the boys in the class had a secret crush on the glamorous Miss Varrin. She preferred figure-hugging black clothes, especially dresses worn with high-heeled pumps, high-heeled strappy sandals, or pointy-toed stiletto boots. When she was not walking around the front of the classroom, she preferred to sit on her desk with her legs crossed, often exposing just a glimpse of the lace-top thigh highs or stocking tops that she wore with garters. When visible, her slightly long toenails were always lacquered a sexy red. Her long fingernails were always painted to match her toes. Her lipstick made her full lips look very kissable, and her high cheekbones gave her an exotic air. One could hardly picture her digging around in the dirt in some far-off country on an archeological site. And her enticing appearance often made it difficult for Devin to pay attention to the lesson.

"Mister Devin!"

Her voice, low but commanding, brought his attention back to the lesson. He was mesmerized by her toes and he had been caught.

"To my office, please, Mister Devin."

Miss Varrin always addressed the students politely even when punishment was on the way. It was part of her charm that she never need raise her voice. A politely voiced command was nonetheless a command, and it was to be obeyed.

Devin rose from his seat and left the classroom. He walked slowly down the hall, his head down, while he thought about the infraction that earned the coming punishment. He had been paying much more attention to Miss Varrin's red-lacquered toenails and her narrow aristocratic feet in her lovely strappy high-heeled sandals than to the lesson. And now Miss Varrin was going to paddle him for his inattentiveness. As he dragged his feet toward her office to wait for her, he could hear her telling the class not to laugh at him because next it could be anyone else's turn to await her, and her paddle, in her office. She opened the classroom door and went out into the hall, catching up with him on the way to her office. She stepped in front of him, gestured with her fingers that he was to pick up his pace, and led him briskly into her office.

"Do you know why you are here, Mister Devin?"

"Yes, Miss Varrin. I am here because I wasn't paying attention to the lesson, ma'am."

"And you shall receive five hard strokes of the paddle for it. Drop your pants and bend over the desk, feet apart. You are to count out each stroke for me, Mister Devin, and thank me for each one."

Devin did as he was bid and after unbuckling his belt, he let his pants drop to his knees. He knew his thin cotton boxer shorts would offer no protection from her paddle. And Miss Varrin was deceptively strong for so slender a woman. Miss Varrin let him stand there, in that humiliating position with his pants down around his knees, while she opened her desk drawer and took out her favorite paddle. It was made of walnut, and the handle was encased in purple suede with black vinyl lacing wrapped in a design around the suede. Miss Varrin made sure he saw the paddle, and she smacked it gently against her hand a couple of times, as if testing it for suitability. Then she slowly walked behind him, the paddle dangling from her hand.

She started by rubbing his bottom almost caressingly with the paddle, round and round on his cotton-clad cheeks. He could feel the coolness of the wood, but that was just another deception. That cool paddle could make his bottom feel like it was on fire. The feel of the paddle immediately made his member erect. Sometimes he thought that he drifted in class just so that he could, and would, be punished. Through his open legs, he could see her dainty feet with their brightly painted nails in their open-toed shoes and her well-muscled calves. How he wanted to suck those lovely toes, how he wanted to take each one in his mouth and worship it! He became more aroused. Then, suddenly the paddle was withdrawn as Miss Varrin brought her arm back to deliver the first blow.

Thwack!

She hit him hard across the bottom of both cheeks. His toes curled inside of his shoes with the blow. But he could not take his eyes off her toes nestled against the suede insole of her shoe. "One, thank you, Miss Varrin," he said obediently, stunned by the hardness of the blow.

Thwack!

The second blow was harder still, and her left heel lifted slightly off the floor as she swung. "Two, thank you, Miss Varrin," he said, his voice a little strained.

Thwack!

The third blow made him rock forward onto his toes, a groan barely held in behind his tightly closed lips. "Three, thank you, Miss Varrin," said Devin, between clenched teeth.

Thwack!

With the fourth blow, Miss Varrin swung the paddle as if she were a tennis player delivering a good backhand stroke. Her heel came almost completely off the floor as she let fly. Devin could not keep the groan of pain out of his voice as he said, "Four, thank you, Miss Varrin."

Thwack!

The fifth and final blow made him cry out loud. She had swung the paddle like a baseball batter trying to hit a home run. And in her own way, she did. "Five, thank you, Miss Varrin." Devin's voice was weak and his knees were on the verge of collapsing.

"You may go, Mister Devin," she purred from behind him. Just those five smacks had made his bottom a misery of red soreness. He ran for the men's bathroom, and locking himself in a stall, he touched himself, the hot, burning redness of his sore cheeks heightening his excitement. He thought of the rise and fall of her arm as she brought the paddle down on him. He thought of her delicate toes in their high-heeled sandals, the red lacquer of the polish glimmering in the sunlight streaming through the ofice window. He thought of the high arch of her lovely feet, of their high instep that just begged for high heels.

With a great sigh, he released himself all over his belly. He used the toilet paper in the stall to clean himself off; then he returned to the classroom where his classmates struggled to conceal their smiles.

"Mister Devin, I didn't expect to see you here so soon after your last infraction," Miss Varrin purred at him, reminding him of a big cat. "What have you done this time, or need I ask?"

Devin stood in front of her desk, but he was too ashamed and excited to look at her, so he looked down at the floor instead. He wished he could see her gorgeous feet, but they were hidden under the desk.

"Please, Miss Varrin, I'm so very sorry. I won't do it again, I promise." He was so nervous that his knees were almost knocking together.

"So what is it you have done? Don't make me ask you again." The purr in her voice was deeper now, a sure sign that she was becoming impatient with him and that she wouldn't tolerate any insolence.

"Well, ma'am, in Miss Woodhouse's art history class, she was sitting on the desk and she dropped her shoe. I picked it up for her."

"Go on, Mister Devin, you are not here simply because you picked up Miss Woodhouse's shoe." The purr in her voice deepened to a soft growl.

"Well, before I slipped it back on her foot, I kissed her arch and then put her shoe back on. That's all, ma'am." Devin hung his head in shame. He knew that his "that's all" was the worst thing he could have said but the words were out of his mouth before he even realized he said them.

"That's all? That's all? Is that what you just said to me?" Miss Varrin hissed at him, reinforcing his impression of her as a great big cat, a lioness or tigress, just waiting to devour him. "You kissed her arch? You kissed her foot? Right there in front of the class? Just because you wanted to?" Miss Varrin acted more shocked than she really was. After all, Devin had been at the university for three years now, and she knew his proclivities quite well.

"Yes, ma'am. Yes, Miss Varrin. So Miss Woodhouse sent me here."

"Mister Devin, you have been sent here more times than I can count, and always for the same reason. I can see now that you need more discipline than I can give you here." Miss Varrin wrote something on a piece of paper and handed it to him.

He was afraid to lift his eyes, to see her face, so he just reached out his hand and managed to grab the piece of paper. He couldn't even look at it to see what it said.

"I want you at this address at six o'clock this evening, and you will stay until eight. And don't be late. Six sharp. Tardiness will be severely punished. Now you may return to your class, Mister Devin."

Feeling lucky to have gotten off so easily, yet strangely disappointed that he did not receive the expected paddling, Devin returned to Miss Woodhouse's art history class. As he entered the classroom, he got many curious looks from his classmates. No one ever returned from Miss Varrin's office so quickly. Miss Woodhouse pretended not to notice him and continued with the lesson. Although she was presenting an interesting slide show of famous sculptures, Devin's eyes were riveted on her feet in their black leather pumps and on the movement of her calf muscles as she leaned forward with the pointer to emphasize her words.

The hours dragged by until his classes were over, and the entire time he was tingling with excitement and dread about his six o'clock appointment with Miss Varrin.

After showering, washing his hair, and putting on fresh clothes, he paced his room until it was time to leave. Remembering Miss Varrin's admonition, he was nervous about being late, so he arrived a little early at the address she had written on the slip of paper. Then he became nervous about being early, so he went back down the steps to have a look at the house. It was a lovely old Victorian, two stories high with an attic, shutters on either side of the windows, and a large porch in front that wrapped around to the side. On the porch, there was a white double-seater swing, a large white wicker chair, a white wicker end table, and some potted plants. The house was painted a saddened lavender and the shutters were a dark gray. The overall effect was lovely. He had never been inside a house like this.

Glancing at his watch, Devin saw that it was only one minute before six. He mounted the stairs, crossed the wide porch to the wooden door with a stained glass window above it, and rang the bell. The door opened almost immediately, and Miss Varrin herself was standing there. She motioned him in and he crossed the threshold into her domain. It was dim inside, and it took his eyes a few seconds to adjust to the low lighting. When he could see clearly, he looked at

Miss Varrin and his eyes opened wide. Her long auburn hair was in an updo, with strands of hair escaping here and there, and glasses sat on her nose. At the university she must wear contacts because he had never seen her in glasses before. She was wearing a long dress with a flowing skirt, a high collar, and long, lace-trimmed sleeves. Beneath her skirt, he could just see the toes of her lace-up boots. A cameo graced the center of the high collar, and around her waist was a tightly laced corset. Her waist looked impossibly small; so small, he imagined that if he could put his hands around it, his fingers would touch.

While Devin was eating up her outfit with his eyes, he did not notice that Miss Varrin was observing him closely, too. Of course she noticed that he had showered, washed his hair, and changed his clothes. She also noticed the smell of his cologne, which she did not like. It was not personal. Miss Varrin did not like any cologne at all and never wore perfume herself.

"Before we start, Mister Devin, I want you to go into the bathroom and wash off as much of that cologne as possible. I do not like it. Follow me."

When she turned, her flowing skirt billowed around her and swayed with each step she took down the hall. Devin didn't know that such clothing could be so exciting; he had never even seen anyone dressed this way, except in movies and books. Miss Varrin stopped in front of a wooden door far down the hallway, opened it, and gestured him inside. Of course, it was a bathroom but this was something else he had only read in books. Although it was only a half bath, no tub or shower, it did have a small set-in window on which sat a small vase of fragrant flowers whose variety he did not recognize. The old-fashioned pedestal sink was glazed with cracks. The toilet did not have a flush handle, but he surmised that the chain dangling from the ceiling next to it was for the same use. Immaculately white, fluffy towels hung from a rod next to the sink. A bar of white soap sat in the soap dish, awaiting his use. Hurriedly, Devin stripped off his shirt, pulling it over his head rather than wasting time unbuttoning it, and set about to washing every place he had splashed cologne. He quickly dried himself, pulled his shirt back on over his head, and stepped out into the hallway.

Miss Varrin was awaiting him. After stepping up to him and sniffing him loudly—which was unexpectedly stimulating—she announced that he smelled much better. Telling him to follow her, she led him to a room at the front of the hallway. He found himself inside a large ornate sitting room furnished with Victorian antiques and good reproductions, wall-to-wall carpeting covered by Oriental rugs, a huge fireplace with a marble mantel, and several wooden tables. A large vase full of blooming flowers, red roses, Star Gazer lilies, and big, fat, white carnations, sat on a table right in the front window. On one wall, hanging from individual brass cup hooks, was the strangest looking collection of instruments. It took Devin a minute or two to absorb the room, and during that time Miss Varrin settled herself into a wingback chair and arranged her skirts.

"So, Mister Devin has an obsession for shoes and feet." Her voice brought him back from his observations. "Mister Devin likes to touch them and caress them, does he?"

"If you say so, ma'am."

"I do say so, Mister Devin, because you are frequently in my office, the complaint being that you are more attentive to shoes and feet than to any class you are in."

Devin hung his head, knowing it to be true. Although he was twenty-one, he was an innocent, and he didn't know that there was a whole society of foot and shoe fetishists in the world and that he was one with them.

"Since you are such a devoted admirer of ladies' feet and shoes, I am going to teach you how to care for them and worship them. I am going to train you to become a proper personal foot slave. Maybe this will release your little inner demon, and you will actually be able to pay attention to the lessons being taught in class. It is quite simple. I use the Reward and Punishment system. Reward for good behavior, punishment for bad. Is this clear? Do you wish to proceed with this? Good. Then we shall begin."

Tossing a cushion on the floor, Miss Varrin began to tell Devin the rudiments of his training. The cushion would be where she expected to find him whenever he was not performing a service for her. It would also be his spot when giving a foot massage. Then she instructed him that he was not to speak unless spoken to; if he needed to use the bathroom, he was to beg her pardon for speaking out of turn before he asked permission to leave the room. His eyes were to be kept downcast unless told otherwise, and he would do nothing except what she ordered him to do. He was to execute all her commands enthusiastically and to the best of his ability, and service would not be limited to satisfying only his desire for feet and shoes. He was to remain small, silent, and unobtrusive while he was not in service.

"You are a fetishist, Mister Devin, a foot and shoe fetishist to be specific, and there are tens of thousands of men like you around the world who have much experience in serving the lady in order to be rewarded with the object of their obsession. So you are not alone. But since you have no experience and are so new, so raw, so innocent, I will allow you a little leniency until you learn all of my rules." She saw a look of relief pass over his face when she said this and hoped that her words had validated his need for the objects of his affection. "Your first lesson will be the proper position for a slave to assume while he awaits The Mistress's pleasure. Stand up, take off all your clothes except your underwear, and tuck them neatly out of sight. Then get on your knees on the cushion."

Confused at having to strip, but somewhat relieved by being allowed to keep his underpants on, Devin was very excited by Miss Varrin's words. Thousands of others just like him! He undressed hurriedly; out of personal habit he folded his clothes neatly and put them out of the way. Then he knelt on the cushion as he had been told, and was rewarded with a smile from Miss Varrin for having done this without further instruction. But he was very embarrassed by his erection that was visible even through his undies, so he closed his knees.

"Now I will teach you the correct position to assume. First, your knees should be open as wide as possible." Miss Varrin kicked his knees apart for emphasis, but Devin resisted her. Miss Varrin calmly rose from her chair and walked to the wall full of the curious implements Devin had noticed earlier. She selected what appeared to be a riding crop. Returning to the chair, she pushed Devin's head down onto the seat cushion and held his head there. Then she beat his back with the crop for twenty-five strokes.

"Remember: reward for good behavior, punishment for bad behavior." She pulled his head up off the chair by his hair and sat down, leaning the crop next to the chair. "Next, your hands should be either on your thighs or behind your back. Today I want them behind your back. Grasp one wrist in the other to assume this position properly."

Devin did as he was told, remembering the pain of the crop across his back. But the more Miss Varrin said to him and the more she did to him, the harder became his erection. He blushed. This did not escape Miss Varrin's notice and she took advantage of his embarrassment. Through his tight jockey shorts, she played with his erection with her foot, pushing it left and right and onto his belly with her shoe. Smiling, she withdrew her foot and picked up the crop she had used on his back. She used the flapper on the tip of his head and used the rod part on his shaft as if she were playing a violin. She even hummed *Eine kleine Nachtmusik* as she played her penis violin. Devin's embarrassment was slowly replaced by a feeling of relief, and he relaxed as she played with him. He was too naïve to know that he was surrendering to her and giving up his control and power to her. All he knew was that this felt so very good and it was what he had been seeking all his life.

"Very good, Devin. You did well. So now we can proceed to your second lesson, how to give a lady a proper foot massage. When a lady is allowing you the pleasure of massaging her feet, she should never have to work at holding her leg up. Take my foot in one hand and remove my boot. Now use your strength to hold my leg up as you massage my foot. Show me your massage technique. And I like it hard, Devin, no soft rubbing or tickling. I am not ticklish anyway. Remember that my other foot is in close proximity to your lowly face. If you annoy me . . ." she trailed off, feeling there was nothing more to say about that.

Devin began to massage her foot firmly, as she had told him to, but it was clear to Miss Varrin that other than the necessary firmness, he had no technique at all.

"No, no, no!" The crop came down across his back. "You have a natural talent for the necessary firmness, but that is all you have. It is clear that you will have to be taught everything from the beginning. Start at the toes, massaging them first all together with one hand, then each toe individually. When you get to the end of the toe, give it a firm squeeze and a slight pull before moving onto the next toe. And remember, what you do to the one foot must be the same as you do to the other, so pay attention or else you will receive more attention from the crop."

Devin obeyed Miss Varrin immediately; he did not want the less-than-tender attentions of her crop across his back. He found himself wanting to please her very much and he listened carefully to each word she said.

"Much better. Now, the ball of the lady's foot carries her entire weight when she is wearing heels, so it is very important to massage it deeply—and don't forget the area right underneath her toes. For this, you are to use your thumbs."

Devin did as she instructed, loving every second he held Miss Varrin's narrow, delicately boned, aristocratic foot in his hand. He was thrilled to his soul and this was reflected in his raging erection. Out of the corner of his eye, he could see her overturned boot; it had an exotic pagan look to it that excited him further. Miss Varrin's next words brought him out of his reverie.

"Now, you will be taught how to massage the instep. Hold my foot in one hand and make a fist of the other. Run the knuckles of your fist up and down the instep. That's right, like that. A few more strokes and we will progress to my heel. That's enough. On to my heel. To massage my heel, you will hold my leg up by the calf. Form your other hand into a cup and massage my heel in a circular motion, squeezing it firmly. Yes, that is correct." Miss Varrin allowed Devin to continue for another minute before proceeding to the next and final steps.

"Devin, there are other parts of my foot that need to be massaged. The first would be the blade of my foot. The blade is the outside of my foot. To do this, you will start at my heel and work your way up to my little toe. Place your thumb on the bottom of my foot and the rest of your fingers on the top. You will actually be using the palm of your hand, assisted by your fingers, to massage this area. Give it a try." Much to Miss Varrin's surprise, Devin picked up on this right away, even giving her little toe the same treatment as the blade of her foot. Perhaps Mister Devin did have some potential after all.

"Very good, Devin, very good." She purred, once again reminding Devin of a big cat. His erection bobbed and throbbed between his legs at her words of praise. "Now I want you to take my leg by the calf and with the other hand rotate my foot. Four times to the left and then four times to the right. Excellent. Place my foot on your thigh so that it does not get cold. We are going to move on to the other foot."

Having Miss Varrin's warm bare foot on his equally warm and bare thigh stimulated Devin so much that he had to make a real effort to stop himself from coming. He did this by thinking about her anger and the crop coming down on his back repeatedly as his punishment. To his relief, it worked, and he gave his full attention to Miss Varrin's other foot. Remembering what he had done on her left foot, he did his best to duplicate those techniques on her right foot. Only once did the crop come down across his back when he forgot to do the area right under her toes. He corrected his oversight immediately, apologizing to her most sincerely before continuing. After rotating her right foot, the final step, he placed her foot on his thigh and awaited further orders, head down.

"You did much better than I expected, Devin, and learned your lesson well. So I will reward you. The reward is not only a reward but also a further lesson. Lift my leg. Now, using your teeth I want you to take the ball of my foot in your mouth. Very gently, I want you to use your teeth on the ball of my foot. Take large amounts of it and bite down; slide it through your teeth and off my foot. Ah! That's right, just like that!" Miss Varrin leaned back in her chair and enjoyed the attention she was receiving. It was nice to relax after all her hard work. Devin was ecstatic at having her beautiful foot in his mouth and, closing his eyes, gave his entire being over to pleasing her and himself. "Now the other foot," Miss Varrin commanded him. He eagerly did as he was told and was rewarded with the same sigh of pleasure.

"Enough, Mister Devin."

Devin obediently placed her foot back on his thigh, wondering what was going to happen next. This had been the most incredible day of Devin's life.

"You have been amply rewarded for your service to me by being allowed to take my foot into your mouth. And you have been taught a valuable lesson today as well. But let's not forget the reason you were summoned here. You must be punished for kissing Miss Woodhouse's foot. Your punishment will be a beating with the crop."

Devin cringed at the thought of the crop. Miss Varrin rose from the chair and walked around behind him. "Now stand up and lean over the chair, your hands gripping the arms. You will receive fifty hard strokes on the buttocks."

He did as he was directed, gripping the arms of the chair so tightly his knuckles turned white. He braced himself for the coming onslaught. Miss Varrin flailed his buttocks with all her strength, repeatedly bringing the cruel crop down on him. At first he tried to count the strokes, but the cropping was so painful he lost count. Miss Varrin was determined that not one inch of his buttocks be missed. He bit his lip to keep from crying out, but at the end, he could not help himself. Each time the crop came down on him, he cried out in pain. Miss Varrin seemed delighted by his cries and increased her efforts. Finally, the cruel beating was over. His buttocks were on fire and he was sure there were welts on it.

"You may kiss my foot, Mister Devin."

Devin had not even noticed that she had not ordered him to replace her feet in their boots, and at the sight of them, he gratefully fell to his knees and began to kiss her feet, holding them lovingly in his hands as he planted many firm, dry kisses on each one. His erection was painful, more painful than his recently beaten buttocks.

"That's enough, Mister Devin. You may take your clothes and go to the bathroom. When you are dressed, you are to report back to me."

"Yes, Miss Varrin," he replied humbly. As he collected his clothes, out of the corner of his eye he could see her smiling. He hurried off to the bathroom at the far end of the hall, not only to dress himself, but to relieve himself of his painful erection and to have a good look at his buttocks. His release into a wad of tissue was like an explosion of mind and body. When he looked at his buttocks, he saw he was right. They were covered by welts, welts that would not go away in a day or even two or three. A reminder of this afternoon spent with her. When he was dressed and his hair combed, he returned to the sitting room where Miss Varrin awaited him. She was seated in her chair and the cushion was in place in front of it. She pointed to it and he fell to his knees, remembering to keep them open, even though he was dressed. She had a small smile on her face, and he was sure she knew he had masturbated in the bathroom, but she said nothing about it.

"Mister Devin, did you learn something today?" she inquired politely, as if they had just had tea.

"Yes, ma'am! Yes, I certainly did. Thank you, Miss Varrin, thank you," Devin said with all his heart.

"Good! Then you may go, Mister Devin. Remember this day and what I have taught you. And maybe I will no longer see you in my office." With that she dismissed him.

He rose and made his way to the front door, Miss Varrin right behind him. He let himself out, and as he walked across the porch, he heard the door being bolted, locking him out of his dream.

Foot Felon

The closet where The Mistress kept her shoes opened without a squeak, certainly a good sign that his mission would succeed. He crouched on his knees just outside of the closet, his eyes wide at the sights inside. He took a quick look around to make sure he was alone and reached one tentative, slightly trembling hand into the treasure chest. Pair after pair of pumps, boots, sandals, slides, and mules, and a pair of pumps he had yet to see her wear. They all had high slim heels and pointy toes, were neatly arranged, and held him fascinated. But he knew exactly what he was looking for at the moment: the crystal low-platform pumps with the beige suede insole, an insole that had been flattened smooth into the shape of her lovely foot. Even in the shadowy closet, he could see them gleaming at him from their orderly places on the floor. His efforts to control himself ceased abruptly. Almost with an emotion akin to worship, he withdrew one shoe from the closet, then the other. One hand touched the imprint her toes had made on the suede. His other hand touched himself. He brought the shoe up to his face slowly, testing how close to his face the shoe had to be before he could catch her scent. He smiled as he caught the delicate aroma and then rubbed. . . .

". . . his nose on the inside! I could swear I heard him sniff it, and then, he licked it with that snaky tongue of his," The Mistress said in a disbelieving tone.

She was upset but very slightly amused at the same time. He assumed her amusement was because her friend Mistress Meris was there to witness his humiliation and because of the punishment she was going to inflict on him for invading her privacy and disobeying her. His Mistress had dragged him into the kitchen by the ear, and there he knelt on the floor, his head down so far, his chin was on his chest. He was so excited at having been caught and at having another Mistress witness his humiliation that he thought he was going to explode. Mistress Meris was sitting at the table, her legs crossed.

Occasionally, she would pump her leg while his Mistress paced back and forth and vented about the horrible behavior of him, her slave. His Mistress's bosom rose and fell as she went on about him and his disobedience and audacity; the look on her face was one of astonishment. But from his position on the floor, all he could see was his Mistress's gorgeous feet in her high-heeled shoes and the open-toe, high-heeled sandals of Mistress Meris.

Crossed at the ankle, one bent knee exposing her calf through the skirt's slit, Mistress Meris's feet and legs tantalized him. The straps of her shoes laced up over her ankle and down over her foot, making her feet appear to be in delicate bondage. He allowed his eyes to stray to her shapely toes. Their red enameled nails glinted wickedly in the sunlight pouring in through the kitchen window. Oh, such terrible torture! Such sweet agony! The feet of his Mistress as they paced back and forth *and* the mesmerizing pumping of Mistress Meris's leg made him almost giddy, and he felt his cock grow even harder in his pants.

He blushed red with shame at the thought of what had happened: They had returned earlier than he expected from their shopping expedition, and he was caught in the act by his Mistress. Sitting just outside the closet, with his back to the door, he held the prized crystal pump up to his face. Sensing something was not quite right, she glided in silently on bare cat feet, grabbed his ear and twisted it as she "helped" him to his feet and out into the hall. Still using his ear, she dragged him to the kitchen, where the stunning Mistress Meris was smoking a cigarette and making tea. Once inside, she used his ear to force him to his knees. And now here he was. Mistress Meris expressed her sympathy with his Mistress but seemed highly amused at his plight. The teakettle whistled impudently and Mistress Meris prepared the pot of tea, listening to his Mistress continue her tirade about his major infraction of her rules.

"He knows better than to try tricks like that! To think I have wasted all this time on him! His house privileges will be revoked, and he will never be left alone in my home again!"

That last utterance really hurt him. His house privileges revoked? Never to be left to guard her home again? He never thought that he would be caught, let alone receive such a punishment.

"Come, Claudia, sit down and have your tea. It will make you feel better and calm you down some," said Mistress Meris.

"Yes, you're right, Meris. Tea and a cigarette or two will help, although I might be sorely tempted to put the live ember out on his tongue so that he won't be able to lick anything at all for quite some time."

Finally, his Mistress did sit and sip her tea in between drags of her fragrant clove cigarette. They both ignored him as he knelt there on the floor but continued to speak of him as if he was not there. With a start, he realized that to *them*, at this moment, he did not exist. He might as well be a piece of the linoleum.

"Well, you can be sure that more than just his house privileges will be revoked," his Mistress said. "He will need severe physical punishment, one that will remind him of my displeasure on a more immediate basis and stay with him for a few days to come!"

"But of course," Mistress Meris said coolly, "he should expect some punitive action. Something like what he has done should not be handled lightly." Finishing her tea and cigarette, she continued, "And now I'll go and leave you to it. Let me know what happens!"

That last was said almost gaily, and he felt a blush creeping up his neck to his face. Stubbing out her own cigarette, his Mistress saw Mistress Meris to the door, then closed and locked it behind her. She returned to the kitchen and gave him a swift hard kick in the butt before reseating herself at the table. His Mistress did not move, say, or do anything, anything at all, for what seemed like a short lifetime to him. His fear, the silence, her bare legs, and her feet in their sexy pumps made his thighs tremble. Finally, she stood up and walked around him several times; he could feel her eyes on him, sizing him up and down. Inside of himself, he grew smaller and smaller each time she circled him. Her high-heeled feet held him in place as surely as if he were rooted to that spot.

"Stay," his Mistress commanded him.

He saw her shod feet leave the kitchen and disappear down the hall. Shortly her high-heeled pumps reentered his limited view.

"Crawl after me," his Mistress said as she turned on her heel and headed off to the living room.

He struggled to keep up with her so that he wouldn't anger her further, but in spite of his efforts, he fell behind. With a speed he didn't imagine could be attained in such high heels, she was suddenly behind him, kicking him in the butt to impel him forward. His Mistress stayed behind him and with each forward motion he made, he received another hard kick in the butt. She kicked him all the way into the living room, and when he was in front of the sofa, she ordered him to halt. She arranged herself comfortably in the middle of the sofa and put a pillow in her lap.

"You are a disobedient, brazen slave and need to be put in your place. I shall have to break you in by hand. Get up! Unbuckle your pants and drop them just enough to expose your cheeks. And I don't want to see anything else of yours except for that butt," the softness of her voice told him exactly how displeased she was with him. The more displeased she was, the softer and gentler was her tone.

He thought he heard some slight amusement in her voice. Nevertheless, he did as she commanded, and it was not until then that he saw what she held in her hand. It was the black plastic hairbrush—the implement of punishment he hated the most. He stood there feeling embarrassed and scared.

"Now, lie across my lap, make sure to position that insulting member on the pillow, and take care to keep yourself in your pants!" With some difficulty he positioned himself on her thighs, holding up the front of his pants with one hand.

"Cross your wrists at the small of your back."

As he complied, she grabbed his wrists in one of her hands and held them in place. Without any warm-up, the first vicious blow let him know that this was real punitive punishment, and there was to be no pleasure in it for him. With that first blow, he jerked up, clenched his cheeks involuntarily, and struggled against any further punishment, but her grip on his wrists held firm. The first hard blow of the hairbrush had landed on the high, round top of his cheek and stung sharply. Each blow was successively harder than the one before it. The Mistress rhythmically covered every inch of his cheeks, high and low, top and bottom, until his whole bottom was warm and pink. He could not control himself; he rubbed against the pillow.

"Insolent," his Mistress growled at him.

The next blows were harder, landed blows, making the previous blows seem like love taps in comparison. She wielded the hairbrush as if it were part of her hand as she tortured his bottom. Each blow made his teeth rattle, jarred him, and threatened to make him lose his balance and fall off her lap. All that held him was her firm grip on his wrists. And the blows kept coming. His cheeks had progressed from warm and pink to hot and red. He struggled not to cry out, biting his lip, his own warm, hot blood on his tongue for a fleeting moment. Then when he could stand it no longer, a strangled cry escaped his lips, but he fought against losing control and screaming out loud. Still The Mistress persisted in the cruel punishment to his cheeks with her hairbrush. The blows came faster and faster until he finally did lose control and cried out for mercy. Then, The Mistress pushed him off her lap. He knew his cheeks would be on fire all night and sore for at least a couple of days, a reminder of his disobedience and his Mistress's displeasure.

"Now, get out of my house! When I want you, I will call you."

He struggled to get his pants up over his sore cheeks and at the same time not to expose himself to her, risking her further displeasure and more punishment. When he was suitably dressed, she showed him to the door and slammed it behind him. It rang with an air of finality that made his heart sink. He wondered how long it would be before he was allowed back into her presence. He hoped it was not too long, but with his Mistress there was no telling. It could be a day or a week or even a month. As he drove home, the weave of his underwear rubbed against his lambasted cheeks. Shame, pleasurable, delicious shame overcame him, and he became aroused at his humiliation in front of Mistress Meris and his subsequent punishment by his own Mistress. By the time he got home, he had a raging erection in his pants. He barely made it through the door before erupting into his shorts. Through the haze of his shame, humiliation, and release, he wondered if his Mistress was on the phone right now, relating to Mistress Meris what had "happened," as she had so gaily put it.

Girl-Doggie

He knew she would be gone only a short time and there was a good chance she might catch him invading her privacy, but he could not resist temptation. He entered her bedroom and knelt in front of her dresser. The dresser drawers held all her delicate woman things, and the drawers hung open displaying an abundance of lacy underthings, rows and rows of bras, panties, G-strings, thongs, garter belts, and dozens upon dozens of long silk stockings. The stockings were the old full-fashioned kind with the seam up the back and the extremely sexy Cuban heel that required a garter belt to hold them up. As each new piece of finery caught his eye, he moved from one drawer to the next, touching and fingering her things and raising especially fine pieces to his nose, sniffing them lovingly.

She knew something was wrong as soon as she entered the house. Things, meaning him, were much too quiet. She took off her shoes and padded up the stairs in her stocking feet, being careful to avoid the creaking board midway up. She tiptoed down the hall and squatted down outside her bedroom door. The door was almost closed, but she could just see through the crack. His back was to her, but she could see him going through her things, touching them, sniffing them. And wait, what was that he had on his head? Her new French silk-and-lace panties! How dare he?

Angrily, she slipped her feet back into her pumps, stood up, and pushed the door open hard, so hard that it slammed into the wall behind it. He spun around, still on his knees, the panties still on his head, and froze at the sight of her. She was magnificent. Her eyes flashed fire as she crossed the room in long strides. She stopped in front of him and glared down at him. She snatched the panties off his head and shook them in his face. He cowered at the rage in her eyes and whimpered softly in the back of his throat.

She barked. "Get up."

When he hesitated, she grabbed him by the shirtfront and hauled him to his feet. One of his buttons popped off and flew across the room. She laughed, a deep, wicked laugh and ripped off the rest of the buttons. She tore off his shirt and flung it across the room. Then, still laughing demonically, she fell upon his trousers. When she had them down to his knees, she pushed him. He stumbled backwards a few steps, lost his balance, and toppled onto the bed. Before he could scramble away, she had him by the feet. She roughly pulled off his shoes and socks, then quickly removed his trousers. Grasping his undershirt in her hand, she pulled him to his feet and slapped him several times across the face, as hard as she could. His cheeks stung from her open palm, but this was a small tax to pay for the pleasure he had enjoyed in her brief absence. He did not yet know that this was not to be all his punishment. He was a fool to think he would get off so lightly for such a serious breach of her rules.

She glared at him and said, "I knew you couldn't be trusted. Just who do you think you are? Do you think you mean something to me? You are nothing, less than nothing. You are not even human in my eyes. So now you have to be punished. And I have the perfect punishment for the likes of you. You, who likes to sniff things. Don't move."

She went to the closet and returned with a length of slender rope and a black crop. Placing the crop between his teeth, she told him to hold it, not to let it drop. Then she used the slender rope to tie his privates between his thighs, anchoring the rope like a G-string around his waist, giving him a smooth front, just like a girl's. This was very painful for him in his current condition; he had an enormous erection, and it was very exciting to be abused and punished like this. She handed him a pair of thick pantyhose and ordered him into them. He struggled with them but finally got them up. The thickness of the pantyhose concealed his body hair and held his privates tight to his body. She handed him lacy panties and motioned him into them. When they were on, she tossed him a bra. Smiling, she crossed her arms over her chest and watched as he wrestled his arms into the delicate straps.

"Stay," she commanded, as if he were a dog.

She went again to the closet, and she returned with a big frilly petticoat and a pair of shoes large enough to fit him. His mouth fell open and he dropped the crop. Her displeasure was obvious, and he quailed under her glare as he bent to pick up the fallen crop.

"No, pick it up with your teeth," she snapped at him.

He dropped to his knees and bent his neck to the floor. He picked up the crop with his teeth as she had commanded and stood to face her. She dropped the petticoat on the floor; it landed in a perfect circle with the elasticized waist hole gaping open like a mouth surrounded by red frills. She motioned for him to step into the petticoat and pull it up. Then she dropped the shoes to the floor and diddled her fingers at him, then at the shoes. He slipped his feet into them and turned his ankle. She laughed at him and dragged him to the mirror by his arm. Unsteady on his heels, he stumbled after her. She stopped in front of the full length mirror and pushed him into its view.

"Stay." Again the dog-like command.

She rummaged through one of her drawers and returned with a lip-stick and hair clip. Grabbing a lock of hair that had fallen down over his forehead, she clipped the barrette to his hair so that it stuck straight up in the air. Then she took the crop out of his mouth, grabbed his cheeks between her fingers and forced his mouth into a pucker. Uncapping the lipstick, she drew big red lips on him and let his face go, laughing at her handiwork. He stood alone in the mirror and beheld himself. His bound-up privates fought and raged against the rope she had used on them. The petticoat and the smear of lip-stick had made him into a caricature of a woman. He was humiliated, totally and completely humiliated by what she had done. Or so he thought, until she forced the crop back into his mouth.

"Get back down on your knees. Now crawl to me," she com-manded. "Don't think for one minute that I'm through with you."

He obeyed, dropping to his knees and crawling to her on all fours. When he was at her feet, she took a dog collar and leash out of a drawer. She buckled the collar around his neck and attached the leash to it. Then she began to drag him around the room. At first he resisted.

"Heel!" she commanded, and followed the command by stepping behind him and giving him a good hard kick in the butt.

She laughed at the astounded look on his face as he realized what his full punishment was to be. Obviously he had no idea of how seri-ously she would take his infraction and just how far she intended to bring him down to put him in his place. But now he knew—and he also knew he was in no position to do anything about it. She held the leash close to her body, with the excess balled up in her hand, and took off around the room. He scurried after her on his hands and knees, trying hard to keep up with the brisk pace she set. If he wasn't in the proper "heel" position, which was next to her right leg, with his arm close to her leg, she tugged brutally on the leash. When his per-formance was particularly unsatisfactory, she took the crop from his mouth and hit him on the backside with it. Then she forced it back into his mouth. After several circles around the room, which included glimpses of himself dressed up as the caricature of a woman and being walked like a dog, he was starting to get the hang of what she expected of him. But she wasn't through with him yet.

She dragged him over to her boudoir chair, and told him to "sit and stay" a couple of feet in front of it; then she sat down. Looking at him, she decided that no dog in the world ever sat the way he was sitting—Indian style—and that he needed to be taught how to behave like a dog. She took the crop from his mouth and thwacked it against her hand.

"You have finally gotten the idea of how to walk properly on a leash, but dogs don't sit like that! From now on, when you are my dog, you will sit with your backside on the floor, your feet flat on the floor with your knees bent and as close to your body as possible, and with your hands on the floor in between them." He looked at her blankly and this made her very angry. She hit him across the face with the crop; something she would never do to a real dog. "Do it, do it now!"

He did as he was told but had some difficulty getting into and remaining in that position, especially hindered as he was by the frilly petticoat. As he struggled to sit the way she had ordered, she emphasized her instructions and displeasure by frequent use of the crop. At last, she announced that she found his position to be "satisfactory." After putting the crop back between his teeth, she told him her plans: He was to be taught ten dog commands that he was to learn by number, instead of by name. This was because she did not want "others" confusing him by using words as commands; after all, the average intelligence of a fully grown man and a fully grown dog was about the same: the best one could expect was about fifteen years. "Sit" was position one, so when she called out "one," she expected him to sit the way he was sitting now. "Two" meant he was to "stay," and this command would be accompanied by a gesture: the flat palm of her hand being brought down an inch or two from the end of his nose.

The command for him to "heel" was "three," and he had already had some training at this. "Four" meant that he was to get up on his hind legs and "beg" by putting his two front "paws" together and moving them up and down. When she wanted him to "lie down and be still," she would say "five." "Six" meant that he was to "roll over," which would usually be followed by "seven," which meant "play dead." As she taught him each of these commands, she was enormously amused by the look of humiliation on his face. The impact of his dress combined with dog training was not lost on him. Continuing with the command count, she told him that "eight" meant she wanted him to stand on his hind legs and walk in a circle. "Nine" meant she wanted him to "bark," and "ten" meant she wanted him to "sing." Seeing the look of confusion on his face at that one, she explained that "sing" meant he was to throw back his head and howl.

"Let us begin. Four!" she commanded, knowing this command to beg would be the most awkward one for him to execute from a sitting position. As he fumbled in his attempts to get into the position, she used the crop on his back and his thighs to show her displeasure and spur him on to execute the command. Eventually he managed to get onto his hind legs and move his paws in the required manner, but not until after several blows of the crop. Next she called out "five," which meant he had to lie down, requiring him to get back down onto the floor. "Nine," for speak, followed "five," which at least he could do from his lying-down position, and thankfully, "six" and "seven" followed "nine." After "nine" came "one" and he scrambled to get into the awkward sitting position. "Eight," the command for stand and dance, followed "one," and once again he scrambled to stand up. When he was in position "eight" she called out "ten," but he did not know what to do. His limited dog brain was confused. He had memorized the commands in numerical order, and she was calling them out randomly.

She brought the crop down on him and informed him sternly that when "nine," to speak, or "ten," to sing or in this case to howl, was combined with one or more commands she expected him to execute all the commands one after the other or together. "Eight," "four," and "ten" meant to stand, beg, and sing; "one" and "nine" meant to sit and speak; so in this case, "eight" combined with "ten" meant he was to stand on his hind legs, walk in a circle, and howl at the same time. Which he did, looking and sounding ridiculous. So ridiculous that she burst out laughing and couldn't stop, which meant that he had to continue executing commands "eight" and "ten" simultaneously, and that made her laugh even more. The red frilly petticoat was the finishing and most humiliating touch. He looked like one of those giant white poodles that have been dressed up in human clothes and made to perform silly tricks. Finally, she was able to gasp out "one," and release him temporarily from any further humiliation.

Gratefully he collapsed to the floor, the frilly petticoat again hindering his progress and making him look very foolish after finally getting into the correct position. She rose and commanded him to "stay," bringing her hand down so close to his nose that he almost jumped back. She left the bedroom and returned with a placemat and a bowl; she filled the bowl with water from the bathtub and placed it on the mat. Then she told him he could have a drink, but he had to lap it up with his tongue just as a dog would. As a seeming kindness, she told him that he would be more comfortable if he drank his water in position "four." This was the preferred position for large dogs. His thirst overrode his humiliation, and he bent his head to the bowl and began to lap at the water. His efforts were sloppy, and he got more water on his face than in his mouth, eliciting more laughter from his trainer. He sincerely hoped that the offered bowl of water was to be the end of his humiliation but it was not.

For the remainder of the afternoon, she drilled him in his numerical commands until he was able to execute each one at random and in order almost perfectly. Finally, she seemed satisfied at his progress and his humiliation, and she removed the collar and leash. She allowed him to take off his woman's attire but sharply commanded him that he was to drive home with the large smear of lipstick still on and the silly barrette in his hair. When he got home, he was to call her and beg to be allowed to wash off the lipstick and remove the barrette.

Knowing how far he lived from her, she guessed he must have broken every speed limit to get home in such a short time. So she denied him her permission to remove the lipstick and barrette. He was to call her in the morning at eleven thirty and to make sure his camera was turned on so that she could see that he had obeyed her and left the lipstick on and the barrette in his hair overnight. She chided him that she would know if he had tampered with either one, and the next time they met, his punishment would be much more severe. She ordered him to memorize each command count, in order and independently from the other and assured him that today would not be the last time he would be made into her dog. Then she hung up.

The next morning her phone rang at eleven thirty sharp. There he was on her computer monitor with the lipstick smudged on his face and the barrette clinging to his head by a few hairs, but it was obvious that he had obeyed her. She graciously gave him her permission to remove both the lipstick and the barrette. He timidly asked her if he was to be allowed to come, and she told him coldly no. She added that he had been caught invading her privacy, and there would never be a reward for such terrible behavior, no matter what punishment he had undergone.

Then she had added flippantly, "A dog's reward is to sniff . . . and you have not earned any sniffing privileges."

L'Homme Cache

As The Mistress, I am usually very conscientious about locking the closet in the playroom in which I keep my special things. But I left in a big rush and locking the closet slipped my mind, which led to his lucky day. When I returned earlier than he expected and caught him in the act, so to speak, this is the tale he related to me, kneeling before me, naked and with his head down.

As soon as he was sure I was gone, he crept into the playroom on cat feet. His mind barely registered a long, low object covered by a black velvet cloth, so intent was he on the contents of the oh-so-tantalizing closet. His hand trembled as he reached for the closet door-knob. He pulled the door open slowly, savoring each second, his nostrils dilating to soak up the scent of latex and shoes emitting from the closet. Then, in a burst of exhilaration at entering the forbidden zone, he flung the door back so hard that it slammed into the wall behind it. Inside the closet were my things, my latex catsuits, skirts, tops, dresses, little leather teddies, thongs, and bras, but best of all, the floor of the closet was stacked high with box after box of my shoes.

He said that the sight of all those lovely shoes and boots thrilled him. When he discovered all my shoes, he allowed himself a little whoop of victory and cradled as many of them as he could in his arms. In his pants, his member did its own little dance of joy. But he knew exactly what pair he was looking for—the black patent leather fetish pumps with wickedly pointy toes and dangerously high six-inch heels. When I wore these particular shoes, he had to carry me from one place to the other because the heels were too high for me to walk in. Sometimes, I rode on his back as if he were a pony; at other times, I allowed him the pleasure of carrying me in his arms. Yes, those were the shoes he wanted to play with. As he rooted through the closet looking for them, boxes of shoes tumbled this way and that, the shoes themselves spilled out onto the carpet in a jumble.

Finally he found them. Delightedly, he raised one shoe to his face and stuck his nose inside it. The faint aroma of my delicate feet floated into his nostrils, and he inhaled deeply, loving the scent of me. Then he hooked the inner heel of my shoe on the top of his nose; the instep was lined up perfectly with his nostrils, and the toe of the shoe was tucked under his chin. He had positioned the shoe in the same way that I did when I tied the shoe to his face. He clutched the shoe to his face and lay back on the floor, his hand wrapped around his engorged member. Slowly, gently, and erotically making the most of this forbidden experience, he began to stroke himself as he panted into my shoe.

He was near to climaxing but managed to balance the one shoe on his face as he groped for its mate. He had the notion that it would be very nice to come in my shoe—something I never allowed him to do. He told me he became totally obsessed with the idea, never once thinking of the consequences. His hand closed on the other shoe. Holding the one shoe to his face, he stroked harder and faster, the second shoe positioned just so on his belly to receive his pearl jam. He released into my shoe with a great groaning sigh and began to laugh, giddy at what he had done.

"Do you think that is funny?" I asked him in a stern and angry tone of voice.

He sat up in alarm; he had been so engrossed in breaking one of my strictest rules that he never even heard me come in. The giddy joy of a minute ago was dispelled by the displeasure in my voice. When he sat up, the shoe on his face somersaulted through the air and landed with a dull thump on the carpet. The other shoe, the recipient of his nectar, slid into his lap, its contents dribbling out one side rather unappealingly. My expression was mocking yet predatory. He cowered on the floor; his heart was pounding so loudly in his chest that I could almost hear it. He was at a total loss for words, with a terror so great that his mouth went dry and his lips stuck to his teeth. After seeing the look of righteous fury on my face, I could see that he resigned himself to whatever punishment it would please me to mete out.

"How dare you? Get that disgusting mess out of my shoe," I commanded.

My voice was deceptively low and cool, a sure sign of danger. He scrambled to rise, to find something to wipe out my shoe with, but I read his mind.

"No, no rags, no tissues. Lap it clean with your tongue."

He sat there thunderstruck. Angry that he did not comply immediately, I crossed the room in a few long strides and repeatedly slapped him hard across the face, forehand and backhand. Hurriedly, he picked up the soiled shoe, worked his cheeks in an effort to muster up some saliva, and began to lap at his own juices. By the look on his face, I could see that his pearl jam tasted most unappetizing, but one look at my face convinced him to go on. He licked and licked and licked under my careful scrutiny until not a drop remained. When I held out my hand, he presented me with the shoe for my inspection.

I inspected the shoe carefully, peering inside it until I was satisfied he had lapped up every drop of his mess. As I did this, he stared up at me under his lashes. Did my dark red hair set off my light olive complexion? Did my high Eastern European cheekbones match my straight Roman nose? How did I look to him when I was angry? No matter. I was in street clothes but still every inch The Mistress. I could tell his nerves were singing and sending shivers of pleasure and fear down his spine. I think that he knew then that on every pleasure, every joy, there was a proportionate tax. And he had only paid a small part.

I dropped the shoe to the floor as if I was still offended by it. I crossed the room to the long, low, black-velvet-encased object that he'd said he barely noticed earlier. Grasping the cloth, I uncovered the object with a flourish. It was a cage, with its bars painted glossy black. Six feet long and somewhat narrow, I had designed it myself to give its occupant a minimum amount of space. Five of its six sides were bars like those you would find in a prison; the sixth side, the bottom, was a thinly padded board covered in black leather. He looked amazed and fearful. He still didn't realize what his fate was to be. My lips curled into a sensuously sadistic smile. I just love this kind of surprise. Makes life so much more rewarding, don't you agree?

One of the short ends of the cage had a latch and a padlock dangling from it. I opened the cage door, and with a grand, sweeping gesture, I silently commanded him to enter it. He started to crawl in, head first, and scraped his spine painfully against the upper bars. Because of the red blush creeping up to his face from his neck, I knew he was humiliated when he realized he would have to slither on his belly like a reptile to get inside. I kicked him impatiently; I wanted him in there, and I wanted him in there right now. He used his elbows to impel himself forward, aided by his hands gripping the bars to pull himself along. As soon as his feet were inside, I slammed the door shut and padlocked him in. Next, I dropped the black velvet cover over the cage, incarcerating him and leaving him in semidarkness. Then I shut off all the lights and left the room, committing him to full darkness and total containment for three hours.

Later on cat feet, I returned to the room and turned on one dim light. Suddenly, with one smooth action, I ripped the black velvet cloth off the iron cage. Lost in the darkness and mist of his own thoughts, he had not heard me enter the playroom. He felt a cruel and erotic joy emanating from me as I towered over him. His member was hard, and his face told me that he was painfully aware of his erection. My eyes missed nothing. I thought I looked magnificent in my red latex miniskirt and matching, low-cut red top. My corset nipped in my waist, and my lace-up patent leather boots rose up to my knees. My hair streamed over my shoulders. I felt like a demon angel, things springing to my mind that I had never thought of before.

He whimpered in the back of his throat, overcome by my sadistic eroticism, overwhelmed by my power. He muttered incoherently, trying to put into words the feelings of awe and love I enkindled in him. I put my finger to my lips, and he fell silent at my unspoken command. Behind me was a tall stool. I picked it up in a show of strength, placed it close to the cage, and arranged myself on it. My eyes held him in thrall. Mesmerized, he watched as I slipped off one of my boots. My delicately boned foot descended through the bars above his face. Almost immediately, his mouth fell open as if he was expecting some kind of reward. I used my foot to push his mouth closed and then cruelly mashed my foot into his face. I stuck my big toe into his ear; I gripped his nostrils between my toes and held them closed as well as I could to cut off his breathing. I used his nose to push and pull his head, and I repeatedly slapped his face with my foot as hard as I could through the bars. As I did this, I showed no anger or malice; it was casually done, making an object of him which I knew he found to be very humiliating.

I withdrew my foot from the cage and slowly put my boot back on so that he could watch my every action and try to anticipate what his next punishment would be. I stood up and bent over. While I was doing this, I was gathering up a good mouthful of saliva. I mustered up a cough to add to the mix and spat on him. It landed directly on his face, just as I had planned. My aim was true.

"Have we learned our lesson?" I asked in my husky voice.

He told me he loved my voice; that it flowed over him like melted butterscotch. He said that he loved my imagination and cruelty and that I could read him so well. In a welter of passion, his eyes responded eloquently as he answered my query. I rewarded him with a small smile.

I released him from his cage. He squirmed out as gracefully as he was able, groveled at my feet, and whimpered in gratitude. His swollen flesh surged with desire, only to be ignored by his cruel mistress. After a while, he told me what his feelings were while he was imprisoned in my iron and velvet darkness. He heard my footsteps moving away from him, saw the lights go off, and felt total darkness descend, and then he heard the door close behind me. Alone in the velvet darkness, he contemplated his fate.

He told me that to him, my innate cruelty offset by my beautiful smile and cool tone of voice seemed beautiful things; he loved them and he found in them an exotic paradise that he made his own. The darkness and bars that surrounded him heightened my cruel eroticism, and his mind turned to the rich, forbidden delight he had indulged in earlier. While in the cage, he said he came to a better understanding of his submission to me and to glimpse his own eternity—*me, The Mistress, his Mistress*. Yes, he deserved this punishment of isolation and darkness; the memory of his lost freedom burnt brightly in the blackness behind the bars of his submission to me. He lost all track of time in his black iron-and-velvet prison; he wallowed in his punishment and realized that the torture one desires the most is the cruelest torture of all.

I commanded him to dress. I could see the strain of his erection in his face, and his hard-on was making a tent pole in his pants. As part of his punishment and part of his reward, I ordered him to drive to the shopping mall about half a mile away and park the car in a far-off corner. The puzzled look on his face was very gratifying to me; this game was a new one to him. When he got there, he was to call me from his cell phone for further instructions. When he called, I spoke to him as his Mistress, making sure he knew why I was displeased with him. I made him recite his infractions back to me. Ensured that he understood why he had been punished, I told him that now he could masturbate himself there in the car in the public parking lot. He was to do so on the count of ten. I would count, and if he came before I said *ten*, he would be severely punished when I next saw him. I assured him that I would know if he came before my command; he was noisy when he came and could not hold back his come groans. He never could. Even with a gag, he still managed to be very noisy.

If he came exactly on the count of ten, then there would be a reward waiting for him during our next encounter. As I slowly counted, I could hear him trying to control himself and wait for ten. To prolong his agony just a little longer, I made the interval between eight, nine, and ten very long. But he hung in there, and when I said *ten*, I could hear him moaning and almost screaming "Oh god, oh god, yes, please, oh god." I knew he had exploded like a rocket. I hung up, smiling to myself.

The Mistress's Treadmill

The slave was waiting in the dungeon when The Mistress arrived. Although music was playing softly in the background for a calming and sexy effect, he was very nervous because this was the first time he was seeing a mistress. He had gotten there early to make a good impression, and he spent that time looking around the room. Neatly arranged on cup hooks on the walls was an array of floggers, crops, paddles, canes, spankers, leather wrist and ankle restraints, blindfolds,

gags, nipple devices, cock-and-ball torture devices, and other implements of torture whose use he could not imagine. There was an Oriental cabinet whose contents he was intensely curious about. But
what aroused his curiosity most was a set of upside-down, U-shaped
black pipes set into the floor about two and a half feet apart. The
longest part of the upside-down U measured about seven feet, and
underneath it was a leather-covered plank. He barely even noticed
the small wooden chair in the corner, the kind one would use as a
desk for a child. She was fifteen minutes late, but he knew she would
not even think of apologizing for her tardiness. He was a first-time
slave, after all, and just a casual one at that, and he knew that no
explanations would be forthcoming. What he didn't know was that
The Mistress had spent that time reviewing his application.

When she entered the room, he was excited by and amazed at how
she looked. He had never seen anyone dressed in such clothing
before. The tall, slender yet buxom Mistress was wearing a floor-
length white latex dress with bra cups and lingerie straps, a black
latex corset that made her waist very small, black latex opera gloves,
and what he was to later find out were called "court shoes." The
shoes had a two-inch platform and six-inch heels and featured two
straps around each ankle. The toes were a rounded point, and the
heels were thin but not stiletto thin. Her long auburn hair was curled,
and a tiara sat on her head; her curls tumbled down her back and
over the sides of the tiara. The Mistress looked most elegant and very
intimidating. He sat there gaping at her as she closed the door, locked
it, and turned to face him.

The first words The Mistress said to him were to order him out of
her chair. He realized he was sitting in a large, comfortable black
leather armchair (the only real chair in the room) that The Mistress
used as her throne. Of course, he realized too late that he should have
been sitting in the wooden child's chair to await her. Quite foolishly, he
had seated himself on the throne and incurred her displeasure immediately. He looked surprised because her tone of voice was cold and
carried an implication that she considered him brainless for sitting
there. This caused him to hesitate, but The Mistress's eyes flashed
fire, and he beat a hasty and embarrassed retreat into the child's chair.

As she walked to the leather chair, he noticed the peculiar swish-
ing sound that only latex makes. He had never heard it before, and the

sound of it would stay with him forever. He watched her as she took her time settling herself in her throne, crossing her legs, and arranging the folds of the latex dress just so.

She turned her attention to him and said in a no-nonsense tone of voice, "The rules: You are never to appear in my presence without performing the proper rituals of bathing, washing your hair, using deodorant, and brushing your teeth, tongue, and gums. You will not wear cologne or aftershave in my presence. You are to keep your eyes downcast. I never want to see you eyeballing me again. Your head will be kept respectfully down."

As soon as The Mistress said these words, he put his chin down close to his chest and looked at the floor. He immediately felt deprived of power because he wanted to drink her in with his eyes, but he soon discovered the secret of looking up at her through his downcast eyelashes. But he was enormously relieved that he had performed on his own the "proper rituals" she required.

"You are to address me as 'Mistress.' You are not to speak unless spoken to except if there is an emergency. An emergency would constitute biological functions, needing attention for medical problems, limits being pushed too far, or the premises catching on fire. The words "Mercy, My Mistress" are what you will say in the event of an emergency. Do you understand?"

"Yes, Mistress," the slave said softly.

"You will perform all duties assigned to you cheerfully and to the best of your ability. You will become an object when I desire it of you. You will accept punishments and thank me for them. You will listen carefully when I correct you, which will be for your betterment as a slave, and make every effort to perform to my satisfaction. And last, your cell phone is to be turned off when in my presence. Breaking any of these rules will result in swift and severe punishment of the punitive sort. Are we clear?"

"Yes, Mistress," he said, still surreptitiously looking at her from under his downcast lashes.

"Now rise and come here," The Mistress commanded him, pointing to the middle of a round Oriental area rug about three feet from her throne. He rose from the child's chair and stood where she pointed.

"First, you will strip for me. Remove you shirt first. There are hangers on the back of the door for all your clothing. You will hang each piece after I have ordered you to remove it and return to the spot you are in now."

He obediently removed his shirt, hung it up, and returned to the middle of the area rug.

"Next, remove your shoes and socks, and place them on the floor underneath your clothes. Remove your wristwatch, and put it in one of your shoes. Now, remove your trousers."

The slave did as he was told, one thing at a time, necessitating many trips to the door and then back to the carpet. He expected to be told to remove his jockey shorts, but to his surprise, tinged with a little fear, The Mistress did not command him to remove them.

"Stand up straight, clasp your hands behind your neck with your elbows straight out. I am going to inspect you."

At first she did nothing but observe him. When her piercing gaze obviously discomfited him, she rose and stepped up to him. First she ran her hands all over the unclad parts of his body, testing his nipples for sensitivity and tickling him to see if this had any effect on him (which it did not). Then she stepped around behind him and ran her long red nails down his back. He didn't see the smile cross her face when this small, simple action raised goose bumps on his flesh. Nor could he know of her pleasure when red stripes appeared where she had raked her nails over him. The Mistress's next action caught him completely off guard. She quickly grabbed the outer sides of his jockey shorts and pulled them tightly up the crack of his ass, making them into a thong. She tugged them up hard and, holding them in one hand, she began to experiment with different spanks on his ass. This action surprised him more than hurt him. He stood very still as she continued with her spanks.

As suddenly as she had started, The Mistress stopped spanking him and let go of his jockeys, returning them to their original position. Then she stepped around to face him and, looking him directly in the face, roughly and humiliatingly pulled his underwear down to his knees. She used her court-shoe-shod foot to step on them until they were on the floor, like cotton panty ankle restraints. He felt the red stain of humiliation creep up his face, but he kept his chin on his chest and his eyes downcast. He had the urge to cover himself from her probing eyes, but he didn't dare move. Did he pass her inspection? He could not know the inspection was not complete. The Mistress rearranged herself in her throne, taking her time, making him wait for he knew not what.

"Keeping your elbows perpendicular to the floor, I want you to turn 180 degrees then stop."

He did as he was told.

"Now, bend at the waist, reach back, and spread your cheeks," The Mistress commanded next.

Glad that she could not see the humiliation he knew was so obvious on his face, he reached back and spread his cheeks a little. A swift kick in the butt by those beautiful shoes let him know he had not pleased her.

"Spread your cheeks as far apart as you can. Expose yourself to me. You are to have no shame or modesty in my presence; you will have no privacy, just like a house cat or dog. When you are with me, all that you have, all that you are, belongs to me."

He pulled his cheeks farther apart until he could feel the warm air of the room on his ass-hole. The Mistress did nothing, but he could feel her eyes on him as if she was counting each of his hairs. Suddenly, a cool stream of air hit his opening. He felt his asshole open then tighten in surprise, and then he heard a wicked and delighted laugh from The Mistress.

"Release your cheeks, stand up straight, clasp your hands behind your neck, your elbows out straight, and complete your turn to face me," she commanded.

Humiliated and feeling as if she had stripped him of his power, when he turned to face her he turned the wrong way. Quite calmly, The Mistress rose from her throne, stepped toward him, and slapped his face.

"I said 'complete your turn!' Now, on my command, I want you to turn around again and this time, complete your turn correctly."

Then she sat back down and let him wait. She looked him up and down, not failing to notice his erection. She leaned forward and gave it a hard slap. He groaned in pain but held his position.

"Now turn around 180 degrees."

He obeyed, expecting her to order him to bend and spread once again, but to his great relief, she did not.

"Complete your turn!"

This time he got it right. He was relieved to hear The Mistress say, "you'll do." Then she added, "just," somewhat insultingly.

She pointed to a spot on the floor at her feet. He obeyed her unspoken command and dropped to his knees. She then ordered him to massage her feet and calves. He unbuckled and removed her right shoe and, supporting her leg, began to give her the deep massage he had painstakingly learned from foot reflexology books and had practiced repeatedly on himself. His fingers searched out her pressure points and worked on releasing the tension from her entire body through her narrow, aristocratic, delicately boned feet with their long red glossy nails. He was thrilled at her occasional soft, sexy moans of pleasure because of his ministrations; he was determined to prove himself worthy in some way. When it came time to massage her calf, he placed her foot on his shoulder so The Mistress did not have to work at holding her leg up to give him pleasure. She seemed pleased and surprised that he had thought of this; it was an action she usually had to order the slave to do.

"Now do my left foot and calf. It is getting very envious of the attentions you are paying to the right one. And you must never leave The Mistress lopsided," she said, her tone gentler now than it had been earlier.

He replaced her right shoe so her foot wouldn't get cold and buckled the double straps back into their original holes. Then he gave the same attention to her lovely left foot as he had given to her right. He was happy that all of his practice had ensured that each foot was massaged in exactly the same way and order as the other. After the foot massage, he placed her left foot on his shoulder, just as he had done with the right foot, and massaged her calves. Although once again, The Mistress did not say anything, he knew by her soft moans that he was pleasing her. When he was finished with her left foot, he replaced her shoe as lovingly and as carefully as before. But still he did not receive a word of praise from her. She lounged in her throne, her eyes half closed and let him sit there unnoticed for a few minutes. From under his downcast lashes, he feasted his eyes on the long, shapely legs only inches from his face.

"Remove my shoes, then lie down on the floor in front of my chair, face up, with your chest under my feet," her deep velvet voice broke in, and he hastened to obey her.

He quickly and efficiently unbuckled her shoes and put them next to her throne. She rested her buttocks on the very edge of the chair and placed her bare feet on his chest. As soon as the soft skin of the soles of her feet touched his chest, his erection stiffened and bobbed with a mind of its own. The Mistress worked her feet up and down his chest, using her toes to harden then squeeze his nipples. When she had tired of this, she used her feet on his member. She captured his member between the soles of her feet and slapped it back and forth between them, squashed it against his body, and then began to push his sack around with them. She separated his nuts with them and pushed hard on them, one foot to a nut. He was very aroused by all of this and the pain that it caused him, and her cool toes on his hot member heightened his excitement.

The Mistress removed her feet from his person and looked down at him. With deliberation, her dainty right foot descended to his face. Playful after her initial remoteness, she grabbed his nose between her big and second toes and turned his head this way and that. She mashed her foot into the skin of his cheeks; she placed her foot so that her toes were on his forehead, her instep resting on his nose, and her heel on his mouth. Then she used her toes to push his lips around, laughing at the contortions her toes made of his face.

"Open your mouth," she ordered.

He had been holding his breath, and on hearing her command, expelled it in one long sigh. He parted his lips, his eyes wide and focused on her delicate foot as it descended toward his face. The Mistress thrust her foot into his mouth, and he opened wide to receive her. She worked her foot deeper and deeper into his mouth, not satisfied until he accepted all her toes and the ball of her foot. When his mouth was completely gagged by her left foot, she ground her right foot mercilessly into his genitals. His erection was painfully hard, and both The Mistress and he knew it. From the heights above him, her laughter rang out, mocking him. Suddenly, she withdrew her foot from his mouth, making him feel that his mouth was a big gaping hole in his face. The foot on his genitals was gone just as suddenly.

"Dry my foot with your hands and replace my shoes," she directed him.

He dried her feet as she had bid him and fitted each shoe back onto her graceful feet, sorry to be deprived of their divine presence. She stood and stepped on his chest as if he were part of the floor. She walked the few steps over to the pipes imbedded in the floor that had puzzled him earlier. The Mistress crooked her finger at him, and he scooted over to her on all fours. She pointed to the toe of the court shoe that she had extended and gestured for him to kiss it. He kissed it adoringly and hard enough for her to feel it through the thick patent leather of the shoe. Withdrawing her foot, she pointed to the padded leather board between the two pipes.

"Lie down face up and be quick about it," she instructed him. He laid himself out flat between the two pipes, face up as she had ordered, and noted gratefully that there was some padding under the leather.

With a wicked laugh filled with glee, The Mistress stepped up to the top of the apparatus, where his head was located, and grabbed a pipe in each hand. Using the pipes to support herself, she stood on his chest in her elegant court shoes. She carefully placed a heel on each of his nipples then she began to dance on his chest to the music playing in the background. All through her dance, she looked intently at his face to see his reaction. Pleased by what she saw, she began to dance more energetically, moving her feet up and down on his chest and swaying her body sexily to the music. When the song segued, she spun on one foot, doing a 180-degree turn on his chest. Still using the pipes to support herself as she walked on the squishy, uneven surface of his body, she began to walk carefully down to his stomach, wiggling her gorgeous ass with each step until she was standing on his genitals. He reveled in the exquisite humiliation of being used as her doormat. Then she turned to face him.

Standing on her toes, she began her dance again, alternating her steps between his cock and his balls, stepping on his cock with both feet while lifting her feet up and down in ballerina steps. He groaned aloud in pain turned to passion and abandoned himself to the exquisite pleasure of this exciting and wonderfully novel experience. Much to his delight, The Mistress chose to continue this sublime form of torture for several more minutes before climbing off him and returning to her throne. She took a cigarette from the drawer of the table next to her chair and lit it. The smell of cloves filled the air as the smoke curled from her lips and shrouded her in an air of mystery. He used this time to savor his experience and imprint it, and her, on his memory. She let him remain there until she had stubbed out the cigarette.

"Come here, slave," she called out to him.

He rose with some slight difficulty, still lost in the experience of her. He crawled to her on all fours and then knelt humbly, adoringly, at her feet.

"You have performed better than I expected, considering how badly you started," The Mistress said. "Because you have redeemed yourself, I shall reward you. Lie down, face up."

Delighted to have won her approval, he quickly did as he was told.

"Now grab your cock."

He was even quicker to obey this command.

"Stroke yourself."

He grabbed his throbbing manhood in his right hand and began to stroke himself in the old familiar way. He was stunned when she bent over his cock and generously spat on it.

"That is part of your reward, to use my spit as lubricant."

Turning on her elegant heel, she strode from the room, leaving him to finish himself off alone. As he gushed onto his belly, he knew he had found the Foot Goddess he had been searching for.

Nectar of the Goddess

Although the Mistress did not need a new slave, she agreed to see the new petitioner at eight o'clock in the evening. She knew immediately that he needed a great deal of training and was not sure if she wanted to go through the trouble of training what was obviously a complete newbie. He had no concept at all of the proper protocol; he did not keep his eyes down but eyeballed her as she glided in to the room; he did not drop to his knees when she entered the room; he had no gift for her, not even a cheap bouquet of flowers or bottle of wine. And his personal hygiene left something to be desired: wrinkled shirt, ill-fitting trousers, and, worst of all, deck shoes. But he was already there; she was dressed and ready and, also, a bit bored. Perhaps he could at least provide her with some small amusement, she thought. The Mistress sat in the high-backed black leather chair she used as her throne and ordered him to strip. When he sloppily began to rip his clothes off, she held up her hand and stopped him. Men!

"You will undress in the order that I tell you. First, this is your mark. You will return to that spot when you have finished executing my commands." She pointed to an invisible spot on the floor. "Now, off with your shirt. Hang it up on the back of the door. Return to me. Now take off your shoes and socks and place them out of my way, in the corner by the door. Now, take off your trousers and hang them from the belt loop on the hook on the back of the door." This was The Mistress's routine and ritual strip, and she was so bored with going over it with the new slaves that she considered writing it up and having them memorize it before they even entered her presence.

After each piece of clothing had been removed and put in place, he returned to his mark, as The Mistress had instructed him and stood awaiting her next command. He still had his boxer shorts on, and she could see the battle of the tent pole going on inside them. The Mistress hid her smile.

"It is plain to see that you have no idea of how to behave in front of The Mistress, so I will give the instructions once, and once only, in the proper protocol. You will not look me in the face unless I instruct you to do so. You will not speak unless it is to answer a direct question. Your word, if you need to say it, will be 'banana.' You will use this word if you need to use the bathroom or if our play gets too heavy for you. You are forbidden to use it to interject your opinion, and you are forbidden to blather on when spoken to. If I ask you if such-and-such a place is on the way to our ultimate destination, I do not expect road directions when a simple 'yes' or 'no' will suffice. I expect silence, unobtrusive service, and enthusiastic obedience from you. Punishment for infractions will be swift and hard, and not particularly to your liking. Is any part of these rules and instructions unclear?" The Mistress had stated these rules so many times to so many slaves that she felt like a broken record. The idea that this, too, should be included in her new written instructions to first time slaves seemed very appealing.

"Yes, Mistress," he said softly with his eyes now downcast. There was a slight hint of fear in his voice, as if he was suddenly afraid of what he had gotten himself into.

He was still clad in his shorts but getting more nervous by the minute. How delicious! The Mistress arose and stood about eighteen inches away from him, making sure he would have a good, long look at her attire. She wore a long purple latex dress with lingerie cups that showed off her voluptuous breasts to their full advantage. A black latex waist cincher nipped her midsection, making her breasts and hips look even fuller. Up the back of the dress was a double zipper so that the dress could be worn loose or as a hobble skirt. She preferred it loose so that it did not restrict her movements and also gave the slave the occasional glimpse of her beautiful legs. Open-toed patent leather pumps graced her feet. Opera-length black latex gloves clung to her hands and arms, and she wore a large amethyst ring on her left middle finger over her glove.

After she was sure he was impressed with her finery, she walked around him, taking her sweet time, making sure he knew he was being assessed for his worthiness and possible use. She returned to her chair and made a big show of arranging herself in it for his benefit and to keep him waiting. Then The Mistress commanded him to remove his boxer shorts. His face slowly turned bright red as he hooked his thumbs into his boxers and pulled them off. After he had placed them neatly with his other things, he stood on his mark and awaited her pleasure, which was to inspect him both visually and physically. She told him to place his hands behind his neck and turn in a half circle, 180 degrees.

When his back was to her, The Mistress ordered him to bend at the waist, reach back, and spread his checks. She let him stand like that for a moment; then, she blew a cool stream of air toward his hot red opening. It startled him so much, he jumped and made a strangled noise in the back of his throat. His embarrassment was obvious and quite delightful to her. This, too, was part of her ritual strip and gave her some indication as to the desires of the slave. After all, they weren't always truthful about expressing them; sometimes they didn't even know that that was what they wanted, and other times they were just too embarrassed to admit to them. It was The Mistress's opinion that, in the end, all men wanted to experience some sort of anal penetration.

The Mistress ordered him to rise, complete his turn, and kneel at her feet. In a coolly disinterested voice, The Mistress asked him what service he thought he could perform for her or of what use he could be to her. All he said was that he hoped The Mistress had room for him in her stable. She considered this for a moment.

"I really don't have an opening for a new slave right now, nor do I have the time it takes to train someone like you. I have two foot slaves, three household slaves, two sissy maids, a cook, a bath attendant, a driver, and several specific duty slaves on call. What special service do you think you could perform for me that would make it worth my while to train you? Someone with no special expertise? Someone who misguidedly thinks that this is all about him, and not about me?"

He had no reply except to beg The Mistress to take him on as her slave.

"Well, since you are already here, I should at least amuse myself with you while I think what use you could be of to me."

The Mistress reached out and began to slap his breasts and pinch his nipples really hard. Then she pinched them and pulled on them, watching his face closely for signs of rebellion or distaste. All she saw there was the pain that her manual torture of his nipples was causing. She was happy with that for the time being. She slapped his face a few times, forehand and backhand across both cheeks and spat in his face. Becoming bored with that, she turned her attention to his genitals. He was erect from the fear and joy of her presence, and that was gratifying to her and no less than she expected of any of her slaves. Then she ordered him to lie on the floor face up and to spread her legs. The Mistress trod on his genitals with her high-heeled shoe, grinding his member into the carpet, poking at his hairy sack with the pointy toe of her shoe. To his credit, he bore it stoically, even though she stomped on him with no care at all for him or his feelings.

Then it occurred to The Mistress what use he could be of to her.

"I have need of a toilet and you will do nicely."

He looked horrified at the thought, and she laughed in his face.

"You said you wanted to serve me in any capacity I saw fit. You said you wanted to be my slave but admitted you have no special talents, nothing to offer me. All I have need of right now is a toilet and you refuse? Get up, get dressed, and get out."

He begged The Mistress to allow him to stay, but her mind was made up.

"Either you become my toilet or you go."

She saw his confusion and humiliation, and his erection. He didn't want to go, but if he could not serve her in the way she had demanded, he knew she wasn't going to waste another minute on him.

"Answer me, slave." She kicked him.

He didn't move from his spot on the floor. His chest heaved with the effort it took him to make up his mind. The Mistress was losing patience with him; after all, he had come to her looking to serve her, and now that she had found a use for him, he was unhappy with it.

Spitting in his face, she said sternly, "Leave now. You disgust me."

He made no move to go; instead, he said, "I will do anything you desire, Mistress."

"You are learning your proper place in my life, slave. What took you so long?"

He had the good sense not to answer her.

"Follow me; no, remain on your knees. I expect you to crawl after me."

With that, The Mistress led the way down the hall, and he scrambled after her on all fours. She took him to the room she had made especially for the purpose of toilet training. It was a bathroom of sorts but with no sink or tub, just a bidet in the center of one wall and a shower nozzle in one corner. The whole floor was tiled, and there was a drain in the middle. A large toilet seat on legs was mounted over the drain.

The Mistress diddled her fingers at him, silently commanding him to lie on the floor. Nudging him with her foot, she made him position his genitals under the toilet. Then she lifted her skirt and took off her panties. She climbed onto the toilet seat and spread her legs wide. His erection was enormous and actually quite impressive. The Mistress began to laugh. Did he think *she* was going to do something with it? Well, she would do something with it, but certainly not what *he* was expecting! He would soon find out.

"You may take that big hard thing in your hand and stroke yourself as I empty my bladder onto it. My nectar will be your lubrication. But you do not have my permission to come."

She began to sprinkle on him, just a few drops at first. Of course, since The Mistress's aim was so accurate and her control so excellent, the first few drops were just to humiliate him. He looked very surprised and embarrassed, but he obeyed her. Then she gave him a few more drops. They doused his member and his hand as he stroked; her warm, yellow juice bathed him in her sweet nectar. She gave him a little more, this time drenching his warm hairy sack with yellow ambrosia. Obediently he continued to stroke himself as she looked on. She withheld her fragrant stream from him for a minute and then showered him generously, her stream splashing on his engorged member.

She stopped her stream suddenly and said, "Now let's try something a little more intimate, which will provide me with better service from you, shall we?"

His bright eyes looked askance.

"Move up here so that your face is under the opening."

He hesitated for just a nanosecond before he slithered into the proper position.

"Open your mouth so I can empty my bladder onto your face, and I expect you to drink as much of my nectar as possible."

The Mistress resettled herself on the seat and gave him a short steady stream, her yellow juice bathing his face in her nectar, hot and straight from the fount. She stopped to give him a mere second to swallow all he had collected in his mouth, and then she showered him generously, letting go of her never-ending yellow stream, holding nothing back, not one single drop. Her stream splashed on his whole face and into his open mouth. Her nectar dribbled down his chin and pooled underneath his neck. She let him have it all and to his very great surprise, he loved it.

The Mistress could tell by his face he was enjoying being her toilet more than he had ever thought he would. His hair was wet and fragrant with her ambrosia. The rapturous look on his face told The Mistress that she had found the perfect toilet slave and that she could use him in this manner anytime she so desired.

He deserved to be rewarded for accepting her dominion over him, learning to exhibit the proper respect due to The Mistress and accepting his place in her stable. She called in one of her assistants, a fresh, petite fireball of a redhead, named Nadine. Nadine was to supervise his self-administered reward and call The Mistress when he was finished.

The Mistress was quite pleased with the quantity and color of his ejaculation, and the ropy design it made on his chest. Then she gave him permission to shower and, under the guidance of Nadine, join the rest of her slaves in the basement. A bunk would be assigned to him, and he would be there to be The Mistress's toilet bowl whenever she required him. What had started off as a more-than-possible waste of time had turned into a good acquisition indeed. It was time to unpack the acrylic potty chair and put it to good and frequent use with her new slave.

The Night's Entertainment

It was The Mistress's favorite kind of evening for playing—the clouds boiled in the sky, and thunder rumbled erotically in the distance. She called down to the dungeon and commanded that a male slave be brought to her forthwith. Of course, her order was obeyed immediately; a handsome submissive stood before her awaiting her inspection.

The Mistress's eyes raked over his naked body. He was about five feet ten, and 170 pounds, nicely muscled, and well endowed. Of course, The Mistress noted that he was extremely aroused in her presence, just as she required of all the slaves in her stable.

"You'll do," The Mistress said coolly.

The slave thanked her humbly for deigning to notice him and dropped to his knees. She played with him, using her foot on his nipples and his private parts while she thought about what she would like to do to him. A loud peal of thunder made him jump; a flash of lightning illuminated his face and *torture* sprang to The Mistress's mind.

"Remain on your knees, crawl to the cabinet, and bring me the red toy box," she commanded. On all fours he scurried to do her bidding. Returning to his spot on the floor at her feet, he raised the toy box in his outstretched hands like an offering to her, his Mistress. He continued to hold it in that manner as she slowly picked through its contents. She noticed that his arms began to tremble from the effort it took for him to stay in that awkward position and took a little longer in her selection to prolong his discomfort. Then she laughed at him cruelly.

Choosing a set of Japanese clover nipple clamps with half a dozen magnetized weights, several lengths of thin black latex ropes, and six one-pound fishing weights, she told him he could put the box aside. Then she called out "At-ten-tion!" He sprang up, lifting his buttocks up off his heels, but remaining on his knees, and clasped his hands behind his neck. He hung his head, not daring to look at her, knowing it would anger her. Free to do as she pleased, it pleased her to torture him.

His nipples stood erect, as did his engorged manhood. His full sack dangled between his legs. With her long red nails, The Mistress pinched his nipples; with her pointy-toed stiletto shoe she poked at his throbbing member. His moan of frustrated pleasure excited her, and she reached for the clover nipple clamps. Before she applied the clamps, she played with his nipples, pinching them very slowly, building up the intensity; imagining that if she pinched hard enough, her two fingers would meet as if there were no skin between them. After his nipple was as erect as she could get it, The Mistress applied the left clamp and waited for the pain to sink in. She knew what he would be feeling: first, the clamp would bite into his skin causing him exquisite pain, and then a slight numbness would set in as the flow of blood to the nipple was cut off.

After playing with the right nipple as she had with the left, The Mistress applied the other clover clamp to his right nipple so she, and he, would have the pleasure of a second dose of pain. When the second clamp had done its work, she moved on to bigger and better things, saving the weights for later.

The Mistress took a long piece of latex cord and unwound it under his downcast eyes so he could see what she was doing and tremble at the thought of what she had in mind for him next. His gasp of mixed pleasure and fear was most satisfying to her. Ordering him to lie on his back and spread his legs, she took the latex cord and first wrapped it tightly around his full sack. Of course, the latex cord stretched as she did this, and both The Mistress and the slave knew the cord would tighten up even more as the evening progressed. She knotted it tightly and gave his taut skin a nice hard slap. He cried out in pain and she was pleased. But The Mistress was not through with him yet.

Selecting another piece of latex cord, she again bent her head to his privates. She wrapped it around each hard nut, separating them from each other, tying them up individually. The skin of his isolated nuts glistened and his hairs stood out from his skin. Reaching over to the red toy box, The Mistress took out a leather strap with snaps to keep it closed and several D rings. She snapped it tightly over the latex rope encompassing his sack and then attached the six one-pound fishing weights to the strap one at a time. Now only his engorged and throbbing manhood was unbound. She slapped it back and forth with the open palm of her hand as hard as she could and heard his satisfying, exciting groan of pain. The Mistress laughed wickedly, delighted at her power over him.

Then she commanded him to stand up. She knew this would not only be difficult for him with the weights attached to him but also humiliating. The Mistress loved this kind of play. When he was on his feet, she took a length of nylon rope from the toy box. She was going to use this to encircle his manhood, leaving only the tip exposed. She started this by leaving a hand's length of the rope down his shaft, but her rope trick would start at the top. Bringing the rope up to his head, she began twining the rope around his throbbing member, starting right under the lip of his red and engorged head, catching the excess rope underneath it. She twined the rope all the way down his shaft, not leaving the least little bit of flesh exposed, with no pinching at all. When she had completely encircled his shaft with the rope, she tied it off tightly at the base with the hand's length of rope she had left there at the start. He looked so beautiful dressed in her finery that The Mistress could not help but to torture him some more.

Then she remembered the magnetized weights! Perfect! Slowly she attached one after the other to the nipple clamps, sometimes using the opposite force to move the clamp around as it dangled from his nipple. Then she quickly stuck it to the clamp, each time eliciting a delicious groan of pain from him. But he was a good slave; The Mistress had trained him herself, and he bore his torture heroically.

Next, she ordered him to march around the room keeping his hands behind his head, elbows straight out to the side, and with each step, he was to draw his knees up high to his chest. His member bobbed and waved in its rope, the fishing weights clinked together merrily, and the magnetized weights pulled on his nipples cruelly—The Mistress was in heaven. She especially loved to hear the sound of the weights clanging together as he marched at her command. His pain registered on his face but not a sound escaped him. He was a very good toy and had entertained her well. The Mistress decided to reward him before sending him back downstairs to the dungeon.

She called him to her and pointed to the floor in front of her. He dropped to his knees and, again, pain registered on his face as the weights dangled from him. First, she removed the rope from his engorged member. As The Mistress pulled on the rope, his member bobbled round and round crazily as it exposed his flesh. This was quite amusing to her, that was why she did it, and she laughed in genuine amusement at the involuntary antics of his member. The rope had left deep imprints on his skin; a tiny clear bead of juice glistened on his tip. Next, she freed his left nipple, the one she had captured first. The rush of blood returning to it caused him to moan and groan—it was music to her ears. She waited a few minutes for the pins and needles to set in; then she played with the newly exposed nipple to the music of his moans. Even her slightest, lightest touch elicited sighs, groans, and moans from him, and her back-and-forth slaps made him scream softly. The Mistress delighted in the sound. After that nipple had become less sensitive, she turned her attention to the right nipple and freed it. Again, his chorus of moans and groans serenaded her. The Mistress gave the same special attention to the right nipple until it was no longer sensitive. Feeling generous because of the entertainment he had provided her with, she thought he should be rewarded for his good service to her.

The Mistress ordered him to lie on the floor and removed the leather strap with the fishing weights hanging from it. Then, one at a time, she freed his balls from the latex cord. After his balls were free, she freed his sack from their imprisonment. The slave moaned and groaned as feeling came back into his genitals. The Mistress took her seat and used one toe of her stiletto to poke his sack, and with the other foot, she pumped his rock hard member as if it were a gas pedal or a brake. The slave was writhing on the floor with pain, metamorphisizing it into great pleasure, just as he had been doing all evening. It was time for his reward. He knew, of course, that The Mistress liked her slaves to come on her count to exert her control over them further, and he was ready to obey her.

Slowly she began the count, kicking him in his scrotal sack to emphasize each number she called out. The slave held back until the count of ten, knowing that if he did not his punishment would be severe. It could be two days and nights in the stockade or two days and nights in the coffin or a severe flogging administered by her assistant. He would not even have the pleasure of The Mistress herself beating him. Since The Mistress had not used him for some time, and no slave was allowed to touch himself without her permission and in her presence, he was aching to come. After the final kick on the count of ten, The Mistress was pleased with the volcanolike explosion. His spurt of pearl jam, as she liked to call it, was generous and looked like glistening ropes on his belly and chest. The Mistress's pleasure with him danced on her face.

"I had almost forgotten about you. You are a fun toy. I shall have to call for you more often," The Mistress said pleasantly.

The slave was delighted when she said this; he felt honored and pleased yet humbled at the same time. Then she called for her assistant to take him away. He would be allowed to clean himself before being returned to the dungeon. That night, as he slept on his bed of straw covered by a blanket, he dreamed of her, The Mistress who had looked into his soul and given him what he feared and wanted the most.

Of Needles and Nails

Although The Mistress was very excited about seeing this male creature, she didn't particularly like him; she liked his scene and enacted it with verve, with more sadism than she showed to most of her other male toys. Why didn't she like him yet enjoy seeing him so much? She disliked him because he drove up in a Rolls-Royce wearing his expensive Bally shoes, and she knew that the clothes on his back cost more than the session. But did he bring her even the cheapest bouquet of flowers or the smallest box of chocolates or ask if she needed milk or cigarettes when he called from the corner phone booth at the prearranged time? No! And he'd the absolute nerve to try to haggle with her over the donation every time he called, even though she needed special and often hard-to-get equipment to enact his session.

So why did she see him? Because he was a full-out masochist; a rare creature indeed, and one that every Mistress dreams of having at least one of and all agree that there are far too few of them in this

world. No role-playing, no begging or groveling, no insincere pledges
of undying devotion, no idiotic wardrobe requests from him, no silly
"girl-friend" cross-dressing enactments, no fumbling or inept service,
no contest of wills or mind games were required; she was Madame
Sadist and he was the object of her sadism. They started as they
meant to go on. With him, she could unleash and release her inherent
sadism full force, and she could be as cold, mean, and uncaring about
his pain as she pleased. No limit was imposed on her pleasure in
indulging her sadism and hurting this walking male appendage.

He arrived, empty-handed of course, and did not even remark upon
her outfit. The black latex ball gown with the lace-up back, her elegant
black patent leather court shoes, and her wrist-length black latex
gloves went unnoticed by him. She promised herself that one day she
would answer the door in jeans, sweatshirt, and sneakers to see what
his reaction was then! After the minimal courtesies had been
exchanged, he tried to walk right past her into the chamber. The Mistress grabbed him by the arm and pointed to the silver donation
plate. He reached into his pocket as hesitantly as if she had pointed
to a trail of burning coals she wanted him to walk over barefoot. The
donation was already folded up and he began to walk away, but she
knew this character better than that. Again, she grabbed him by the
arm, and right in front of him she counted out the donation, something she did not do with anyone else who was a regular. But he had
shorted her before, so now she always made sure he had donated
the correct amount before letting him enter her chamber. Leaving him
standing in the foyer, she squirreled the donation away in her bedroom before leading him into her dungeon.

He followed her into the chamber and took off his clothes while
The Mistress sat on her throne. At least he respected her rule of not
throwing his clothes around the room and put them in a neat pile in
the corner without having to be told. The lights were dim and exotic
music with a Middle Eastern flavor to it emitted softly from the
stereo. The medical examination table, complete with electronic foot
pad to elevate the top of the table, was all prepared with a fresh sheet
of white paper pulled down over it, tucked under, and taped firmly to
the end of the table. A pile of black towels stood at the ready, as did
a first aid kit and a styptic pencil. A side drawer containing a large
box of surgical gloves and the other special equipment she needed

was open just enough for him to see what was inside. What did arouse his curiosity was a large heavy wooden chair with arms and a cloth-covered table next to it that was never in the chamber before, but he didn't say anything about it. All the better that he didn't ask her about it; this way her plan for him later on would come as that much more of a shock. Deep inside, The Mistress smiled with sadistic glee, which she knew gleamed in her eyes if he'd bothered to look.

When he had stripped down to his bare skin, she looked at him with barely disguised disgust. He was overweight, but at least his belly did not hang down so far as to conceal his genitals. Rising from her throne, The Mistress led the way to the examination table and gestured him onto it. She humiliatingly laughed aloud at his difficulty at climbing up onto the table, but after all, if he was not overweight, getting onto it would not have been a problem. Finally he was settled on the table with his feet in the stirrups, knees spread wide. She left him to lie there splayed open while she selected a whip from the large collection hanging on cup hooks from the wall behind her. She chose a cruel little thing: short in length, it was made up of many strands of $1/8$-inch latex cord, with diagonally cut ends, and carried quite an impact. Just right for whipping his genitals! He needed no warm up, so she let the whip fly with a considerable amount of force.

He winced in pain at the first blow, and although he had his word, he had never once used it. So she continued along on her merry way and brought the whip down hard on his penis and scrotum until she became quite warm in her latex and had a good squish factor going on. Heaven! Giving pain to an all-out masochist and having a good squish factor going all at the same time! She was feeling better already, and the festivities had hardly begun.

Enjoying herself more with each passing second, The Mistress roughly pushed his legs apart, climbed up onto the table, and knelt between them, whip in hand. Her target this time was his "man-boobs" and nipples. Because he was overweight, his man-boobs were more like breasts: large and meaty. But his nipples were the real delight. Not small and shy, not tiny or inverted, his stuck out proudly and made excellent targets. She went to work on them with the same gusto as she had on his genitals, and soon, in her excitement, she dropped the whip and began to use her hands on him. She slapped his fat man-boobs as hard as she could, forehand and backhand, one at a time, both at a time, whatever means took her fancy; she pinched his red nipples slowly, imagining that they were mountains that she could crush between them. Both his genitals and his nipples were quite sore when she was through with them.

As much as The Mistress was enjoying these activities, it was time for the real action to begin. After she had gracefully climbed down from the table, she took some of the black towels and placed them under his genitals. Then she walked to the front of the table to face him. She took several of the black towels and stuffed them partially under his chest near his nipples, making sure that half of each towel was under him and the other half was wadded up next to him. He may bleed, and she did not want this mess on her table or her Oriental rug; the towels would soak up the blood, the paper would protect the table, and the table could be sterilized thoroughly afterward. Leaning over, she looked into his eyes but said nothing. With one hand, she reached down and opened the slightly ajar side drawer wide enough to pull out two pairs of the surgical gloves. Dropping the gloves on his chest, she put her hands in front of his face and snapped them on one at a time over her black latex gloves.

She smiled coldly as she reached down and pulled out a row of a dozen individually wrapped disposable insulin needle points for him to see. He groaned loudly and thrashed his head from side to side, but she knew it was nothing more than a display of his fear and excitement and that the needles were exactly what he wanted. Laying the row of needles across his heaving chest, she took a blindfold down from a hook on the wall and made sure she gave him a good show of cleavage as she bent over him to deprive him of his sight. This was also part of his masochism: to know she was going to pierce him with the needles but not to see where the needles would be placed. After he was blindfolded, The Mistress did what she had to do. She turned the lights up as high as they would go and retrieved a pair of reading glasses from one of the examination table's drawers. His last memory of her would be of her lovely face, framed by her auburn hair, and her magnificent breasts almost bursting free of the black latex dress. There was no need for The Mistress to destroy her mystique by letting him know about the bright lights and reading glasses, was there? And they were essential to what came next.

Dragging her nails up his chest, she lifted the row of needles, detached one, and dropped the remainder back on his chest. Holding the package right next to his ear, she ripped it open. He moaned at the sound of the paper ripping; it was one of his turn-ons, even though he never had a hard-on. The Mistress did not care about whether he had an erection; his purpose was to serve as her pin-cushion and he did that very well. She started with the left nipple since she was already at that side of the table. Pulling it out as far as she could, she used her fingertips to feel for the nerve, which she wished to avoid. This was easier than it appeared in spite of all the gloves because she had so much practice at it. Pushing the nerve to one side with one thumb and forefinger, she jabbed the needle through his flesh, right up to the hilt of the blue tube that would have been attached to the barrel of the needle if there had been one.

His groan was, as always, music to her ears. Ripping open another package, she jabbed the second needle through his nipple; then a third, a fourth, a fifth, and a sixth in a circular pattern. His groans came faster and louder as she jabbed each needle through his already sore chest. When she was through, the blue tubes made a lovely pin-wheel design that she was quite proud of; she was so proud of it that she brought out the instant camera and took a picture of her handi-work, being careful to leave his face out. Now, onto the other nipple! She stepped around to the opposite side of the table to get a better angle and closer view. Once again, pulling his nipple out far from his body, she felt for the nerve, located it, avoided it, and went to work on the nipple with relish. The Mistress was very careful to duplicate the same lovely pattern on his right nipple that she had made on his left one. Two more photos were taken: one of the right nipple alone and the other of both nipples together. The camera obediently spat out the photos that she put to the side until they developed.

Smiling at her pinwheel design, and absolutely delighted by his low and constant moaning, she began to think of what she could do to his penis that would equal the artistry of what she had done to his nipples. The Mistress decided to make the design on his shaft a con-trast to the design on his chest: instead of a circular pattern, she thought that a straight pattern, with the blue tips in alternating direc-tions, would be quite nice. Opening the side drawer, she removed two more rows of a dozen needle points, twenty-four in all, also tipped in blue. Wishing to avoid the tiny capillaries in his penis, she pulled a floor lamp closer for more illumination, but she knew she would inevitably hit some of them and there would be some blood loss. Who would think that those tiny capillaries could bleed so profusely? But that was what those towels were for, and they did their job well.

The Mistress stood between his legs, still in the stirrups, and began at the top of his shaft. Pulling out the topmost layer of skin, she inserted the first needle and was enormously gratified to hear a strangled scream from the slave. She used the remote control to make the music louder in case he became noisier. But his scream was the real music for her. Ripping open the next package quickly, she pulled out his skin again and jammed the second needle through his flesh in the opposite direction. The third was jabbed into his shaft in the same direction as the first, the fourth in the same direction as the second, and so on, down his shaft until all twenty-four needles with their blue tips decorated his penis. She was quite happy with the neatness and precision of her work and with the pleasant contrast the pinwheels on his nipples made with the aligned needles through his shaft. Then The Mistress took a picture of his shaft alone and one of his nipples and shaft together.

But there was more to be done, more torture and torment for her to inflict on this creature who lay so voluntarily helpless on her table. There was the final piece of needlework to be done and the surprise she had in store for him with the wooden chair.

She moved the floor lamp and walked to the head of the table. Before using the foot pad to elevate him into a sitting-up position, she could not resist the urge to flick her fingers at the needles protruding from his nipples. Flicking gently at first, as his moans excited and incited her, she flicked harder and harder until he was almost screaming when she flicked cruelly at both nipples at once. She knew just when to stop; she did not want him to word up on her and spoil her fun and, more importantly, deprive her of her surprise ending for the session. From the first drawer in the side of the examination table, she removed another dozen needles, and from another drawer, she removed an eight-inch-square, two-inch-thick piece of white Styrofoam. Then she commanded him to take his feet out of the stirrups. Only then did she use the foot pad to elevate him into a seated position.

The Mistress moved back to the end of the table and sat on the

small doctor's swivel stool that had previously been pushed out of
the way. Carefully she positioned the piece of Styrofoam under his
scrotum and over the towels and then positioned his thighs and buttocks to hold the Styrofoam in place. Next, she placed his large and
rather loose scrotal sack over the foam board. She took a minute
to look at his pinwheel nipples and his straight-angle shaft and to
decide what would be a complimentary design for those two. In a split
second, an idea came to her that pleased her very much. With another
slave, she would have had to tie him down to perform this action, but
with this one, she needn't bother. This was the pain he craved, this
was the main reason she kept seeing him, and this is what she enjoyed
so much, even though she didn't care much for him.

The Mistress's idea was to pin his scrotum to the foam board in
an alternating pattern, like a starburst. To make sure "things" would
end up even, she pulled out both of the far sides of his scrotum as far
as she could and jabbed a needle into each side, right up to the hilt
of the blue tip. He almost screamed, but in fact, if one avoids the
"nuts," the real business in the scrotal sack, the skin of the scrotum is
not very sensitive. His almost scream was more one of surprise than
pain, but she took great pleasure in it anyway. Then, moving from one
side to the other, she carefully pulled out the skin about an inch less
than the two overstretched needles on the far sides of his sack and
the one in the middle. He continued to moan and groan and thrash
his head from side to side. But she knew that he was escalating the
pain in his mind, and that although somewhat painful, it was not as
painful as he was pretending it to be. It was a mind game he played
with himself and she let him continue. It gave her pleasure, too, and
was not against her wishes.

Alternating between the overstretched, pinned-down skin and the
one inch shorter pinned-down skin, in no time she had accomplished
the starburst effect on his scrotum. She admired her artistry and
more pictures were taken; this time one of his sack alone, his sack
with his penis, and his entire torso showing off all three pieces of her
"needlepoint." There were two photos left in the camera, and she was
saving them for the *grand finale*: the wooden chair surprise.

It was time to remove the blindfold, but first she removed her
glasses, lowered the lights to their original dimness, moved the swivel

stool out of the way, cleaned up the flurry of plastic and empty paper needle packets, and tossed the soiled towels into a plastic bag, hiding it in a black box for laundering later.

Then she stood tall in front of him and lifted the blindfold, greeting him with almost the same view she had given him when she deprived him of his sight. He looked down at her handiwork and gasped aloud. It was impressive, and The Mistress had done a remarkably good job at missing those pesky capillaries, especially those in the scrotal sack, so blood loss had been minimal. Gingerly he touched each of his nipples in turn, making himself wince. Then he bent over to take a good look at his pierced cock and finally at his starburst sack impaled on the foam board.

"Oh my god! Oh, Mistress, look at how beautiful it is!" he exclaimed with the most enthusiasm and passion that The Mistress had ever heard from him.

She gathered up the now fully developed photos and handed them to him, upon which he began to exclaim anew and compare them to the real artwork right before his eyes. The Mistress let him enjoy himself while she went to the first aid kit and brought out the items she needed, gathered up more clean towels just in case, and collected the little red biohazard box and the stinging styptic pencil. It was time to remove the needles and move on to her much-anticipated surprise.

When she felt that he had admired himself and her artistry long enough, she took the pictures from him and placed them to one side. "The last shall be first," she thought to herself and decided to unpin his sack and work her way up to his nipples. This decision was also influenced by the fact that his sack was more likely to bleed than his shaft or nipples, and she wanted the styptic pencil to have as much time to work its cruel stinging magic as long as possible. She rolled the swivel stool back into place between his spread legs and put her supplies on the shelf that pulled out from underneath the examination table. Then she began pulling out the needles, one at a time, taking out the shorter-placed needles first to maximize the pain of the longer ones. As she removed each one, The Mistress dabbed the pinprick wound with alcohol to sterilize it, and if one bled, she dabbed it dry of the alcohol and applied the styptic pencil. To her great delight, she was "forced" to apply the styptic pencil to three of the first six removals and hear his shrieks as the pencil stung the wound and stopped the blood flow. Another three applications of the cruel pencil were needed when she removed the final six needles from his sack, and again she was immensely gratified to hear his shrieks.

Now, it was time to remove the needles from his shaft. She made him hold his penis firmly down against his protruding belly while she removed one needle at a time, prolonging the moment, prolonging his pain, and prolonging her pleasure. Several times he almost let his penis go, but at a sharp word or two from her, he held it in place as she had told him to do. Finally, the last needle was removed from his shaft, with only four mere occasions to use her stinging styptic pencil. Oh well, she thought, four times was better than no times at all, and the best, the wooden chair (which he seemed to have completely forgotten about), was yet to come. She stood to remove the needles from his nipples, and this proved to be a little bloodier than the previous removals. For dramatic effect, she let the blood flow in little rivulets onto his overstuffed belly before taking any action to either clean him up or staunch the flow. This made him scream for her to help him and to stop his torment.

"Wimp," she said aloud in a tone of voice that made him think she was thinking to herself: "What kind of masochist who asks for this treatment would get so alarmed at the sight of a little blood?" She laughed aloud before attending to him. Whatever would he make of the chair? She would soon find out and was looking forward to the experience with sadistic relish. She did give him a few minutes to compose himself while she cleared away the new batch of soiled towels, the little red box of used needles, the alcohol, and the miscellaneous cotton balls she had used.

After The Mistress was through with her little chores, she helped the overweight slave get off the examination table, took the slave by the hand, and then led him to the wooden chair. She positioned him in it carefully, making sure that his scrotum sat fully on the seat of the chair. The look on his face showed some curiosity, but he said nothing, so she said nothing. Her first action was to wrap his wrists to the arms of the chair in black hand towels and to duct tape the towels closed. Then she spread his knees wide and did the same thing to his ankles on the legs of the chair. He looked a little more curious now; this was completely new to him. Next, she took out four pieces of short chain, each with a double clip hook on one end. The Mistress firmly wrapped the chain around each wrist and ankle; she had guesstimated right, they fit perfectly over the towels, with just the tiniest bit of play for comfort, but no possibility of escape. By this time his fear and astonishment was clear on his face, but she had one more piece of apparatus to use on him before she continued.

The red ball gag was on the wall behind her, not under the cloth-covered table to the side of the chair. Gently she placed it in his mouth and not so gently she gave the two leather ends a hard yank to secure it firmly in his mouth before tightly buckling the ends together.

"Listen to me," she said to him in a casual tone of voice as she placed a red bandana in his right hand. "If you have a problem, I want you to drop the bandana immediately. Do you understand me?" He nodded yes.

With a dramatic flourish she just could not resist, The Mistress yanked the cloth off the side table like a magician would uncover the "sword impaled" lady. His eyes flew to the table and opened as wide as saucers. The table held only two objects: a hammer and a long, $1/8$-inch-thick nail in a small bowl of sterilizing solution that had been boiled and whose point she had honed herself. He looked from her to the table and back to her again, but the bandana remained in his hand. Maybe he did not yet understand what she was going to do, but in a minute he would. She hoped like hell he held onto that bandana. She had been looking forward to this for so long!

She picked up the nail first and held it before his unbelieving eyes. She wanted to do this so much, yet she knew this was new to him and had taken a chance by not discussing it with him beforehand. The red bandana remained in his hand, although he was nervously clutching it tightly. Then slowly she picked up the hammer with her other hand. It wasn't a big, old, mean, ugly, man-sized hammer. It was brand new, as was the sterilized nail, small and ladylike; The Mistress wanted nothing that would swing wild because of its weight when she hammered in the nail. Actually she was more afraid of hitting her own fingers and making a fool of herself than of what she was going to do to him!

Still holding the hammer in one hand and the nail in the other, she looked pointedly at his scrotum and then at his face until she was certain he knew what she was going to do. A slight nod of his head told her to go ahead, and his brow broke out in a sweat. Kneeling before him, she pulled his sack midpoint and stretched it out as far as she could. Then she carefully positioned the nail well away from any of the flaky white remains of the styptic pencil. She looked at him again and at the hand that clutched the red bandana. To The Mistress's great joy, consent was in his eyes and the bandana still in his hand. She brought the hammer down six times in rapid succession and drove it through his sack directly into the hard wood of the chair. She could hear him scream from shock from behind the gag, and his chest was heaving as he caught his breath. He looked down at his scrotum and could not take his eyes off it, nailed to the chair as it was. But bless his masochistic heart, he still held on to that bandana.

The Mistress wondered if he realized that what goes in, must come out, and that she would need the hammer's claw to remove it. She let him observe himself for several minutes—long enough to recover from his mild shock and absorb the fact that it didn't hurt nearly as badly as it looked. Helped by the white marks left by the styptic pencil, she had missed every capillary in his sack and, of course, his all-important nuts. As yet there was no bloodshed, just the terrifying nail holding his scrotum to the wooden chair.

After some minutes had gone by, she brought her first aid supplies over to the chair. She made the thumb-across-the-throat sign to mean that it was time to remove the nail. He nodded his head yes, and she showed him the claw end of the hammer. Once again, his eyes became saucerlike as he realized that this was the only way to remove the nail, but what choice had he? It was either to use the claw end for removal or to remain nailed to the chair forever! Hesitantly, with more real fear than he had ever shown before, he nodded his head that he was ready.

The Mistress braced the head of the hammer against the chair and held it there with one hand. She intended to remove the nail quickly and in one smooth motion so that she could immediately staunch any blood flow and release him from his bonds as quickly as possible. Hammer in hand, she looked up at him to see if he was ready. He nodded yes. She had practiced this using two pieces of plywood and had drilled herself in the nail's removal until she could remove it twenty times in a row in one swift motion. Quickly she positioned the claw over the head of the nail, braced the hammerhead against the chair, and pulled. All of her practice had paid off; the nail came out quickly and smoothly in just the one pull.

He did scream then, really scream, but by the way his head lolled on his chest, she knew it was a scream of relief, not one of unbearable pain. Rapidly she washed the double-sided wound in Betadine solution and applied liberal dabs of triple antibacterial ointment to them. Then she gently placed a thick, sterile gauze pad on each wound. As fast as her fingers could fly, she released him from his gentle yet no-nonsense bonds, ankles first, so that he could close his legs if he wished, then freed his wrists. She removed the gag and told him to call her if he needed her. She quietly left the chamber to give him some time alone.

Still in her latex ball gown but minus the double-layered surgical gloves, she was sitting at the dining room table having a relaxing cigarette and a glass of iced tea when he emerged from the chamber fully dressed. She rose, went to him, and looked deeply into his eyes before she showed him out. She saw deep satisfaction there, and then he surprised her by lifting her hand to his lips and kissing it.

The next time he returned, he presented her with two dozen long-stemmed roses.

Shaving Snoozy

The Mistress received a call from a Southern gentleman, visiting her city from his home state of Texas. This gentleman spoke in slow, languid tones about his fetish: a ritualized shaving scenario he wished to enact the next day. His requirements were few: he loved The Mistress to wear latex and wanted the session to take place in a medical examination room but did not want any doctor/nurse overtones. The Mistress was pleased with this scenario because she had the perfect chamber for his fantasy and she did not like playing "nursey." The chamber she had in mind had an en suite bathroom, an antique wheelchair, a steel floor, a gurney, a gynecological table, a doctor's stool, a glass case full of very intimidating looking equipment, and best of all, a fully mirrored ceiling. As they spoke, he was so laid back and so mellow that The Mistress nicknamed him "Snoozy" during their phone conversation. She thought this to be very amusing because his description of himself totally belied the nickname: at six feet three inches tall, 225 pounds, this thirty-six-year-old blond, blue-eyed Texan was a tall drink of water, bearing no resemblance at all to one of the seven dwarfs.

Although he had not asked that The Mistress wear white, she thought that it would be appropriate to the fantasy if at least part of her outfit was white. None of her white latex remotely resembled a nurse's uniform or doctor's lab coat but instead consisted of a catsuit, balls gowns, and white blouses. She chose something she had just received as a gift: a white mock turtleneck blouse that zipped up the front, a red "waspie" waist cincher, and a floor-length black hobble skirt with a double zipper up the back. Wrist length black latex gloves and regular black patent leather pumps completed her outfit but not her look. Being somewhat nearsighted, she pulled her auburn hair back in a French twist to keep it out of her face and wore her tortoise-framed glasses, which she would definitely need for such close-up, delicate work. Wouldn't want any shaving cuts in such a sensitive area, would we?

Snoozy arrived promptly at the appointed time and presented her with a two-pound box of Godiva chocolates. How lovely! So few slaves had such nice manners these days (an air of entitlement was more prevalent than manners or the little niceties), but then, in her opinion, Southern gentlemen learned manners as they were being brought up. Their rude Northern counterparts, who had very few manners at all, wasted a lot of a Mistress's time training them in the manners that should have been ingrained in them from childhood. With a Southern gentleman, The Mistress did not have to spend endless and unnecessary hours teaching him things he should already know. She was pleased with Snoozy already.

She beckoned him to follow her and led him into the medical examination room. She had prepared everything in advance and had a pair of scissors, a pile of big fluffy towels, a number of disposable razors, a twelve-foot piece of rope, and a bar of creamy soap. She never used shaving cream because she was allergic to the smell of it and also because most shaving creams contained camphor that could cause skin irritations, especially in one so fair skinned. Besides, using a bar of soap ensured cleanliness. As they walked down the hall, she was highly aware of, and amused by, the difference in their height and of his gangly, loose-limbed walk compared to her graceful glide. As he entered the room, she gave him a moment to take it all in. After he had surveyed every piece of equipment, she pointed to the mirrored ceiling; the last place anyone ever looked at, if they looked up at all. His big face broke out in an ear-to-ear smile as he realized that he would be able to see everything that was going to happen. Then, she sat on the gurney while she made him perform the ritual strip and inspection, which he seemed to enjoy, although some fetishists did not. But she had to get their clothes off them some way, didn't she? Left to their own devices, well, they were clueless, and as The Mistress it was her right to show her power over them. The ritual strip and inspection did a wonderful job of establishing her authority.

Once Snoozy was stripped and inspected, she made him kneel while she made him repeat these words after her: "I, the fetishist Snoozy, humbly ask The Mistress to denude my genitalia of body hair. I implore her to shave off all the hair on my groin, on my root, on my sack, and up my crack. I leave it to The Mistress to accomplish this in any way she sees fit. Any shaving cuts or worse will be the result of my disobedience, my squirming, or other misbehavior on my part, and I take full responsibility for them before The Mistress begins."

Having said that to her satisfaction, she pointed to two bowls, a large one and a small one, and told him to go into the bathroom and fill them with cool water, not hot water. Hot water could cause shaving bumps on his fair skin, and she did not want the smoothness of it to be marred by them. Sliding gracefully off the gurney, she piled towels underneath where his genitals were to be, pointed to the lower end of the gurney for the placement of the water bowls, and told him to lie down. At least he didn't ask, "Which end do you want my head at, Mistress?" An extremely stupid question asked by many slaves. Once she had told one to put his head near the water bowls and the fool did. But then she had the pleasure of verbally humiliating him, making him get up and bend over for twenty hard smacks on the ass with the heel of her shoe before telling him in insulting detail exactly how to lie on the table. But Snoozy seemed to have brains as well as manners, and he positioned himself correctly over the piled-up towels without knocking over either bowl of water and awaited further instructions.

The Mistress immediately saw what the problem was. Most of the slaves were short and fat, which made them eye pollution, but at least they fit easily on the table. Snoozy was a long-limbed fellow, and even with his head as close to the top end of the table as it could get without hanging off, he barely fit on it. But slender people are more limber than their overweight counterparts, and Snoozy was able to bend his knees far apart and brace his feet on the sides of the table, giving The Mistress plenty of room in which to work. The Mistress let him lie there and look at himself in the ceiling mirrors while she retrieved several surgical gloves and snapped a pair on over her black latex ones. First she began by cutting his hair down to a manageable length to prevent razor drag and make her job easier. After that she dropped the bar of soap into the large bowl of water and then used her cupped hands to pour water over his genitals. Quickly reaching for the soap, she worked up a rich lather on the front of his body and began to slowly shave off his pale reddish-blond hair, dipping the razor frequently into the smaller bowl to rid it of hair and prevent razor drag. The more hair in the razor, the less effective it was.

The Mistress took her time shaving Snoozy, not only because she liked what she was doing, not only because she was a perfectionist, not only because he was so clearly thrilled by it, but because those light reddish-blond hairs were a bitch to see even in the bright light of the medical examination room! She had gotten into a rhythm: stroke, stroke, dip, stroke, stroke, dip. More water, more lather, stroke, stroke, dip, she thought to herself, her hands moving in time to her thoughts like some sort of strange sea chantey. She moved his penis around as necessary to get at every hair on the front of his body, even bending her head to his body level and turning it this way and that to look at him from different angles to make sure not one errant strand had been missed. She could see Snoozy smiling, but she dissembled and kept a straight face, knowing he would see her mirth in the mirrors above. A ritualized shaving scenario was no scenario for sudden outbursts of laughter.

Satisfied that his body was denuded of hair, The Mistress proceeded on to his member and sack. First she mowed down the hair at the base of his shaft with the scissors to make it easier to shave off. Then, much to Snoozy's delight, she blew on the base of his member to whoosh the snipped hairs away, and then she brushed it with her gloved hand to make sure no loose hairs remained. His member was sizable and very hard for all the attention that area of his body was receiving, and as she pushed his member aside to shave the base, it grew harder still. She knew that because of his erect state, having his member pushed aside and held there was not comfortable, but since his erection got even larger, she knew Snoozy was enjoying it. The Mistress picked up a new razor and set to work removing the coarser curlier hairs at the base: again, stroke, stroke, dip, stroke, stroke, dip. She manipulated his member, sometimes holding it down with her arm to keep it out of her way. When she did this, she pressed down on it very hard and was gratified to hear him moan.

Once The Mistress was finished shaving the hair at the base, she pointed out to Snoozy that his member looked at least an inch longer without all that unsightly hair at the base. He thanked her for adding an inch to his length and spread his knees farther apart in gratitude. Then, she cupped her hands and rinsed off his body and base. She used her gloved hands to pluck at these freshly shaven areas to make sure no hairs had been left behind. On finding one, she applied the razor to it, and soon it, too, was gone. But there was still a great deal of hair to be removed from his tight sack, his taint, his inner thighs, and, of course, his crack. Being the most interesting and humiliating part to shave, The Mistress was leaving the crack until last.

Preparing to shave these parts, she used her cupped hands to re-wet the area and generously lathered his taint and inner thighs. The Mistress knew Snoozy enjoyed this immensely because his member began to bob and wobble around of its own will. But this bobbing and wobbling would interfere with her work, so she moved the doctor's stool that she was sitting on to the side of the table so that she was leaning over his body rather than sitting between his legs. Again, she used her arm to hold his member in place and began to shave his sack. After the first stroke, stroke, dip, she found that this task would be more easily accomplished by standing up. This also gave Snoozy a great view of her lovely round ass tightly encased in her hobble skirt. Leaning over him with her head between his legs, The Mistress got to work on his surprisingly hairy and ridged sack.

Usually blonds weren't quite this hairy, and the ridges of his sack made her task more difficult but she did not mind. More fun for her! Falling back into her stroke, stroke, dip rhythm, the careful shaving of his sack had her complete attention.

She stretched his sack out as much as she could, pulling and pushing it if need be and meticulously shaved each hair away until his sack was as hairless as his lower body and his base. Tilting her head to the side, she looked at it from different angles to ensure that his sack was completely denuded. Pleased with her job so far, she cupped his sack in her hands and squeezed it, then used her hands to bat his hard-on around, slapping his member from one hand to the other and using just one hand to give it good hard slaps. Snoozy moaned and groaned and even gave the occasional yelp as she manhandled him, but he stayed erect, a sure sign of his enjoyment. And manhandling him, or anyone, gave The Mistress so much pleasure. But this was a shaving ritual, and Snoozy still had much more hair that would soon find its way into the dipping bowl under her nimble ministrations.

Next, The Mistress turned her attentions to his *taint*. She called it the "taint" because it wasn't his sack and it wasn't his crack but that length of skin in between them. Hence, since it "tain't sack" and it "tain't crack," it became the taint. The taint was a fun part to shave, and its sensitivity varied greatly from person to person. Some were very ticklish there. She was eager to find out how sensitive Snoozy's taint was. Applying more water and lather, she lightly dragged the razor up his taint. To her great delight, he squealed with laughter, but very aware of the sharp instrument between his legs, Snoozy didn't move the lower part of his body at all, although his head thrashed from side to side as he laughed. Ticklish submissives delighted The Mistress, and she took her sweet time shaving his taint just because she could and added a little tickle torture to the scene. But laughter was infectious, and soon she was giggling at Snoozy's litany of "no, stop, please, don't, stop . . . ," knowing that he meant just the opposite. Finally, and a little to The Mistress's chagrin, Snoozy's taint didn't have one single hair left on it for her to shave off and hear more of his laughter.

She rinsed his taint of loose hairs and relathered his inner thighs, preparing them for her razor and full attention. Pushing his left leg as far down as it would go, The Mistress applied her blade and tried to make quick work of ridding Snoozy of the reddish-blond hairs on his inner thighs. But dear Snoozy was quite ticklish there too, more so than on his taint, and denuding him of the hairs there took a bit longer than The Mistress expected. As she shaved this area, she had to hold Snoozy down with her body to keep him in place as he tried to close his leg. But she won out in the end and was able to keep him restrained by her weight and a gentle reminder that a sharp object was very close to things he would rather have uncut. She pointed out that he was *cut* already, and one such cutting should be enough. Finally, she finished the left inner thigh and let Snoozy's laughter subside before giving the same treatment to his right inner thigh. Snoozy's right inner thigh was not as ticklish as the left, so although she still had to restrain him by partially lying on him to keep him down, the right side did proceed at a somewhat faster pace than the left. The Mistress rinsed him well and went on to the next step of her plan.

After that, all that was left to shave was his crack; The Mistress's favorite place to render hairless. She needed Snoozy to have a good spread for this; so taking the twelve-foot piece of rope she had brought into the medical examination room prior to the start of the ritual, she bound him in a way to give her best access to his puckered and delicate anus and crack. Looping the rope under his back and tying it tightly over his chest in a secure square knot, The Mistress then used the two separate ends of the rope to pull his ankles as close to his chest as she could get them. She looped the rope around each ankle twice and tied it off with a double hitch knot. Then she went and stood at the end of the gurney to see if this had the desired effect. It did. Snoozy's cheeks were spread wide, and in his excitement his anus was clenching and unclenching as she looked at him. His eyes were glued to the ceiling mirror, and he seemed unable to look away. Perfect! The Mistress knew his eyes would take in every stroke of the razor and that he would witness his own denudement and humiliation at her hands. And just thinking about the poking and itching stages he would undergo when the hair started to grow back in gave her thrills.

Soaking his crack well, she then worked up a luxurious lather there, on her favorite area, his anus. Taking a new razor, she decided to begin at the outermost reaches of his hair and work her way in toward his anus. She bent in close and began to shave him using many passes of the razor in small areas, stroking and dipping, stroking and dipping, prolonging her pleasure and his humiliation. As she shaved him, the clenching and unclenching of his anus each time the razor touched him amused her. This could be used to her advantage, so she began to stroke and dip with pauses of different lengths between each pass of the razor. This uneven tempo excited him further, and his moans became steadier and steadier until he was moaning continuously. Greatly enjoying this, The Mistress began to vary her stroking and dipping as well: three strokes, a dip, and a short pause; two strokes, a dip, and a long pause; and quickly stroke and dip, stroke, and dip. One long slow drag and then a quick dip was followed by a series of short strokes and a dip.

The Mistress continued in that fashion until all the hair had been shaved off his cheeks, leaving only the lesser amount of hairs right around the pink and puckered ring of his anus. This she would draw out as long as she could by trying to shave off only one or two hairs at a time and lathering him over and over again. She knew this would drive him crazy and kick his endorphins into high gear, increasing the pleasure for both of them. The more he enjoyed it, the more she enjoyed it. The Mistress just hated a slave who was a blob, but Snoozy was no blob. She bent in close and began to breathe through her mouth. She was close enough so that he could feel her hot breath on his anus in contrast to the cold steel of the razor blade. Then she applied the razor for the first time. Although she did not cut him, all of the combined sensations made him cry out to release the pent up feelings inside him. The cry was, as usual, sweet music to her ears, and she sighed in satisfaction.

Then she went back to work: lather, stroke, breathe, dip. His anus was doing a crazy dance of puckering up and pushing out with each action she performed, and its crazy dance began to fascinate her. She wished there were more hairs to shave off, just so she could continue to use her power over him to continue the dance. Much too soon, all of his reddish-blond hairs were gone.

Using the ropes to tip his butt back toward his head, she piled a couple of more towels underneath him. Then The Mistress went into the bathroom and dumped the soap bowl and refilled it with clean warm water. When she returned, she noticed that Snoozy's eyes were still glued to the mirrored ceiling, as if he couldn't get enough of seeing himself in this way. His member still raged, untended, untouched, and virtually unnoticed between his legs. Slowly she tipped the bowl and let the warm water flow over his newly shaved flesh. His skin looked so tender, so pink, so vulnerable without its protective covering of hair, rather like that of a very large, very well developed newborn babe. He sighed and moaned as the water washed over him, rinsing away any strands of hair and any remaining soap. Seeing him there, so vulnerable, so open to her touch, The Mistress couldn't resist removing her gloves and touching him with her bare hand. When Snoozy felt her bare hand on his genitals, and her fingers exploring his crack, tickling his taint and inner thighs, inspecting his sack gently, and finally brushing her hands against his member as she caressed his base, his groaning became a plaintive wail to be released from his bonds and be allowed to come.

The Mistress extricated him from the ropes and gave him a minute to stretch out his long, gangly limbs. She gave him her permission to explore the newly shaved parts of his body while she counted to sixty—he had one minute. His hands busied themselves with his genitalia and spent several seconds of his minute touching his crack and anus. All this while, his hard-on raged between his legs with a mind of its own. He continued to plead and beg for permission to release. She took out a bedpan, a silver kidney-shaped metal bowl, which hospitals used for patients who could not walk to the bathroom, and handed it to him.

"You may come into that bowl, but only if you promise me you will lick up every drop. If you will not lick up every drop, you will not be allowed to release in my presence. What do you wish to do?" The Mistress asked Snoozy.

"I'll come in the bowl, Mistress, and will lick up every drop. I promise, Mistress, I promise, please just let me come," Snoozy pleaded.

"Come, Snoozy, come in the bowl and lick it up. I will watch you as you stroke and make sure you keep your promise," The Mistress said teasingly but in a stern voice.

Snoozy began to stroke, the bowl positioned on his belly to catch his juices. He was so excited that he didn't have to masturbate for very long, and in short order, pearly drops and strands decorated the bowl. The Mistress removed the bowl from his belly and placed it on the floor at her feet. Then she gave Snoozy half a minute to catch his breath and get his legs back underneath him. After that she pointed to the bowl on the floor. Snoozy knew what was expected of him, and he kept his promise, on all fours with hips high in the air, and began to lap up his pearl jam. He grimaced at the first taste of it but determinedly kept lapping it up until every last drop was gone. Then he picked up the bowl as if it was an offering to a Goddess. With arms outstretched and chin on his chest, Snoozy presented it to The Mistress for her inspection. He had gotten every drop; indeed the bowl looked quite clean. The Mistress released him from service by saying, "You have served well and I am pleased. You are now released from my service. You may dress and go."

The Godiva chocolates were as delicious as one would expect and gave The Mistress many nights of pleasure. Each time she ate one, she thought of Snoozy.

PART TWO

Friends

The Boy in Bondage

The chamber was painted a deep, dark blue, as if midnight had long ago entered the room and never left. Thick, soft carpeting, also of the deepest blue, covered the floor and reached halfway up the two long walls. A burgundy leather sofa took up one wall, but he was never allowed to sit on it. Floor-to-ceiling mirrors covered the two uncarpeted parallel walls, gave a good view of the room, and enhanced the feeling of being weightlessly floating in the arms of mother sky. Pinpoint spotlights with bulbs of red, purple, peach, and hot pink provided ambience and illumination, yet kept the room dim and mysterious. Barely discernible in the dim light, soft black ropes littered the floor of the chamber; they hung in a spider web scramble from a thick metal hook firmly imbedded in a beam in the ceiling. The spreader bar was out, and scattered around it were several dildos and vibrators. A long, narrow table, waist high and covered in black leather, was the focal point of the room. On the underside of the table was a series of hooks, and at each corner of the table there was a metal post.

Luke, one of The Mistress's slaves, was lying nude and face up on the table. The Mistress was wearing a clear red-tinted latex dress that showed off her figure as well as the tattoo on her lower back. Seeing her tattoo was a rare treat; she had deliberately placed it where no one could see it unless she chose to display it. On her feet she wore what she called her "Cinderella shoes" made of acrylic, the platform and heel were see-through as were the sandal straps that held them on her feet. They made her look barefoot but as if she were walking on her toes, and she knew they gave her a ladylike air. Opera gloves of transparent latex covered her hands and encased her arms. She was medium tall and slim, with a surprisingly voluptuous bust. Her dark auburn hair was loose and thick and shiny. He could smell the fragrance of it as she moved around him, readying the chamber for her ultimate pleasure. When the room met her requirements, she came and stood at the head of the table and looked down at him. The Mistress wanted to see his face when she showed him the spreader bar in her gloved hands, with its attached ankle cuffs. Satisfied with the glimmer of fear she saw there, she buckled the leather ankle cuffs, taking care to pull them tight.

She trailed her fingers up his leg to his groin, then up his belly, and up his smooth hairless chest. Pausing, she gave in to the urge to rough handle him. Smiling, she let her fingers pinch his nipples, pull them, roll them, but most of all squeeze them between her thumb and index finger. She squeezed them slowly, building up the intensity of the pinches envisioning that there was no skin, nothing, between her fingertips. This was always her intention when she performed this torture, and she loved to do it. She watched his contorted face carefully; nipple torture was not one of his turn-ons. He did it to please her so she didn't do it as hard or as long as she would have liked, but she did do it—she did it just to assert her authority over him. Besides, she enjoyed it and this was about her, too, which most *slaves* seemed to forget. But he understood his position in her world, and so he withstood the nipple torture uncomplainingly, with only the faintest groan of pain escaping his lips.

She released his beleaguered nipples and moved away from the table to gather up some ropes. When he turned his head slightly, he could use the mirror to spy on her actions. As she bent over the ropes, a lock of red hair kept falling in her face, blocking her vision. With one hand, she impatiently pushed it behind her ear. The other hand held tightly to the sleek black ropes she was about to thread around him.

"Hands over your head," she ordered him sweetly. He obeyed. "That's a good boy."

Her grip was surprisingly strong as she attached each wrist to its corner post, her bondage tight. No chance he could break free, even if he wanted to. His legs were spread and attached to the bar, his hands bound to the posts; he was unable to move anything but his head.

But she was not through with him. Next she crisscrossed the ropes back and forth over his chest, and she looped them through the hooks on the underside of the table. His whole torso was woven with ropes, which she had pulled tight. She threaded her rope through the eye hook in the spreader bar, then through the eye hook imbedded in the ceiling over his head. Taking the rope in both hands, she pulled hard and then pulled again. She hoisted his bound, spread ankles up to the vicinity of his shoulders and secured the rope. She stepped back to look at him, her toy, her handiwork. Now he was hers, immobilized, with every part of him exposed and helpless. She loved to see him this way. His cock was rock hard and she could see it throbbing. She slapped it a few times, then administered quick slaps to his balls, enjoying herself immensely and spurred on by each of his moans.

She walked over to her staging area and selected an item he could not see. She turned and approached him, a bright red ball gag in her hand.

"No, mistress, please," he said, feigning distress, "please don't gag me."

"Luke, do you remember your safe signal?" The Mistress said in her velvet growl of a voice. Then she placed a large set of keys in his hand.

"Yes, Mistress," he said, "I am to jingle the keys."

"That's correct. Now open your mouth."

She inserted the red ball gag and strapped it to his head. Now he had only his eyes to plead with and his safe signal to stop her. She stepped away from him, as she usually did, before she began to play with him. She used this time to impress his helplessness on him and allow him to reflect upon it. Sometimes she spoke to him, other times not. When she did speak, it was to describe to him how he looked to her, how the ropes, leather cuffs, and spreader bar made him appear. She called it "dressing him in her finery." Sometimes she would tell him how humiliated he must be to be spread and helpless before her. Occasionally she would tell him in loving detail what she had planned for him that evening.

But tonight she was silent as she sat on the sofa and smoked her cigarette. Somehow, she managed to make her utter silence more humiliating to him than if she had spoken. Her cool disregard of him, the languid way she puffed her cigarette and pumped her leg back and forth in its crystal shoe, told him she didn't spare a thought, or a care, for him. Bound to the table, his nipples still tingling with pain, with the spreader bar holding his legs apart, he was left there to contemplate his fate. Just a toy, he thought to himself, that's all I am to her, just another toy. And when I no longer please her, she will discard me with no thought at all. When she walked over to her collection, cigarette still in her hand, his eyes followed her. She carefully selected a dildo to use on him. She turned to him and smiled—the dildo dangling from her gloved hand. Then she ground out her cigarette in a crystal ashtray and walked toward him. Standing very close to his face, she made sure he got a good look at the dildo, which she called "Big Blackie." It deserved its name. He whimpered in the back of his throat but could not turn his head away or tear his eyes from it.

He watched her slender, latex-clad form walk to the far end of the table to which he was bound. She settled herself on a high stool between his legs. All he could see of her was the top of her head, even when he lifted his head up and craned his neck. He heard the unmistakable snap of surgical gloves being put on over her latex opera gloves. He moaned behind his gag when he heard the top being snapped off the tube of lubricant. When her lubricated finger entered his anus, he tried to call out but his gag prevented him. The finger only stayed there a minute, to be replaced by something small and cold and slippery. She had filled up a syringelike tube with lubricant and was inserting it into his rectal passage. He felt the cold gel turning to warm liquid in his rectum and tried to clench his cheeks. A sharp slap on each buttock made it clear that no clenching was allowed. He relaxed as per her physical command; he knew it would be easier, and so much more pleasurable, her way.

The finger entered him again. It stroked him, this finger, and probed him and stretched him just a little. Then another finger joined it. At first they were playful, gentle fingers, but then these fingers began to stroke him harder, probe him more deeply, and stretch him more. Her third finger entered him, twisting and turning, stretching him more and more; his chest heaved with excitement and the act of turning pain and humiliation into such delicious pleasure. He was humiliated and fascinated and excited by the mental picture he presented to himself: tied to a table with his ankles spread, legs hoisted up to his shoulders, cock hard, anus exposed, and a woman torturing his rectum with her fingers and hand. His hard-on throbbed; his cock engorged with blood tortured him further. Her fingers were relentless in their quest to stretch him, probe him, and humiliate him. He conquered the desire to scream and fought the desire to come. He was happy she had gagged him.

The Mistress stood up and smiled at him from between his legs. It was a wicked smile, an icy smile, and his heart pounded in his chest. She stepped out from the end of the table and allowed him to see that she was holding the dildo over her pudendum and stroking it just like a man would stroke his cock. Taking a large dollop of lubricant, she slowly and pointedly rubbed it up and down the dildo, smiling at him the whole time. He knew she was going to rape him. She resumed her position at the end of the table, still smiling. He felt the cold, slippery tip of the dildo touch his tender anal opening, and he let out a gasp. She used the opportunity to push into him with the head of her cock. He strained at the ropes for a second then relaxed, resigned to his fate. She pushed into him a little farther, and then withdrew the two inches she had given him. She immediately stroked into him, giving him more than two inches. He knew this game. She would enter him repeatedly, giving him a little more each time, until he could take the whole dildo.

Over and over, she entered him, and reduced him little by little to a mindless thing hanging limply from the end of her cock. When he was totally quiescent, she took her time and stroked into him like her dildo was a real cock. She fucked his ass the way a man would fuck a pussy, going hard and deep, then soft and shallow, or making circles inside of him with her cock. She stroked him every way she could remember a man ever having stroked her an eternity ago. She varied her strokes, their rhythm and their depth, wishing she could really come inside of him with her fake cock. She rocked into him and watched his cock grow harder with each stroke and felt all his resistance finally melt away. She was very pleased that he was one of the few male creatures she knew that could maintain an erection during anal penetration. Excited by this, her hands gripped his thighs and pulled them to her as she sexed him. She pumped him and pumped him until his opening was loose and her thigh muscles ached from the effort of pounding into him.

The Mistress pulled out of him, vacating him slowly, leaving him feeling empty after her invasion of him. She let the dildo drop to the floor before she flung herself onto the sofa and assumed a languid pose. Then she just looked at him for a little while, which humiliated and stimulated him further. He didn't know what she had in mind for him and her face was unreadable as she reached for her cigarettes.

After taking a long deep drag, she said to him, "I want a little entertainment for my efforts on your behalf. Release yourself in front of me."

Wisps of smoke eddied and whirled around her face as she spoke. Then she got up and untied one of his hands. He was deeply humiliated at handling himself in front of her, but a slave has no choice but to obey. Obediently, he wrapped his hand around the base of his cock and began to stroke himself slowly. He tried to forget that she was watching him but he could not. He felt her eyes on him, hot as coals, and it spurred him on. She made him wait for her permission.

"Please, mistress, may I? May I come? Please, mistress?" he begged.

"No, no, you may not," she said laughingly, through a haze of smoke.

She loved to hear him beg for it almost as much as she loved to see the pearly ropes of his desire splashed across his belly and chest at her command.

"Please, Mistress, please, my Goddess, I adore you. Please may I come?" Luke was breathing heavily and practically gasped out the words.

The Mistress let him go on in this vein for several more minutes, prolonging his torture and her enjoyment. Finally, she relented.

"You may come, slave."

"Thank you, Mistress, thank you."

His words and face were contorted with the effort of thanking his mistress and obeying her command at the same time. When she was satisfied with the quantity and quality of his pearl juice, she untied him, bid him to rejoin her in the living room, and then she left the chamber. It was his job to restore the room to its original order. As he worked at cleaning up after their play, he thought about her and what she had just done to him. His thoughts thrilled him, and he had to pause more than once to get a grip on himself. When he was finished performing his chores, he dressed to go. According to The Mistress's instructions, he entered the living room where she awaited him. He got to his knees in the position of the universal homage for mistresses everywhere and kissed her foot.

The Mistress escorted Luke to the door, and he heard her bolt the door behind him. The sound carried an air of finality to it, but Luke knew that was just an illusion. He would be back; he knew it, felt it in his body and soul. Luke had known The Mistress a long time, and he also knew that she enjoyed having him as one of her toys.

Caught in the Act

Music wafted through the crack of her bedroom door, a crack just big enough for him to see through. He pressed his eye up against it eagerly and scanned the room. She was in the corner by the chair; her dark red hair was up on top of her head, and she was wearing a sheer, sexy robe. Her high-heeled mules with the marabou fur on the toes slapped against her heels as she walked to the dresser. Opening one of the top drawers, she rooted through it and finally took out a pair of long black stockings, a white cotton bra, and a tiny white panty girdle. She twirled on her toes in time to the music, floating and twirling her lingerie like a dancer would use her ribbon. She stopped in front of the boudoir chair and dropped into it in a fake swoon, her arm thrown back over her face. She giggled and smiled and sighed, very unaware that she was being watched.

The unsuspected spy was delighted by this unconscious, uninhibited, feminine display he was witnessing. He was enchanted with this beautiful woman-child, the child-woman he met so many years ago and began to call "Mistress." What was it now? Fifteen years? She was still his beautiful Goddess, always young in his eyes, always desirable to him. Her smile still lit up the room and had, indeed, grown brighter over the years. He had never regretted being her slave and had never strayed from her or even thought of it. She was a dream-life partner, his friend, his playmate, his seductive tormentor; she was the "stuff" all of his dreams were made of, and with her help and understanding, they had played out all his dreams together.

He heard a noise from the room and stopped his woolgathering. She rose with the beginning of the next song. She untied her robe, and to his utter disappointment, she turned her back to the door before letting it fall open. Had she seen him? No, she would have done something by now if she had. She dropped the bra and hose on the bed, shook out the tight white panty girdle, and then checked the garters. Bending, she stepped into it and pulled the girdle up to her knees. Then she worked it up over her creamy thighs by rocking from knee to knee, easing up first one tender thigh, then the other. When the girdle was just below her buttocks, she dropped her robe. His breath caught audibly in his throat at the sight of her graceful back, but again she didn't seem to hear him. She gripped the girdle firmly in both hands and, doing a little wiggle dance, tugged it up over her buttocks and then past her hips, to settle it firmly and finally around her waist.

Turning slightly, not enough for him to see any more than the outline of her breast, she picked up her bra and hooked it around her waist. The pointy cups of her bra sitting brazenly atop her buttocks made him smile. Suddenly the cups began to move toward her belly, jerking along like someone was pulling on a clothesline. She deftly looped her arms into the straps and with the assistance of her hands, positioned the bra over her unseen breasts. She turned and faced the bed, toward the eye peering through the cracked door. He drew back lest she see him. But she just picked up one silky, sheer black stocking and began rolling it up in her hands. She swayed to the music as her nimble fingers did their work. Sliding one foot out of her mule, she pointed her toe and placed her foot on the bed. She bent down and slipped the stocking over her foot, unrolling it as she went up over her high arch and dainty ankle and then up her shapely calf.

When she reached her knee, she slid her foot back into her mule. With her toe pointed, she gently pulled the stocking up her leg to her outer thigh and hooked it in the little metal garter hanging from the girdle. The inner thigh and garter received the same treatment. Removing her other mule, she again pointed her toe but sought the bed's assistance, and the second stocking was treated as tenderly as the first. From his position in the hall, she looked to be in a picture frame, with only a small part of the bedroom visible and she being the focus of the picture. When she was finished with the last garter and her foot was back in her mule, she started to dance. Small unconscious movements at first, then larger more thoughtful ones as the music took her.

She danced alone to a faster song, whirling and gyrating, shaking loose a few tendrils of her hair, her mules slapping with each step. When a slow song came on, she swayed her way over to their "toy" closet and removed his favorite whip, "The Prague," named after the enchanting city where he had bought it for her. He almost laughed aloud at the memory of the look on the vendor's face as she tested it on the nearest tree. It was black and single lashed. Definitely quite wicked to behold and even more wicked when it bit into his flesh. He shivered in delight, his eyes full of her and his dreams. She cracked the whip to emphasize the music as she swirled around her room, a dreamy look on her face. He wondered what she was thinking and imagined that she was thinking about using that same whip on him later. Mesmerized by her and by his thoughts, he lost his balance and his forehead banged against the door frame. He fell over onto his butt and yelped in surprise. He was caught!

She strode to the door, flung it open, and glared down at him but not at all surprised to find him there. Around her mouth played a small wicked smile. "Spying on me? You know what happens to spies, don't you?" she asked like the Wicked Witch of the West.

With that, she grabbed him by the ear, hauled him to his feet, and pulled him into her bedroom. Roughly she stripped him of his clothes, throwing them around the room in her frenzy to get them off him. She grabbed his ear again and dragged him over to the dresser, and there she withdrew four stockings from a drawer. Still using his ear as a towline, she tugged him along to the four-poster bed. Pushing him facedown, she secured his wrists to the posts at the top of the bed with two of the stockings. Then she stepped away from him so suddenly he felt a small draft. She cracked the whip in the air and left no doubt in his mind as to what his punishment was going to be. She let it fly, and the next thing he felt was the beautiful whip bite into his ass. With only ten lashes of the Prague, she had reduced him to a screaming child, begging to be let off from his punishment.

Releasing him quickly from his wrist bonds, she ordered him to lie down faceup on the bed. His ass on fire and covered with welts, he did as he was told without question. Quickly she grabbed his near wrist and looped a stocking around it. She neatly secured it and then tied the other end to the bedpost, musing aloud about how "that wasn't all he was in for," how he was "going to really get it," and how she was going to "give it to him."

She climbed over him in a flurry of shapely bare arms, white cotton, and long slim legs in black silk stockings. In no time at all, his free wrist was no longer free. And in short order, his ankles were restrained in the same simple yet effective way. She straddled him and smiled playfully. Arching her hands into claws, her red nails glinting, she threatened, "I'll get you, my pretty little boy," and followed it with a fake cackle. Then she fell upon him, her long nails tickling him under his arms. Although his ass was a world of pain, he roared with laughter and squirmed to get away, but he didn't fight very hard. She dismounted and knelt next to him, letting her nails travel his body looking for ticklish spots.

Each time she found one, she would dwell on it lovingly, torturing him with his own laughter and helplessness against her onslaught. She tickled him softly, just running the very tips of her nails or pads of her fingers over his skin. She tickled him hard, digging in to a sensitive spot with mischievous relish. She tickled him and tickled him and tickled him, until tears ran down his face and his sides ached from the strain of laughing. And still she tickled him. Her fingers relentlessly sought out and persecuted his soft spots, and exploited them fully. To his humiliation, he was greatly aroused. He begged and pleaded with her to stop; he even cried "uncle, uncle," through his gasps and hiccups, but she ignored him.

She tickled him until he lay sobbing and gasping on her bed, his wrists and ankles still bound by her stockings to the bed frame. His cock was rock hard, throbbing; a tiny droplet of his juice escaped his glans and glistened on his tip. He was ready and she knew it. She went into the bathroom and emerged with a cup in her hand. Handing the cup to him, she said, "I want you to masturbate into this cup. I want you to keep masturbating and coming into this cup until you can come no more." That said, she reached over and untied both of his hands. He reached down and gripped his cock firmly in his right hand; in his left, he held the cup. To his delight and surprise, her right hand closed on his and pumped along with him in rhythm to his strokes.

In his mind, he relived the exquisite agony of her nails and hands on him, and his helplessness against the bonds of her delicate stockings. His first and second ejaculations happened one right after the other. The third took a little longer under her watchful eyes but slowly, surely, he was obeying her command to fill the cup. He lost count of the number of times he came for her but he came and came and came into the cup until he could come no more. Exhausted from his efforts, he smiled up at her and, with a trembling hand, offered her the cup filled with his semen.

"Thirsty, sweetheart?" she asked him; the kindness in her voice belied by the wicked twinkle in her eyes.

"Yes, dear, I could use a drink."

Wordlessly, she handed him the cup, the same cup he had just filled with his own juices. He took it from her slowly, uncertainty wrinkling his features.

"Drink!" she ordered him, "drink!"

He brought the cup to his lips and tilted it. His thick jism, pearlescent even against the whiteness of the cup, made its slow progress toward his open lips. The first drops passed his lips and then flowed into his mouth. He really didn't like this salty unpleasant taste, but the warm and loving look on her face was all he needed to spur him on. He ignored the taste, thick and viscous on his tongue, but totally his own, and kept on drinking to please her. Finally, the cup was empty and, like a dog, he used his tongue to lap up the final drops.

When he was finished, she untied his legs and growled, "Get up. Get out. And don't let me catch you spying on me again. I know many ways to punish a nosy man."

Getting up from her bed, he turned and fled down the hall into the bathroom. Much to his surprise, her final words to him had aroused him once again. He grabbed a towel then grabbed his cock and began to masturbate. The way she emphasized the words *catch* and *punish* when she kicked him out of the bedroom played in his head like a broken record, exciting him further. He began to grind his hips against the towel until the urge to keep doing so was uncontrollable. He thrust and ground, and ground and thrust, until he felt his juice soak the towel. He groaned in relief and humiliation at what he had just done and hid the come-soaked towel in the bottom of the hamper.

Cuffs and Stuff

The Mistress was very pleased. One of her favorite toys, the handsome, well-built Viggo, was coming over to be her toy for the evening. The prettier the toy, the more she enjoyed playing with it, and Viggo was all a Mistress could ask for. He was six feet tall, about two hundred well-defined pounds, with chiseled features except for big mushy lips, long sandy brown hair, and hazel eyes that took on the color of whatever he was wearing and were mist gray when he was nude; he was quite a desirable toy and playmate. He was also a polite and obedient masochist who understood his inferior position but was not servile or obsequious. Her plan for him tonight was an active one, so she chose a short, zip-up-the-front black latex minidress and black patent leather platform boots with thick heels that allowed her more freedom of movement. She left her long, straight auburn hair loose but tousled and applied very dark eye makeup and deep red lipstick. Her long nails were lacquered red.

As soon as Viggo arrived, she led him into her chamber, sat on her throne, and gestured to him to perform the ritual strip for inspection. The Mistress and Viggo had played together often enough that words were not necessary between them for the opening of the scene. As he stripped, she couldn't help but admire his body and his handsome face. But she kept her feelings hidden, keeping her mystery intact, and maintaining her Mistress persona. When he bent over and spread his cheeks for her inspection, instead of blowing on his anus, she quickly tapped her finger on it twice. Although she knew Viggo was surprised by this break from protocol, he maintained his position until she commanded him to let go of his cheeks, stand up straight, arms behind his neck, elbows out, and complete his turn. When he was facing her, she rose and ran her hands all over him, feeling his muscles, running her nails down his back, pinching his nipples, and hefting his genitals in her hand. She announced that she accepted him for service. She always did. Then she pulled out a pair of handcuffs from the small bureau next to her throne. She stood behind him, handcuffs at the ready.

"Do you like that sound?" The Mistress asked, knowing very well that Viggo did. "Can you hear the lovely metallic jingling that excites you so much? Nothing else sounds like a pair of genuine police-issue handcuffs, you know. And don't you agree that the little clicking noise each notch on them makes as they close around your wrists and restrain you with such an air of finality is so arousing and causes feelings of utter surrender? Of course, you agree. If you didn't, you wouldn't be here! That's why I am closing them ever so slowly around your wrists. And since your hands are behind you and I am standing in front of you, I know the closeness of my body to yours excites you. Standing in front of you enables me to look into your eyes. Each little click is reflected in them, and I can see the intensity of your submission. I so enjoy adjusting the cuffs to the perfect tightness—you know—just tight enough so that your hands cannot squeeze out of them but just loose enough so that I can slip one of my fingers in there to touch you and soothe you as you struggle and labor underneath the cool stainless steel. I especially like to hook my fingers under the cuffs when you are attached to my headboard and I am sitting on you . . . , but that's not what I have planned for tonight, poor Viggo. Tonight you will suffer for me."

Sometimes The Mistress enjoyed talking to him while she set him up, both psychologically and physically. This was one of those talkative nights, at least for now. Although Viggo's hands were securely cuffed behind his back, The Mistress had more in mind for him. She had taken the time to braid red rope into a halter/vest combination for him so she could attach it to his handcuffs. She ran the rope around just the back of his neck, over his shoulders, down underneath each armpit and used the remaining rope to encircle his back and upper chest. By doing it this way, the rope wouldn't choke him, but the whole array was securely anchored and was tight enough to make indentations in his skin, especially around the skin of his underarms. The Mistress enjoyed knowing that she had marked him slightly and that he would sport small reddish-blue lines for a day or two. She had also left a knotted loop at the back of his neck and she knew him well enough to know that he was very curious as to its purpose.

The Mistress could see that Viggo was becoming uneasily excited as he grasped the fact that he was naked and already partially restrained, and that she had completely disabled his upper body. She took another smaller length of rope and slipped it through the loop at the back of his neck and then down his back to catch the chains between the handcuffs. His arms were bent at the elbows and The Mistress tightened the new piece of rope vertically from his handcuffs to the loop at the back of his neck. As she did this, he struggled to deal with the ever-increasing pressure on his shoulders and upper arms that resulted from such an awkward position.

"Get on your knees, slave. I'm going to test your endurance tonight, my dear Viggo, simply for my entertainment and amusement. It has been too long since you have suffered for me, and I am afraid that you are getting spoiled. Now, tell me how much you love it when I test you. Tell me how you long to be the object of my amusement. Not that I don't know these things already. I just like to hear them frequently. And I would strongly recommend that you compliment me and offer me words of worship and devotion now because I have many more things in mind to do with you tonight, slave Viggo. And very soon, my dear, you will be unable to form any words at all with that lovely, mushy-lipped mouth of yours."

Without being sycophantic, Viggo uttered eloquent words of adoration, paying The Mistress one sincere compliment after another. He called her the Incarnation of the Goddess on earth, a true Superior Female, the one and only one who he thought about and who could satisfy his needs, and how he was hers to use as she pleased. He paid her compliments on her hair and her latex, and said many other things he knew she liked to hear. With each word, she felt more empowered; with each word, she felt his power flow out of him and into her. As a small reward for his praise, she grabbed his head and smashed it into the crotch area of her latex. But Viggo never took advantage or opportuned; he kept his head still in her hands, didn't try to rub his face against her, or do rude things with his lips. After a brief moment, The Mistress let his head go, and he immediately returned to his original position without being told.

"What I want you to do now, slave Viggo, is to lie on your side on the floor. Since your arms are bent up at such an angle behind your back, you will have to be very careful when lowering yourself to the floor."

But the clever and agile Viggo had no trouble complying with this request. First, he bent his body over onto his knees. Then he used his head to brace himself as he went into his roll and extended his outer leg as he did so. Done! The Mistress was pleased by his grace and the thought that went into obeying her; many slaves would have just flopped over and probably would have hurt themselves in the process. But not Viggo. She thanked the Goddess for the night they had met at a mutual friend's house party and had clicked right away. Toys like Viggo were rare, very rare indeed, and she intended to keep him.

"That was very well done, Viggo, very graceful. Now turn your face upward, toward the ceiling," The Mistress said graciously. Then she stood over his face, one foot in its black shoe on each side of his head.

"Now, slave Viggo, I command you to look straight up my lovely legs and under my dress as I stand above you. Then I want you to tell me what you see."

Viggo did as he was commanded. Starting with her boots, his eyes slowly took in each of them, then progressed to her cute round knees, and finally to her shapely yet strong thighs. Then his eyes looked up her dress and flew open wide in pleasure and surprise. The sight made him forget about the discomfiture of the handcuffs and ropes, and he moaned with raw, naked desire.

"Mistress, you are shaven!" Viggo exclaimed.

"That's right, slave! Again I have broken with protocol and I am freshly shaven. And of course I didn't do it myself! This perfect job was done just this afternoon by my succulent little female body slave. I hope you didn't think that I would allow you such a pleasure, did you? I should hardly think so." The Mistress said that last sentence with asperity. Then she went on, "Just to torture you some more, I am going to bend my knees just a little and give you a closer look." She did as she said she would and saw Viggo's eyes glaze over. Good! That meant that he was getting further and further into the head space she wanted him in. "So close and yet so far," she teased him, bending her knees just a few inches more.

Much to her surprise, Viggo did something that he had never done before and that she certainly never expected him to do. He stuck his tongue out and began to wiggle it back and forth, as if he was giving her head!

"Put that disgusting tongue of yours back in your mouth! How dare you treat me with such disrespect! There is no way you can reach my secret garden from down there and your piggly-wiggly tongue flapping back and forth is making me sick, sick, and angry!" The Mistress looked very stern and forbidding as she said this, and Viggo had the grace and good sense to obey her immediately and look ashamed.

But The Mistress often had lightning changes of moods, and she had one now. She bent her knees until the bottom of her dress was almost touching Viggo's face. Then she lowered her voice to a coo to tease and torment him. "My pretty pink lips are almost close enough for you to smell my fragrant aroma, aren't they? This is what I call 'sniffing distance.' You'd do anything, endure anything, to worship your Mistress between her legs, wouldn't you? So tell me, do you like what you see? I want to hear you tell me!"

Viggo groaned with desire and began to speak his thoughts out loud. He told her how luscious her pink lips looked, lips that he had only rarely seen when she rode him and how he longed to taste them. He described to her how sweet she would taste, of how he longed to swallow her delicious juices, and of how his tongue would search out her pleasure button and press it over and over again to please her. Although The Mistress was greatly enjoying his words of desire, she abruptly stepped away from him and gave him a medium-hard kick in his butt. She still had many games she wanted to play with Viggo tonight, and there would be more time for compliments and adoration later on.

She addressed him in a casual tone, as if his words meant nothing to her, "Not tonight, slave, and maybe never. But you can always dream! Just think about the two or three times that I rode you for my pleasure. And tonight you have yet to prove yourself worthy. I have other games in mind to play with you. Tell me, are your shoulders and arms aching from the cuffs I have pulled up your back by the rope? Of course they are! That was the point. But look at you! You poor thing, you. You are so tightly restrained and so very vulnerable that I could take advantage of you right here, right now, in any way I pleased if it pleased me to do so."

He began to plead and moan and squirm around on the floor as much as the cuffs and rope would allow. The anticipation of what she would do to him next, combined with his erotic discomfort, was having an extremely arousing effect upon him—and with each word she said, with each action she performed on him, he felt more and more powerless. His begging became constant, almost mindless as he lay there helplessly awaiting her pleasure.

"Don't beg! It is so unbecoming, and it makes me want to kick you." The Mistress did give him one little warning kick in the stomach. "You know, I like the idea of marking my territory, staking my claim, so to speak. I just so happen to have this short, thick, and ugly butt plug here to do just that. Stop that wiggling! I know what you are trying to do. You are trying to rub that thing of yours (his hard-on was impressive) between your thighs. You know you are not allowed to do that without permission and here you are doing it anyway! I am afraid that you have just incurred a serious punishment, slave. Instead of gentle insertion, you will take the plug all in one push. But I will still allow you the lube."

The Mistress gave the ugly, fat plug a quick smear of lubrication and without any further preliminaries or the least bit of concern for his comfort, she bent down, rolled him onto his stomach, spread his cheeks, and very quickly reamed the plug into Viggo's tight, puckered opening. His shout of pain, even though she had felt him push down to make entry easier, didn't bother her in the least. Then she wanted to be sure the mean little thing did not slip out so she decided to crupper it into him. For the crupper she needed more red rope, and besides, she loved the sensuous feel of rope in her hands. And Viggo was very familiar with the fact that The Mistress was very proficient in its use.

She got a piece of rope long enough for the crupper and went to work. She doubled the rope, looped it around his waist twice, and then pulled the two strands down the front of his body. She carefully placed one strand on either side of his sack and then pulled the two strands tightly up the crack of his ass. As The Mistress did this, she made sure that she positioned the ropes directly over the flanged base of the butt plug. Then she looped the two strands of rope under and then over the rope at his waist and did the same action in reverse. First, tightly down his crack and over the base of the butt plug; then she used the two strands in the middle of his sack to separate his nuts; and finally, she pulled the remaining rope up the front of his body and used a double hitch knot to tie them to the ropes at Viggo's waist. This secured the butt plug quite firmly into his anus, had the added advantage of separating his balls, and was very pleasing to her eye. Viggo looked good in red rope; that was why she always used the red on him. She had even cut it into the proper lengths, especially to his size.

"Oh, yes! Yes! What a nice package you make," The Mistress exclaimed. "I just love that gorgeous butt of yours where I have so securely staked my claim. Now, my dear bound and plugged Viggo, you must bend your knees for the next step."

With a rough push with the toe of her boot, The Mistress made sure that his face was completely smashed into the rug. More rope! She wanted more rope! She took her time looping and knotting the rope around his ankles in the classic ankle restraint. She took the strands of rope remaining from the ankle restraint and pulled his bent knees back toward his thighs. There was plenty of rope left to anchor it to the crupper at Viggo's waist so she proceeded to do this with her usual gusto and efficiency. Then she found she still had more rope to use for the greatest effect. She pulled the two strands up to the cuff-and-rope arrangement she had first performed on Viggo's wrists and tied the remaining rope to that. It was not the way to do the classic hog-tie, but it was very creative, very neatly done. The result caused The Mistress to be very pleased with the outcome and with herself.

Viggo began to moan from the strain of the uncomfortable position he was in: his arms and shoulders were aching, his nuts were separated, the crupper was tight around his waist, his puckered opening was throbbing and aching from the butt plug, and his poor ignored cock, his beautiful member, was unnoticed and smashed into the floor underneath him. But The Mistress knew Viggo well enough to know that these moans were still moans of pleasurable pain, and as a good masochist, he would be able to relax into his restraints, get himself further into his head space, and turn his pain into soaring pleasure. And Viggo knew The Mistress well enough not to expect any mercy.

"I don't think you will be going anywhere at any time soon, my little tied-and-plugged Viggo," The Mistress said, her voice dripping with sweet sarcasm. "I can see the physical strain in your shoulders and arms. I find your distress to be quite arousing and very entertaining. And I hope you have not forgotten that I promised you that you *would* have something in your mouth later. But I doubt very much that you and I are thinking of the same thing!"

Having said that, she stepped away for a split second and returned with a bright red ball gag. "Open wide," she ordered him in a coaxing tone of voice, as if speaking to a child. When Viggo opened his mouth, The Mistress inserted the ball gag and quickly buckled it to his head. "That's a good boy," she said. "You wanted something in your mouth, and see how much I care for you? I have granted your desire. It holds your mouth open very wide, doesn't it? You look so very vulnerable, so very helpless wearing all those ropes and the cuffs. And I love the plug up your ass! But you will have to endure that tightness all over your body for just a bit longer while I go take a nice, hot, relaxing bubble bath. I have worked up quite a sweat tending to you. Here, take this in your hand."

She placed a brass bell in his hand; he knew what it was for: he was to ring it if he got into trouble or became distressed while she was in the bath. But the bathroom was en suite so she would not be far away.

"And after my bath, I will be sure to put my boots back on so that later when I release you, remove your gag, and unplug you, you will have something to clean and worship. You can put that piggly-wiggly tongue of yours to use then. If you do a very good job on my boots and show me the proper respect and devotion, I may allow you to masturbate in front of me for my entertainment. I will probably soak for about an hour. If you had been a good boy, you would have been allowed to bathe me but . . . such is life! And Viggo, while I am gone, try not to drool on my carpet."

The Mistress turned on her heel and went into the bathroom, leaving the door open about three inches. Viggo could see into the bathroom from where he was on the floor and knew she had left the door open on purpose. Maybe so she could hear him if he rang the bell, or maybe because she just wanted to tease him some more. She sat on the end of the tub and started the water running, pouring a generous amount of bubble bath under the faucet. Then she sat on the end of the tub and removed her boots. Standing and turning her back to the door, she unzipped her dress and let it fall to the floor. Viggo groaned with lust from behind the gag. Even from the back she was lovely, and he had never seen her tattoo before. On the rare occasions she had ridden him, she had always faced him and kept her clothes on.

After testing the water with one pointed toe, she gracefully climbed into the tub and relaxed into the foamy bubbles. His eyes glued to the slightly ajar door to keep him aroused, Viggo settled down to await her return.

Dinner, a Movie, and Then Some

I just love ropes! Ropes are such very sensuous restraints. Just the nature of rope makes it a more intricate and personal restraint than leather and so much more intimate than the vanilla world could ever imagine. The time and care taken in the placement of the strands and knots, as well as the close contact of the skin to the rope make this a deeply bonding experience in many ways. Soft yet sexy silk and nylon ropes of a slender diameter are my preference for an activity that I enjoy greatly: male genital bondage. I was introduced to it by a well-versed male switch, someone who understood what the male wanted in this aspect; hence, he literally knew "the ropes." Did I ever have fun learning this aspect, which I was able to practice repeatedly on him until I became as proficient at it as he. And did he ever enjoy being the object of such personalized and ardent attention! I find genital bondage intensely exciting and satisfying. With all the male organs bound tightly together and pulled forward, there is just something infinitely vulnerable and submissive about this aspect.

Before we went to dinner tonight, I tied a simple red ribbon onto the base of his rod as a symbol of my domination over him. Because of this ribbon, all throughout dinner he was not only slightly uncomfortable but extremely aware of my dominion over him. Occasionally I asked him how the ribbon felt and was very pleased to see the red blush creep up his neck to his face! After dinner he was compelled to request my permission to remove the ribbon just long enough to make a necessary trip to the men's room. I granted him this permission because I understand that relieving a biological need such as that is one of everyone's inalienable rights as a human being, but sternly admonished him that as my property he was not to play with himself. When he returned to the table, I asked him for his wallet and then signaled the waiter for the check. Out of long habit, the waiter handed the check to my male "companion."

"Give it to me," I said, "he isn't allowed to have any money."

Again I was rewarded by seeing that blush of shame and embarrassment creep up his neck to his face, but he bore it well. It wasn't the first time I had played this little game with him. Adding on a generous tip, we left the restaurant for the parking garage. The minute we were back in the car, I demanded that his organs be put in real bondage; this time it was much more intricate than just the short length of red ribbon he had worn during dinner. I commanded that he fully expose himself to me right there in the parking garage so that I could once again claim that which was mine. I produced a much longer length of red ribbon from my purse. This time, after tightly securing the ribbon around his genital sack and the base of his cock, I left about a three-foot strand that I ran from his crotch, under his briefs, and out of the waistband of his pants. Then I tucked the remaining ribbon discretely into his pants pocket.

Our plans for the evening included a movie after dinner, a recent release we both wanted to see: *Gladiator* starring Russell Crowe. I find sex and violence to be closely related for both of us, and the movie itself was a beautifully filmed costume action drama, with wonderfully realized special effects. The combination of implied sex and actual violence had the desired effect on him, and all during the movie I delighted in reaching into his pocket and tugging on the ribbon. Sometimes I gave it a quick hard tug, other times I tugged slowly to build up the pressure and sensation, and yet at other times, I pulled it gently just to remind him of my control over him. Even though my fingers never touched his crotch, the ribbon acted just like a hand gripping his most sensitive and aroused genitals. I knew that he felt totally owned by me and secure in having my attention.

After the movie, before we undertook the drive home, I once again asked him to expose himself to me in the parking lot. His fear of being seen in the less private lot showed in his face, but being the good slave that he was, he obeyed me. Once he was exposed, I rerouted the ribbon up through his shirt and out through his shirtsleeve. Then I tied the end of it onto the band of his wristwatch. Except during hard turns, this was fairly comfortable as he drove, but as soon as he exited the car, it was obvious that the little bit of slack was taken up by his height. He was compelled to walk somewhat stooped over, with his arm and shoulder sloped down crookedly so that he did not yank off his family jewels. This amused me greatly, and he pleased me very much with this little display of devotion and compliance to my will.

When we got home, I removed the ribbon and gave his sack and rod a gentle slapping through his pants. Then I commanded him to strip for my inspection. I love to inspect him. He finds it so humiliating, so enjoyable. I know just what buttons of his to press, and when I inspect him, I always make certain that his skin is not nicked or irritated before proceeding with more cock-and-ball bondage. I decided that I would enjoy seeing him tied spread-eagle, hand and foot, to the cleverly concealed bondage bed in my living room. To the casual observer, it looks just like a double bed futon that matches the rest of the décor in my living room! But we know better, don't we? The thought of seeing him tied hand and foot, spread wide for my pleasure and use, turns me on. The sight of his fingers clutching the ropes on his wrists, straining at them as I work my tender and not-so-tender ministrations on him is exciting to me. I also enjoy pulling his legs as far apart as they will go, stretching them down with ropes at his ankles, and securely anchoring them to the futon bondage bed.

I like to leave shallow red indentations on his skin with my bondage so that he is marked but only for a very short time. I like seeing my marks on him. So tonight I put him in the spread-eagle position, naked and completely unable to escape. I know his thoughts are about my unrelenting bondage, his complete helplessness, and his total inability to stop any activity I may have in mind for him. I also know that he greatly desires the guiltlessness of the bondage experience and the mind-freeing and mind-blowing effect it has. Because he enjoys this so much and because I want him to see everything that I am going to do to him, I almost never blindfold him. I enjoy seeing the expressions that pass across his face as I work my rope magic. Seeing these expressions is most enjoyable for me and gives me further insight into his deepest fears and desires.

But tonight he will not be able to see very much at all. My plan is to block his vision effectively and to indulge myself and reward him at the same time, with a little face sitting while I attach my final bonds to his genitals. He has but a moment to glance up between my slender yet muscular thighs when I throw a leg over his head and settle myself down on his mouth. I know that he is disappointed that I am wearing plain cotton underpants, but this is still a reward for him, and he does not dare beg me to take them off. As if I would, just because he wanted me to! As I sat, I took special care not to squeeze his head with my legs, and instead I balanced myself by putting my knees on each of his shoulders. Such divine imprisonment!

Upon seeing that he has started to swell and thicken, I lean forward and work quickly to trap the blood inside his cock. Using a length of thin rope that I bought especially for cock-and-ball bondage, I make a double loop of it and capture his sack tightly. Spreading the strands, I separate one ball from the other and tie them apart. Then, after tying this package off at the root of his rod, I use the remaining length to crisscross around his cock, making a single knot and pulling it tightly, then repeating the process so that the last loop and knot are directly under the flared ridge of his swollen purple head. I know he can feel the pressure in that supersensitive area. After I have finished, there is still two feet of rope left, which I use as "riding reins." I wrap them tightly around my hands, just like real reins, and settle in for a good ride. I really enjoy myself and get more and more turned on as he moans into my panties.

He knows his job and I trained him in how I like to be serviced, even if it is through my panties. I start to make small circular motions with my hips, making the most of his tongue as it frantically tries to locate my button through the cotton panties. At this point I sit up straight and begin to press my knees into the sides of his neck. The grinding of my hips becomes more urgent and, almost forgetting about him, I begin to pleasure myself seriously. He is intensely aware of the ropes that I have graced his cock and balls with and that I have pulled quite taut in my own efforts at pleasure. As I begin to combine my hip grinding with a slight bouncing up and down on his face, he becomes aware that I have actually begun to pull on the ropes as if they were the reins of a horse as I ride his face. I can feel that he is struggling to catch his breath as I press down on his face, but I am not worried. Plenty of air can still get in there and still allow him to perform well. My panties became moist long ago, and my moistness urged him on to greater efforts. I know he wants to feel my sticky ooze soak my panties so that he can try to suck it off them.

My eyes are closed as I revel in the pleasure of using him, of taking him with no concern for his needs, only for my own. But then I open them briefly and see that his swollen and aching organ is hugely engorged, and he is responding to each firm tug of my reins. Clear drops of preejaculation make me laugh in wicked delight at his arousal. I am on the brink of coming, and we both know that I could enhance my pleasure by forcing him to release. I lean forward at a 90-degree angle, take just the head of his cock into my hand, and begin to stroke it the way I have seen him stroke himself. I use my square-filed nails to scrape oh so gently across the tip of his fat and swollen head. I can hear his muffled groans from between my legs, and I command him to continue with his service, which in his own pleasure and excitement he seemed to have forgotten about. He obeys me, and my grinding becomes more energetic as he uses his tongue, lips, and teeth to service me the way I like best. My panties are soaked, and I can hear and feel him suck at them to drink up my juices.

As I stroke him, my hands feel the thin ropes I have tied him up with, and this excites me further. The combination of his spread-eagle position, the ropes I have used to control him, and the weight of my body on top of him adding to the restraint of the ropes almost makes me come—but I hold back. All I want him to know is the relentless tugging of the reins I hold in one hand and my other hand gripping his cock. I want to drain every drop out of him, and I want him to lap up every last drop of my juices. He pulses and throbs, and as I feel his juices beginning to course through his rod, I pull my hand away. I love to see the pearly ropes of his jism decorate his belly. I am pleased with the quantity of it and the glistening pattern it leaves on his belly. After he has come, I ride his face to my own spasming end and feel him suck ravenously at my nectar through my cotton panties. Drained, I collapse onto his chest, and we both rest awhile before I have the strength to get up and remove his restraints.

After he cleaned himself off, I escorted him to the door and thanked him for a most pleasurable evening. He dropped to his knees and kissed my feet in adoration, knowing that there will be more exotic pleasures to come.

Drink Your Milk, Dear

One year when I was in my twenties, I took a rare week-long beach vacation with my family. After all, who at that age wants to vacation with their parents? But I went mainly because two other couples who were family friends were going, too, the Sansones and, in particular, the Penzas. The Penzas had a son named Alex who was a couple of years older than I. Alex and I had known each other since elementary school, and when the families visited, the two of us often played together. As we got older, Alex and I began to flirt, but as the families moved or drifted apart and I saw Alex less and less, it never went any further than that. So I hadn't seen him in years, and I was extremely interested in seeing what kind of man he was today. As a boy, Alex had been very handsome, with thick and wavy medium brown hair, the most amazing twinkling sky blue eyes, a strong face, and the budding body of a football player. But all things change with time, and in the river of change, a handsome boy or young man could well have turned into an ugly man. Was this the case with Alex? Or had he just grown more fully from the handsome boy he was into the handsome man I hoped he had become?

I drove to the beach in my own car because if tensions arose, it would be my escape vehicle. I also wore a pretty summer dress, not only for giving me comfort while driving, but for allowing me to be at least presentable when I got there. Arriving at the rented house, I saw it was a lovely old Victorian with a spacious wraparound porch, which the owners had decorated with a hanging swing, white wicker furniture, and old-fashioned oil lanterns. As I pulled into the driveway and followed it around to the back of the house, my attention was immediately drawn to the "fancy." A fancy is a large shed, the 8 × 10 or larger variety, that has been decorated inside and out to make it into a little house. I don't know why they were called fancies; I like to think it was because they were fanciful creations that expressed the child's desire for a little retreat from the parental world.

This one was particularly charming. Electricity had been run to the fancy so it could be used at night. Patio blocks led to two steps up to a front deck decorated with flowering potted plants. On either side of the door was a window. The door was unlocked, so I went inside. The walls were draped with pale lavender fabric that also acted as window coverings. A deeper lavender carpet covered the floor and on top of that was a matching area rug in the Aubusson style. The sofa and chair were upholstered in a white floral pattern, which complemented the purples in the room. There was a small glass coffee table in front of the sofa and a side table next to the chair. A small bookcase held not only books but framed pictures, unusual knick-knacks, and a stereo system. One corner had a Lilliputian kitchen that had a small dormitory-type refrigerator with a small microwave on top of it, and on a shelf above them, there was a small stack of neatly arranged plates, bowls, and the like. In another corner, the floor was tiled, and on it stood a coal-burning stove with its hod of coals and fireplace accoutrements right next to it so that the fancy could still be used on cool nights. I was enchanted by it and knew I would spend many hours there.

It was midafternoon and I was the last to arrive. Enough of the fancy; now it was time to go inside and greet the assembled families. Of course, seeing Alex again was foremost in my mind. I entered by the back door and made my way toward the living room where the sounds of laughter could be heard. As I walked through the arched doorway, someone spotted me and called, "Look who's here!" Immediately ten people rushed me and hugged and kissed me in that extravagant and somewhat abandoned way of many Italian families. Over the heads of the huggers and kissers, I could see Alex smiling at me from a few steps behind the rest of them. Time had been more than kind to Alex; he had grown into a very handsome, well-built man and his eyes were still that twinkling sky blue I remembered. Our eyes met and immediately we began to flirt. But we weren't kids anymore; we were both in our twenties and could do as we pleased. And I thought it would please me very much to play with Alex.

At dinner, Alex and I sat next to each other, and as the other conversations became more animated, assisted by the plentiful and inevitable bottles of wine, we had the chance to speak quietly together. He had done very well for himself: He owned five successful gyms, had a large house with an in-ground swimming pool in the spacious backyard, and drove an expensive sports car. He was twice divorced, but had no kids, and was on excellent terms with his ex-wives. Of course, this wasn't stated as a dry recitation of facts, there was much eye contact, many pauses for intimate little touches on the hand, and once or twice our thighs brushed each other's under the table. I told him I was an author and, of course, he asked what kind of books I wrote. Although I could feel his raw sexuality and see his attraction to me in his lovely blue eyes, I still decided it would be best to tread carefully here. I went into my "cute" routine.

I leaned in close to his ear and whispered, "I write romantic sex manuals." I followed this statement by a low giggle.

"Romantic sex manuals? On what? What do you mean by romantic sex manuals? Aren't they all romantic?" I could see the interest in his eyes and hear it in his voice.

"Well no, not really. Many of them relate in dull terms sex techniques without considering the emotional factors involved in sex. Mine are different, very different," I said in a tone that invited further questions.

"Well, tell me about them. How are they different?" Alex asked, obviously intrigued.

"My books are about alternate love styles," I said, once again inviting more questions.

"Alternate love styles? What do you mean by that? Tell me more," he said, prompting me in an almost conspiratorial whisper.

"Well, an alternate love style is as different from regular sex as night is different from day. My books are about romantic BDSM," I said somewhat coyly.

"You mean like bondage and stuff?" Alex said in a low voice, his blue eyes wide with interest.

"Yes, exactly. I write about the psychological implications of tying someone up, as well as instructing and illustrating how to tie them up. That—and things like role-playing, cross-dressing, corporal punishment, you know, anything that falls out of the category of what is commonly called 'straight sex.'"

I sat back in my chair casually, but all the while I was carefully observing his reaction. It was positive, very positive. He was thinking about what I said, rolling it around in his mind like one tests wine by rolling it around in one's mouth. Except, unlike the wine taster, I knew Alex wasn't going to spit this information out. I had engaged his sexual curiosity. Good! Maybe it wouldn't be such a dull week.

The assembly sat late over dinner, drinking more wine as the dessert and fruit was served. My bags were still in the car and Alex offered to carry them in for me. Of course, I accepted and accompanied him to the yard to unlock the car so that he could retrieve them from the trunk. How nice! A handsome, virile man carrying my bags for me: This was off to a good start indeed. Upstairs, where the bedrooms were, we found that one of the women had put little cards on the doors to signify which room was whose. Mine was a charming little room for one at the end of the hallway with a double bed, wardrobe closet, vanity and stool, a cheval glass, and a bedside table with a lamp. There was an overhead light for brighter illumination, and best of all the room had one window facing south, toward the yard with its charming fancy, and the other facing west so that the morning sun would not wake me too early. I have always been a late sleeper and enjoy lounging in bed for an hour or so before I get up. Alex's room was just across the hall and one door down from mine. How convenient!

Alex placed my bags in my room and turned and smiled at me. I returned his smile and before I could say "thank you," he had crossed the room in two steps and had me in his arms. He angled his head to kiss me and I leaned in to encourage his kiss. Our lips met and sparks flew. He was a very talented kisser, and his strong arms around me exerted just the right amount of pressure to hold me tightly without crushing me. We broke apart like guilty children when we heard footfalls in the hallway, and Alex went to his own room. Now my curiosity was in overdrive, but I had no desire to train this gorgeous hunk of male to be my slave. I doubted very much he would agree to being made into a submissive, but I knew there would be other things I could do with him that he would greatly enjoy. As I lay in my comfortable bed, I stayed up very late thinking by the light of one of the candles I had dug out of my bags of just what kind of kinky fun Alex would enjoy. (I always had items special to me in my bags: my favorite teas, candles, CDs, whatever.) Several ideas had crossed my mind, so I blew out the candle and slept on them, knowing that in the morning, the perfect one would present itself to me.

I woke up a little earlier than usual, most likely because of the excitement of playing with Alex. During the night I had dreamed of a scenario that would be very erotic, very exciting, extremely unusual, and very likely to excite Alex as well. The scenario had elements of submission to it, but it in no way would seem as if I was trying to train Alex as my slave. Wearing only my bathrobe, I padded barefoot down the hall to one of the bathrooms, and did my morning ablutions. I saw no one but smelled bacon frying and heard voices rising up from the kitchen as well as the rattle of frying pans. Breakfast was being served.

After dressing in a thin-strapped, long, flowing summer dress with a high slit, I slipped my feet into my favorite pair of flat-heeled, but very sexy, strappy summer sandals. I applied light, natural-looking makeup and let my long auburn hair flow free. I checked myself in the mirror and, pleased with what I saw, I headed downstairs to the kitchen.

The men were still there but were soon to be on their way out for an eighteen-hole game of golf. They would be gone most of the day. Great! All of the women were busy cooking, clearing plates, squeezing and straining fresh oranges, making coffee, putting a kettle on the stove for tea, and other homey chores. Their chatter and laughter filled the air as they went about their work; this was not work for them, it was just their regular morning routine enhanced and made more enjoyable by the presence of old friends and many hands to share the tasks. They were talking about packing a picnic basket to take to the beach, where they intended to spend the afternoon enjoying the beautiful sunny weather on chaise lounges and under umbrellas. Besides the parental men and women, Alex's younger brother, Ray, was there, as were the Sansones' two kids, who were in their midteens. Soon the three of them were going off to find a volleyball game they could join. But most important, to me anyway, Alex was there. His handsome face split into a smile when he saw me, and he hurried to pull out a chair for me and push me in. Then, laughing, he took a large napkin, shook it out, and placed it in my lap.

"And what will the madam be having for breakfast this morning?" Alex inquired, like a waiter taking my order.

I smiled and said concisely but politely, just as if I was speaking to a real waiter, that I would like two eggs over medium, a side of bacon, home fries, lightly toasted white bread, orange juice, and a pot of Ceylon Breakfast tea. Before he could say they didn't have that tea, I handed Alex the tea bag I had stashed in my bra, with the intention of drawing his notice to my lovely breasts. Of course, this little ploy worked, and his eyes twinkled at this briefest of glimpses. As I spoke, Alex pretended to write my "order" on his hand, then he bowed ceremoniously, and told his mother what I wanted. I was highly entertained by this little game he had invented for my pleasure and amusement, so naturally I played along with it. All the better to set you up later, my dear, I thought to myself like the big bad wolf hiding in grandma's clothes.

Like a good waiter, Alex brought me my orange juice and a pot of tea, as well as cutlery, while my breakfast was being cooked. I chugged down the cold, delicious, fresh orange juice in two big gulps and handed the hovering Alex the empty glass. He understood that the *madam* wanted a refill, and in a snap another full glass was placed in front of me. Then his mother called him to say my breakfast was ready. He returned with the platter in one hand and the smaller dish with my toast up the same arm, waiter style. He served me to the right, which is the proper way, and arranged the dishes in front of me.

"Is everything to the madam's satisfaction?" he inquired solicitously.

By this time, everyone in the kitchen had become aware of his "service" to me and were all greatly amused by it. When he asked that last question, they all started laughing and shaking their heads as if to say "kids!"

"Yes, thank you, it seems to be just fine," I replied.

Then I patted the seat next to me, inviting him to sit down and join me. He got himself a huge glass of milk, and I remembered that Alex was always a big milk drinker. In his younger days, he even drank milk with barbequed ribs and cheeseburgers. Inside, I jumped for joy. His love of milk would greatly enhance my plan. He sat beside me in comfortable silence drinking his milk while I dug into my breakfast. In between bites, we conversed casually about this and that: places we had traveled to, life in the separate cities we lived in—nothing at all out of the ordinary and nothing we wouldn't want the parental units and the teenagers to hear. When I had finished eating, Alex arose and resumed his role as the waiter.

"Was everything to the madam's satisfaction?" he asked, as he removed the dishes from the left side. I nodded and said yes. "May I get the madam anything else?" I thanked him and said no.

Then he efficiently cleared the plates away, smartly leaving the pot of unfinished tea behind. Brawn, brain, a sense of humor, and manners! How very delightful! When he was through putting the plates in the dishwasher, he returned to sit next to me and asked me if I had any plans for the day. I said I hadn't really thought about it; the smell of bacon had lured me to the kitchen as surely as a cobra is lured out of its basket by the sound of a pipe. After catching the aroma of the frying bacon, my thoughts had gone no further than "bacon, I smell bacon" and down to the kitchen I went. He laughed at that; then he said that he had no plans for the day and asked me if we could spend it together. I paused for a moment, just to keep him in suspense, before saying that I would enjoy that. I mentioned my interest in the fancy, and at his puzzled look, told him what a fancy was. Then I casually said that with everyone gone for the day, we would have the whole place to ourselves. By the pleasantly surprised look on his face, I knew he liked the idea of hanging out in the fancy and even better, that the entire property would "belong" to us.

We retired to the living room where I could smoke while everyone else packed up and cleared out. Alex watched me intently as I puffed away; could he have a smoking fetish? I called it correctly because halfway through the cigarette he told me that he found a woman who smoked fascinating. So I turned myself into the Smoking Diva for his benefit, and to keep him interested, I smoked more cigarettes in the time it took for everyone to vacate the house than I normally would, using all the moves I knew to keep him intrigued. I handed him the lighter so he could light my cigarette, I showed him how to hold the lighter so I didn't have to bend into it and possibly set my hair on fire, I held the cigarette in puckered lips right in the middle of my mouth, I blew smoke rings, I let the ash grow very long without dropping it, and I exhaled like Puff the Magic Dragon as we spoke. He couldn't keep his eyes off me. After a short eternity, everyone left the house.

"Let's get everything we need and take it out to the fancy all at once so that we don't have to keep coming back inside," I said. He immediately agreed. "You go into the kitchen and pack up a cooler with a pitcher of ice tea, a lemon and a knife, whatever you want to drink (I knew it would be milk), and some fruit and cheese and crackers while I go upstairs and get some things out of my bag. We'll meet back in the kitchen." Then we darted off in our separate directions to get our *supplies*.

I had more in mind than just getting the CDs, the candles, the massage oil, a fresh pack of clove cigarettes, and a crystal ashtray. I also wanted to change into a different type of dress—a dress I had brought just in case a situation like this arose, a situation I intended to turn into a scenario. It was a very conservative pinafore dress, in black, under which I wore a white blouse. I also had girlish Mary Janes with me, just like the ones I wore when Alex and I were elementary school kids playing together. Although I wore panties, I did not wear a bra. A bra would spoil the effect of how I wanted to appear and the memories I wanted to evoke. I put all of my things into a little satchel and went down to the kitchen to meet Alex, who had already accomplished all his tasks, cooler at the ready, and was eagerly awaiting my arrival.

His eyes flew open in surprise when he saw my new outfit. It obviously turned him on and definitely aroused his curiosity. I could smell his pheromones, and although I was excited, too, I acted as if nothing was different. I led the way out the backdoor to the fancy, following the patio blocks, climbing the two steps, crossing the deck, and waiting to one side for Alex to put the cooler down and open the door. He followed me inside, and without any instruction, he emptied the contents of the cooler into the little refrigerator. While he did that, I filled the CD player with five discs, turned it on and adjusted the volume, placed the candles strategically and lit them, put the ashtray, the massage oil, and my sexy black clove cigarettes on the coffee table, and opened the windows but closed the door so that no one could see inside. Then I reclined on the sofa and lit a cigarette while he finished stowing the things from the cooler into the refrigerator.

When he was done, he came over to me, but since I was taking up the whole sofa, he had no place to sit except across the room in the chair. Clearly Alex did not want to be that far away from me. So I lifted my feet and motioned to him with the hand holding the cigarette that he could sit there. As soon as he had seated himself, I put my feet in his lap. He smiled at me when he sat down and looked at my footwear.

"I remember these," he said. "You wore them all the time when we were in elementary school."

"Yes," I said, "and now they make them for big girls." Then I took a long drag on my cigarette and blew the smoke out in one long leisurely exhalation.

Alex's fascination with me increased; I could feel the electricity in the room, and I must admit that not all of it was coming from Alex. But we pretended that nothing was happening as we spoke, and he casually ran his hands over my shoes and around my ankles. Then I suggested he take my shoes off, saying my feet were getting very hot. He deftly undid the buckles and slipped off each shoe, carefully placing them on the floor next to the sofa. I wiggled my toes and made a sound of relief when my feet, which were, by the way, getting hot, were released from my shoes. He placed my feet back in his lap and began to trail his fingers gently over them. I let him continue this while we spoke some more; then I suggested that he use the massage oil and give me a real foot massage. I asked if he knew how to give one.

"Of course!" he answered with a little asperity, "I get massages at my gyms all the time. Getting one is the best way to learn how to give one." He was certainly right about that.

I told him I liked firm massages, and after pouring some of the massage oil in his hands and rubbing them together, he began to work on my feet with his big strong hands. His technique was wonderful. He did each toe separately, paid close attention to the fleshy parts of my sole by using his knuckles up and down the center of my foot, rubbed the slightly calloused ball of my foot more firmly, and, in general, did a wonderful and relaxing job on my foot. Which, astonishingly enough, he was able to repeat in the same order on the other foot so that I was not left feeling lopsided. As the finale, he gently decreased the pressure, as if he was bringing me down from some high (which he was), and finished off by gently trailing his fingers over my feet, one foot for each hand. By the time he was done, I had thrown my arm back over my head, my eyes were closed, and I know I had a dreamy look on my face.

"That was wonderful," I said from somewhere out in space. "Almost as good as sex. I could go for a cigarette."

We both laughed at the little remark/joke about the cigarette: back in the days when smoking was common, everyone who smoked had a cigarette after sex. It was part of the ritual. Alex leaned forward, took out a cigarette and lit it before handing it to me. What a nice touch, especially since Alex himself had never smoked. I took the cigarette, loving the smell of the clove and lolling back against the arm of the sofa, ate Alex up with my eyes. He had his eyes closed, his head resting against the back of the sofa, and his fingertips were still lazily running over my feet. Dear Goddess, I thought. I could spend three days like this! Then the thought struck me that I really could spend three days like this; we were going to be here for an entire week!

After a while we broke out of our trance, and Alex asked if he could get me an iced tea. Of course he could. He made short work of cutting up the lemon, put a slit in the circular piece of citrus, and hung it decoratively on the side of the glass. He served me my tea before he poured himself a nice tall glass of milk and, for good measure, brought a small plate of cut-up fruit as well. Cherries, squares of cantaloupe, kiwi slices, rounded triangles of peaches, blueberries—very tempting indeed—and temptation is one of the things I simply cannot resist! I sat up and moved onto the cushion next to his. I dangled a cherry from its stem in front of his mouth and when he reached his mouth for it, I moved the sweet fruit up higher. Soon his head was tilted back with the cherry dangling over his mouth. I dunked it into his open mouth and he quickly caught it, leaving me with just the stem in my hand. Then I took a cherry, and after eating it, I put the stem in my mouth and tied it in a knot. I told him to hold out his open hand and deposited the knotted stem into it. He was more than impressed with the deftness of my tongue, and we both almost spilt our sides laughing.

Our hunger and thirsts satisfied, I put my legs back on the sofa and nestled up against his muscular chest; then, he put his strong arm around my shoulder. The fancy had already become our own little world, our secret hideaway, and our place for trysts and assignations, and nothing or no one was going to intrude on it, even if I had to bar the door. Alex and I began to kiss, and I realized that the brief though passionate kiss we had shared last night was nothing, zip, zilch, nada, compared with his skill during prolonged kissing. This man could make me come just from kissing, and I abandoned myself to him. Just because I had a plan for him didn't mean I couldn't enjoy myself in the interim instead of always being the one in tight control of the situation. And that was exactly what this was—a situation and a very pleasurable one at that, not a Mistress/slave scenario.

Time passed very quickly in our fancy. Much too soon we heard voices and cars, and not wanting to let anyone know that we had made this place our own, we quickly blew out the candles and turned off the music. Leaving the unconsumed food in the fridge, we hightailed it out of there before anyone came looking for us.

After dinner that night, everyone stayed up quite late, and it was well after two before people started to head for bed. After the noise from the other bedrooms had died down, Alex crept across the short hallway and quickly entered my room, closing the door behind him just as fast. Kneeling at the side of my bed, he gave me a very long, very passionate good-night kiss that made my thighs creamy.

"Tomorrow, in the fancy?" he asked me.

"Of course," I said. "Where else?" Then he left the room as quickly as he had come in.

The next day, much to everyone's amusement, Alex once again acted as my waiter at breakfast. Some of the daddies gibed him saying things like "you're going to spoil her, Alex," and "if you don't watch your step, you'll be her slave," and other silly things. The mommies had to get their two cents in, too, but their remarks were quite different: "Go for it, Claudia, he comes pretrained," referring to his previous marriages, and "There's a good man you found for yourself, girl." Obviously I found these remarks to be funnier than anyone else did, and as for Alex, he just smiled and waved his hand at them in a humorously dismissive way. But after everyone had gone off to Atlantic City for the afternoon, I asked Alex to wait for me in the kitchen.

Knowing this to be the day I was going to put my plan into action, I had gone down to breakfast in a loose dress and casual open-backed shoes. Of course I did not intend to stay in this rather drab garb, but I didn't want the teenagers and parental units to see what I was going to wear later on. After they had gone, I bolted up the stairs two at a time to quickly and properly dress for the occasion. Unlike yesterday, when I wished to evoke childhood memories and bring Alex up to my present-day womanhood, today I wished to be all woman and a tease too.

I chose a sassy and kind of slutty red, low-backed halter dress that clung tightly to my breasts. The dress was so short it barely covered my derriere when I walked, and I had on no underwear. High-heeled red strappy sandals crisscrossed my feet and showed off my high instep and perfectly shaped toes. Again, I chose natural-looking makeup except for bloodred lipstick that matched the dress. Unlike my unladylike bolt up the stairs, I descended them slowly so that the waiting Alex could hear the click of my high heels on the wooden staircase.

As I entered the kitchen Alex rose from his chair and looked me up and down appreciatively. Pretending I didn't notice, I said that the fancy probably needed to be restocked with milk and breezed by him and out the door into the yard. Alex caught up to me, a fresh quart of milk in his hand, and opened the door to the fancy. Today he had already turned on the music, lit the candles, and opened the windows. He must have done that while I was changing. He closed the fancy's door while I sat in the middle of the sofa, my legs crossed to show them off and make the short skirt of the red dress climb even higher up my thighs. I imagine that it looked like I was wearing a somewhat longish blouse rather than a short dress.

When everything was as we liked it, Alex sat next to me on the sofa, right where I wanted him—next to the armrests. He offered me a cigarette, and as I smoked it, I lay back across his lap, my head on the armrest so that I could look at his handsome face. He played with the smoke rings I blew, sticking his finger through them and blowing on them to disperse them. He inhaled my secondhand smoke, lips to lips like mouth-to-mouth resuscitation, and liked the sweetness of the clove cigarettes. When he gave me a quick but passionate kiss on the lips, he remarked that my lips tasted sweet like the clove cigarette. So I took another drag and invited him to kiss me again. With this kiss, he made sure all the sweetness from the cloves was gone from my lips before he ended the kiss. Since kissing had changed my position in his lap and on the sofa, just the quickest glance down showed to Alex I wasn't wearing anything under the skimpy red dress. I made no motion to cover myself and he made no uninvited advances. Alex was not the grabby and gropey type most women, including myself, disliked. Instead, we lay there comfortably, listening for almost an hour to the sexy and dreamy CDs I had brought along, and I couldn't have cared less if he looked his fill. I wanted him to look.

"Alex," I said softly, "be a dear and get us something to drink."

He helped me into an upright position so that he could get out from under me and get up. I returned to my lounging position, letting him look at me as much as he wanted while he made my iced tea first and brought it to me, then returning to the refrigerator for his milk. But when he reached for a glass to put it in, I stopped him.

"Show me the plates," I said.

His puzzlement at this request was plain on his face, but being the polite and sexually adventurous person that he was, he held up one plate at a time for my inspection. The fifth plate, an old-fashioned, heavy white one with a large lip encircling it, was the one that best suited my purposes.

"Bring the milk and the plate here, Alex," I said seductively, pointing to the table.

Curiosity, sexual curiosity, replaced the look of puzzlement, and Alex hurried back to the sofa with the milk and the plate and put them both on the table. Without getting up from the sofa, I carefully positioned the plate in one of the outside corners of the table and poured the milk into it.

"What drinks milk from saucers and plates, Alex?" I asked him in a throaty whisper. "Don't pussies drink their milk that way?"

Swinging my legs off the sofa and standing, I walked around the table the long way and motioned that he should come and sit on the floor in front of the plate. Then I straddled the plate, lifted my dress, and sat down in the plate of milk. Alex groaned loudly, his eyes glued to my dark pink nether lips in the plate of snow white milk. I pulled him to his knees and started to kiss him, and my passion rose quickly to meet his. He engulfed me in his arms like my labia were engulfed by the milk and went from being the kissee to the kisser. Then I came to know the true adeptness of his kisses. I experienced a wracking orgasm right into the plate of milk. Alex recognized that I had come; he gently broke the kiss, and held me slightly away from him so he could look at my face. My whole body was slack and my head lolled a bit to one side, a dreamy, spent look on my face.

Picking me up in his strong arms, he laid me down on the sofa. My labia still dripped with milk and my own juices. "Eat me," I whispered. "Lick me clean of the milk."

Alex climbed onto the sofa between my legs, and taking one leg in each hand, parted my thighs. Starting with the milk that still ran down my legs, he gently started to lick my thighs clean before making his agonizingly slow, teasing way to my nether lips. When his tongue first touched me there, I had another orgasm. He plunged his tongue into me to lap up my pearly milk; then he began a long deliciously slow process of licking me clean all over.

After I was limp from coming, I managed to gasp out, "You can drink the milk in the plate, too, if you like."

He set himself to licking the plate dry, lapping up the pearly juices that were mixed in the milk. Feeling lazy yet utterly delighted at the success of my plan so far, I was planning another, more intense encounter in my head.

The next day, to my great disappointment, it rained. And since everyone knows that there is absolutely nothing to do at the beach when it rains, everyone stayed home. Wishing to keep our secret place *our* secret, Alex and I didn't even try to slip away to the fancy. Instead, when a variety of board games and a deck of cards were produced, we sat down with the others and joined in. Ray, Alex's brother, and the two Sansone teenagers played Monopoly in the living room while we adults sat at the large kitchen table and played poker by a rotating dealer's call: five-card draw, five-card stud, seven-card stud, whatever. Alex and I sat next to each other so we could play footsie and touch each other's thighs, which distracted us so much we lost many hands that we should have won. Although the other adults seemed entertained playing cards and drinking wine, for us the day dragged on endlessly. Trapped!

We played cards until dinnertime, and since most of the group had been drinking wine all day and then had more wine with dinner, dinner was somewhat raucous, and we sat over the dinner table until almost midnight. Fortunately, the collective parents were so drunk that when they went to bed, they fell asleep as soon as their heads hit their pillows. Someone down the hall was snoring so loudly that if a burglar had decided to break in, no one would have heard him.

I lay in my candlelit room and waited to hear Alex's soft footfall in the hall and the old wooden floor creak in that one spot. He must have crept the short distance across the hall on catlike feet and avoided the creaky board entirely because he was suddenly in my room and kneeling next to my bed as if he had come through the keyhole like a vampire in a puff of smoke.

"I smell cloves," he said in the teasing tone of voice one would use with a child when playing hide and seek.

Then he cradled me in his arms and began to kiss me. The passion of his kiss reflected the torture he felt from not being able to have our tryst in the secret purple world of the fancy. We kissed for a long time knowing from the increasingly raucous snores coming from down the hallway that we would have as much privacy as we wanted. We kissed and cuddled and kissed and cuddled until we had teased each so much neither of us could stand it anymore.

"Let's watch each other come," I whispered in his ear and patted the bed.

He eagerly climbed into the empty space beside me and helped me untangle myself from the blankets. He had an enormous hard-on, and I was already wet from his kisses. His strong hand encircled his cock right in the middle, and as he stroked himself, his hand moved up and down over the head as well. My clit was so large and I was so ready that I had to waste some time avoiding my button so I wouldn't come as soon as I touched it. I played with his nipples with my free hand and was delighted when they proved to be very sensitive and aroused him even more. Just a minute or two after that, I saw his stroke change and knew that he was on the verge.

"Are you ready too?" His voice was a hoarse whisper.

"Yes, very ready," I said passionately.

He stroked harder and faster, and as soon as I saw the first drops of pearl jam spurt from his cock, I touched my button and had a smashing orgasm, my face crushed into his chest. Ropes of pearl jam decorated his belly, and my thighs were so creamy and sticky that they could have glued themselves together. We just laid there for a while, sated and content, and still excited from watching each other come. Alex used some tissues to clean off his belly, but I decided to do nothing and fall asleep enjoying the creaminess between my legs. As it was very late by now, Alex gave me a deep good-night kiss and got up to go back to his own room.

His hand on the doorknob, he turned and asked me, "Tomorrow? In the fancy?"

I smiled enigmatically and said, "Yes, of course. Where else? And we'll probably need fresh milk. Now go, I'm sleepy."

The next day dawned bright and sunny. Donning a long, black sleeveless dress, I went downstairs barefoot and tousled. Breakfast was a quick affair, but Alex still served me, much to the continued amusement of the three pairs of parents and ribbing from the teenagers. The collective parents and kids were going to a local park for a picnic, but I politely declined to accompany them. Protests came from around the

room as the picnic baskets were packed, my own protests gone
unheard, until my mother spoke up. She announced that I had severe
allergies to grass and pollen as well having hay fever and that I would
be miserable the whole time I was there, scratching like a hound and
unable to breathe. Then she added that I was also allergic to bee and
wasp stings, and *she* was not going to spend her day at the hospital
if I was stung. That silenced their protests, and one of them asked
Alex if he was going to join them.

"No," he said, "I think I'll stay here and keep Claudia company."

The parents smiled and the kids hooted but made no further
protestations. Breakfast was cleared away and finally everyone left,
using three cars to carry them and all the picnic baskets. Privacy at
last! I went upstairs to change into something more appropriate while
Alex went out to the fancy to check the supplies. When I came down
in a black top with a set-in underwire bra, a short, black hip-hugger
skirt, and high-heeled, black stiletto pumps, Alex was waiting for me
in the kitchen, basket at the ready. His face broke into a smile when
he saw me, and I smiled back wordlessly. He opened the backdoor
for me, followed me out to the fancy, and then stepped in front of me
to open the door. With a sweeping arm gesture, he invited me to cross
the threshold. Once inside, I saw that while he was out there earlier
checking on the supplies, he had once again gotten our little hideaway ready for our afternoon delight. Everything was as it should be:
the open windows, the music, the candles, and the clean ashtray. As
he unpacked the basket into the refrigerator, including a new quart of
milk for himself and a fresh pitcher of iced tea for me, I massaged his
neck muscles and ran my nails through his hair.

Once the fancy's door was closed, with the music playing and the
candles flickering, the outside world seemed very far away, if it even
existed at all. After getting me a tall glass of sweet and lemony iced
tea, again he sat at the end of the sofa so that I could lie back across
his lap and rest my head on the armrest. The scent of my clove cigarettes filled the air, and Alex made us both laugh by sniffing at it as
I exhaled. As part of my plan, I was sipping on the tea frequently
between puffs and soon needed a refill. Alex didn't notice at all that
I was drinking one glass after another and amiably got up each time I
asked for a refill, sometimes bringing a glass of milk along for himself.

"Don't drink all the milk," I said with a cryptic smile.

This of course intrigued him but he didn't ask any questions. Perhaps he thought today was going to be a repeat performance of the day before, but I knew differently. Similar yet different and something I hoped he was willing to do.

"Let's lie down together," I suggested.

Since the sofa was not long enough to accommodate Alex's height, we tossed the cushions on the carpeting and made ourselves comfortable on the floor. Soon we were in each other's arms, rolling around, sometimes with Alex on top of me and other times I was on top of him. Once when I was on top, I pinned his arms down. He laughed, rolled me off him, and he did the same to me. Then he kissed me, one of those deep, long passionate kisses he was so good at, and with his strong arms holding me down, I felt the creaminess between my legs as my clitoris enlarged. Through his jeans, I could feel him start to grow, and as he did, he gently began to grind his hips against me. It felt wonderful: my legs open, my arms held down, his tongue in my mouth, and his hips grinding against me, and I was loving every minute of it. He stopped the gentle movement of his hips, and we broke the kiss so that we could look into each other's eyes. I knew mine were half-closed with lust and his sky-blue eyes had a depth to them I hadn't seen there before. We held each other's gaze for a minute and then for some reason started to laugh.

He let go of me and rolled onto his back on the floor, extending his arm, inviting me to nestle into the crook of his shoulder. I was a perfect fit, and when his arm encircled me and held me close, a deep sigh escaped. We lay there for maybe half an hour, content just to be together, listening to the music and watching the flicker of the candles. But my bladder was ready to burst, so it was time to put my plan into play.

"Alex," I said, "aren't you thirsty? Why don't you bring a bowl and the quart of milk over here?"

He got up quickly and returned with the desired items, probably thinking of our erotic encounters of the two days before and maybe intrigued by my request for a bowl instead of the same plate. I placed the bowl on the corner of the coffee table and gestured him to come watch. Then I urinated into the bowl. He was completely fascinated as he watched the urine stream from my pussy and inched in closer as I urinated more and more. When I was done, I presented him with my pussy, and without any direction from me, he licked me clean. Then I took the quart of milk and filled the bowl almost to the top. Enthralled, Alex could not keep his eyes off the quickly filling bowl, my urine mixing with the milk and giving it a faintly yellow hue.

Kneeling down next to him, I whispered in his ear, "Time to drink your milk, dear."

I had prepared myself for the fact that he might not want to do this, but I thought the odds that he would were in my favor. I so love it when I am right. Without saying a word, he reached for the bowl, put it to his lips, and began drinking. After the first sip, he smiled at me over the edge of the bowl and then downed the whole thing in one long gulp. When he was finished, he put the bowl down, licked his lips, and sighed "ahhhh."

I let out a little laugh and flung myself at him, kissing his face and then seeking out his lips. As his lips met mine, his strong arms gently lowered me to the floor, his muscular body lay on top of mine, and his handsome face was just inches from my own. Not even thinking about what I was doing, I managed to finagle my hand between our two bodies and began to unbutton his jeans. He caught on to what I was doing before I did. In no time at all, his jeans were off, the tiny skirt I was wearing was up around my waist, and he was inside of me. I cried out as he entered me because although I was very wet, he was very well endowed. He started slowly to loosen me up, and with each orgasm I had, he went in harder and deeper. Soon we were fucking like minks and biting each other's neck. I dug my fingernails into his back, wrapped my legs around his waist. He was as adept a lover as he was a kisser. He brought me to the brink over and over, his own control amazing to me, and finally when I came, I almost fainted. Then I felt him spurt into me, his juices hot and plentiful.

We lay there in the afterglow, side by side, spent, and enrapt by the mind-bending encounter we just had. Too bad there were only two more days left to "our" vacation. We had one more tryst after that, mostly rough sex, and agreed that this was the best family-style vacation either of us ever had.

I never saw Alex again.

Elegant

The special number that clients called on rang for the first time in several days. Most of The Mistress's clients, and her old house of domination, knew she was taking a break from sessioning to write a book, so the phone had been quiet lately. But she was bored and restless and missed her old avocation and antics, so she took the call. To her pleasurable surprise, it was a handsome, young male creature whose company and interests she greatly enjoyed. He asked her, no, almost begged her, to session with him the following evening. He was a fetishist, and his fetish was foot and leg worship. His tone of voice, the respect he showed her, plus the fact that he gave excellent foot and leg massage (she had trained him herself) piqued her interest. She hesitated for just one second before saying yes and giving him the confirmation instructions. The diversion would be a pleasant one.

The next day, he confirmed their session and gave her a contact number, following her instructions to the letter. This pleased The Mistress because it showed that his intentions were sincere and that he appreciated her coming out of her temporary retirement just for him. Because of this, in a rare gesture of kindness, she wore the same outfit that she had worn when they first met many years ago. The outfit was a high-necked, sleeveless, full-skirted black dress; a thick, black suede belt; lace-topped, black thigh-high stockings; and black suede stiletto pumps with the low vamp that showed lots of toe cleavage. She knew he loved toe cleavage. Didn't most foot fetishists?

He arrived right on time because he knew she did not tolerate lateness and that tardiness carried its own "choice" of punishments. A late male creature had three punishment options, and it was his obligation to choose. The first option was that if the male creature arrived twenty minutes late, the session was cut short by twenty minutes, although the donation was still for the full hour. Option two was that the male creature added five dollars for each minute he was late to the regular donation. The final option, one that was only chosen by masochists (who often arrived late because of it) was that the male creature would willingly submit to the hardest caning The Mistress could give. Option two was the most frequent choice of the nonmasochist, and the hit to his finances served well to teach the male creature a lesson in punctuality.

At the ring of the bell, The Mistress opened the door and gestured that he enter the foyer. As he handed her a carton of her favorite clove cigarettes, The Mistress could see that the male creature was suitably impressed and flattered that she had worn that particular outfit. He thanked her with his eyes before bowing his head, but she knew that with his head bowed, he was admiring her legs and her feet in their cleavage-showing pumps. At her hand signal, he dropped gracefully to his knees, put his head and shoulders to the floor, kept his hips held high and his back in a pleasing arch, and placed one hand, fingers closed, on either side of her extended right foot. Then he kissed her shoe ardently to offer the proper homage due her. After he had adored her foot and shoe to her satisfaction, she wiggled her toe inside her pump to signal to him that he had been accepted into her service. Almost pirouetting on one heel so that her full skirt would flare out, she snapped her fingers; the signal that he was to follow behind her on all fours into the adjoining room. The male creature scuttled down the hallway and followed The Mistress through the open door.

The click click of her heels on the wooden floor of the foyer and hallway disappeared and was absorbed by the thick Aubusson carpet as she entered her richly decorated living room. Her favorite flowers, Stargazer lilies and red roses, were in a large vase on a round antique wooden table. Their familiar sweet scent filled the air, music played softly in the background, and his senses became aroused as soon as he entered the room. The carpet was a blessing to the male creature's knees after the hard wooden floors, and he was able to follow her quickly to the pillow-decorated divan where she seated herself and arranged her full skirt. Lounging comfortably and looking stunningly sexy, The Mistress pointed to a spot on the floor, his spot. He hurried to the invisible spot and knelt there, seemingly obedient, but she knew he was consuming her legs and pumps with their enticing toe cleavage by looking at them surreptitiously with his downcast eyes. It was an old trick, and it did not fool The Mistress one bit—but she was enjoying herself, was pleased by his gift of cigarettes, and was interested in observing him, so she gave him a little leeway.

After a few minutes of letting him devour her legs and glamorously shod feet, she began to tell him a story, carefully watching his face. She told him about a college boy who had a fetish for his professor's legs and feet, about the boy's various infractions and about the punishments received from his professor and then from the dean of boys. She knew this type of story excited him, and even though he was still fully dressed, she could see his organ straining against his trousers. As she spoke, she decided to tease him further by rearranging her legs several times into positions she knew to be the most flattering, passing them mere inches from his face when she did so. And each time she could feel the warm expulsion of his breath on her legs a mere second later. Although the male creature did not know it, and she would never tell him, The Mistress found his hot breath on her legs to be very exciting.

Because of the throbbing organ so visible in his pants, The Mistress decided it was time for him to strip for her pleasure. She bade him to rise and ordered him to undress to the music, divesting himself of all garments except his tight boxer shorts. With his well-muscled physique, she liked the way he looked and silently thanked the Goddess for all of the new styles in men's underwear that gave her such visual pleasure. He neatly tucked his clothes away, knowing that this was part of the command to strip, and awaited her next order. She motioned to the same spot on the floor, and he immediately took up his position. Then she continued her tale of the recalcitrant college student.

As the story got juicier, little by little The Mistress began to tease her skirt up her legs until the lace tops of her thigh-high stockings were exposed. His eyes were glued to her legs, and she could have been speaking in tongues for all he cared. Tentatively, his hand reached for the leg nearest to him, but she pulled it away, saying, "You haven't done anything to deserve touching me." Leaning forward, she slapped his face hard, forehand and backhand, for his impertinence. The male creature withdrew his hand quickly and stared at the floor in obvious disappointment. Hidden among the pillows on the divan was a flogger that she withdrew with which to punish him further. She forced his head onto the divan, his face pressed up against her suede-shod feet. The male creature did not like to be whipped, so he was comforted by her feet as she soundly whipped his back as his punishment and for her pleasure.

He accepted his punishment stoically and thanked her for caring enough about him to correct him. The Mistress decided to reward him and to give herself more pleasure by allowing him to give her a foot and calf massage. On hearing this, his hands, warm and strong, slipped off her pump, and then he fell on her foot and calf with a controlled savagery, digging in or caressing as needed. Because she had trained him for foot massage herself, he was doing a very good job, needing little correction and occasional direction to spots that required more attention. As he massaged her, she draped her other leg around his neck as he bent to his task and began to rub the pointy toe of her suede pump on his bare neck. His moan of pleasure delighted her. She began to alternate between the pointy toe of her shoe and her sexy nylon-encased leg. His moans of pleasure increased, and so did the feeling of the power inside her.

But the leg The Mistress was using to tease him with began to get envious of the attention being paid to the other leg, so she ordered him to stop and begin anew on the envious leg.

"Can't leave The Mistress lopsided, can we?" she asked with a teasing smile.

"No, Mistress," the male creature said politely as he slipped her massaged foot back into its pump.

He removed the other pump, and taking the other foot and leg, the envious one, into his warm strong hands, he gave it the same full treatment he had given the first leg. As he did this, The Mistress used the wickedly pointed toe of her other shoe to lift his chin and turn his face to hers. She commanded him to look at her, and she met his eyes and held them as she raised her skirt to her waist. Out of his peripheral vision, he could see what she was doing, but he did not dare break his gaze to look at the objects of his desire. But he could still see the lace tops of her stockings and the enticing soft span of her thigh between the stocking tops and her black lace thong. Then The Mistress asked him what he would do if she gave him permission to worship, as he most desired.

"I would adore you" was all that he said in a reverent tone of voice.

"Then adore me," The Mistress said. "Show me that you know me to be the Goddess I am."

Gently, lovingly, he picked up her right leg and cradled it in his arm. Then he bent his head to her foot and began kissing it, leaving no saliva on her foot because he knew that would anger her. His lips were big and mushy and quite talented. He massaged her leg as he kissed her foot; the combination of soft kissing and hard rubbing was lovely and very relaxing. She slid her foot out of her shoe and dangled her left foot off the divan, placing it on his boxer-shorts-encased organ. Thereupon she began to use her foot to manipulate him, to tease him, to trod on him, and to push and step on his sack. Although his organ grew larger and harder because of her attentions, he did not let her use of him distract him from giving her the worship she deserved and he so desired to give her. Who knew what pleasures might be next? And he did not want to spoil his chances for further rewards. He worked his way up her leg, massaging her with his hands and caressing her with his lips until he reached the lace top of her stocking.

The Mistress still wished to have her fun with him, but her right leg did not reach his groin. So she used her right leg to catch his neck in pincher and then slowly, carefully, watching his face every second, she used her leg to deprive him of air. It was not a lot, not enough to make him pass out, but just enough to make breathing more difficult, especially when he was already breathless and panting from lust. Although she slowly began to tighten her grip on his throat with her leg, he valiantly worshipped his Mistress for several more minutes. His ragged intakes of breath were very exciting to her and she squeezed a little tighter. Although he was being deprived of more and more air, this excited him even more than it did her, and he fell upon her leg with renewed vigor. The Mistress laughed at how easy it was for her to read him and removed her leg from his neck.

She bid him to rise and take off his boxer shorts. As he did so, his organ sprang free. He was well formed, long, and not too thick and looked very sexy clad only in his nakedness. He was rock hard just as she expected him to be, which pleased her enormously. She leaned forward and gave his organ a few playful slaps. Unable to control her-self at his organ's antics, she giggled as her slaps made it bobble this way and that, and she was gratified to hear his groans as each slap landed. To tease him further, she turned over onto her stomach and pulled her dress up, exposing her buttocks. Giving him a few seconds to take in the loveliness of her upper thighs and round firm buttocks, she commanded him to kneel on the floor and pointed to the spot she wanted him on, directly across from her lovely buttocks. He fell to his knees instantly, hoping this was part of the reward he had so long wished for.

The Mistress then charged him to massage her upper thighs and buttocks but told him that if he got "fresh" he would be severely punished and sent home immediately. As commanded, he descended upon her limbs and cheeks like a starving man, but he was gentle yet firm, knowing just how she liked it to be done. Wrapping his strong, well-muscled arms around both of her legs at once, he lowered his head to her thighs and began to kiss them fervently. His lips on the skin above her stockings were silky and soft, and his hot breath sent little shivers down her spine. Occasionally his nose would brush against her black lace thong, and he could not help but notice the effect this had on her. Spurred onto greater efforts by her reaction, he loosened his grip on her thighs just enough to make a small triangle. Her thighs comprised two sides of the triangle and the black lace thong covering her secret garden made the third. Every so often as he nuzzled her, he would brush his nose against her garden gate in a deliberate attempt to elicit the little tremor this action produced. He was delighted when his efforts were so rewarded.

Much to his dismay, suddenly The Mistress turned over onto her back and stopped him by pulling his head up by the hair. Using the handful of hair to turn his face toward her, she ordered him to lie face up on the floor a few steps away from the divan. Then she arose, and facing him, she straddled him and walked up the length of his body from his feet to his neck, pushing her pointy-toed pumps into him as she made her progression. When she reached his neck, she made sure he had an excellent view of her black lace thong and her legs up her dress and gave him a few seconds to appreciate them. Then she quickly sat down on his chest. Using her pumps to turn his face toward hers and imprison it there, she smiled into his hot lust-filled eyes. She laughed at his obvious yearning and was pleased that her laughter had brought a fleeting look of humiliation across his face.

Sliding off his chest to sit next to his head, The Mistress lifted his head and cradled it on her leg, making his head arch back slightly.

Then she draped the other leg across his throat. With The Mistress's permission, he began to touch and stroke himself at the same time she deprived him of air when she thought his efforts on her behalf were not up to her standards. His response to asphyxiation was very strong and quite evident from the increasing size of his organ, so she continued to apply more pressure. He stroked harder, his breath ragged, his chest heaving. When The Mistress's thigh closed on his throat in a final pinch, he struggled to remain conscious and won. He groaned loudly with his final stroke, and thanking The Mistress, his Mistress, with his eyes, he released his pearl jam onto his belly.

Her Booted Highness

He couldn't see her from where he was, so he cowered there with his head on the floor, afraid to move, afraid to breathe without her permission. He could hear her boot heels clicking on the same floor he was lying on, but her actions were a mystery to him. Screwing up his courage, he tried to turn his head to sneak a sideward glance at her. But suddenly his head was clamped into place by her feet in their patent leather thigh-high boots, his ears occupying the space between the arched sole of her boot and the rise of her wicked spike heel. She loomed over him, looking down on him as he lay there, awaiting her pleasure. His stomach felt full of butterflies, and his breath came in ragged gasps as she towered over him. His eyes were drawn to the loveliness of her legs, the delicious curve of her buttock as it merged into her thigh, the curling dark red hair escaping her latex thong.

A quick movement dragged his eyes away from the loveliness between her parted thighs. The black riding crop, the beautiful sexy one he had gotten her from Hermes, was in her delicate, long-fingered hand. She brought it down on his penis—he was as hard as a rock from the nearness of her and her power over him. The sharp stinging pain of it, the braided leather biting into his supersensitive flesh, made him groan aloud before he could control himself. Her dark eyes, wide and dancing with fire, glared down at him from her pale face.

"What did you say?" she said in a threatening tone of voice.

"N-n-nothing, Diva Claudia, I am sorry, Diva," he stammered.

"If you didn't say anything, then why are you apologizing? You know my rule of silence—no open-mouthed sounds allowed, no speaking for any reason. You also know that you are not allowed any modesty before me, nor privacy—all that you are, all that you have or will be allowed to have, comes from me, from the generous bounty of my heart and hand. You were born to serve me, you live only to please me. Even your orgasms are controlled by me—if it pleases me, if it suits my whim, you will be allowed to release yourself in my presence."

She stepped away from him and positioned herself in the high-backed chair she referred to as her "throne." She called him to come serve her. He got up but still crouched as he approached. She motioned him to the floor—a slight diddling of her fingers in his face—and he knelt at her feet, his buttocks resting on his heels. Silently, he waited for her to speak. Instead, she lit a cigarette and blew the smoke in his face. He closed his eyes and held his breath. He didn't like the smell of it and she knew it. She inhaled deeply, held it for a moment and then exhaled forcibly, engulfing him in a cloud of smoke. An ash was starting to form on the end of her cigarette. A small cough escaped him.

"Open your mouth," she said charmingly.

He swallowed hard, realizing as he did it that it was a mistake. His belly knotted; he almost groaned aloud but caught it before it passed his lips. He opened his mouth.

"Stick out your tongue," The Diva said in a coaxing tone of voice.

He knew that would be her next command, but he always waited for her to tell him her desire—it was not up to him to think. Obediently, he stuck out his tongue. He tried to keep it from trembling, tried to hold it still, but it kept moving with a will of its own. She saw his difficulty and kept him waiting just so she could watch him struggle to control his little tongue spasms. As the seconds turned into a minute, she began to laugh at his efforts. Her deep throaty laugh filled the room, echoing humiliatingly in his head. The ash on her cigarette grew longer. She flicked it onto his tongue; a little ember of tobacco burnt him fleetingly before extinguishing itself.

"Swallow it," The Diva said sweetly.

Curling his tongue with its precious cargo back into his mouth, he worked his cheeks in an attempt to muster up some saliva to wash it down. But sitting there with his tongue out while she laughed at him had dried his mouth out even more, and when he swallowed, the ashes stuck to his teeth and gums, leaving his mouth filled with fine grit. He swallowed repeatedly but to no avail. He could feel her eyes on him; she resembled a cat watching a mouse. Was he worthy of such a beautiful, cruel mistress? He swallowed again.

She dropped the cigarette to the floor and her booted foot ground it out. Flicking her fingers at him, she signaled to him to move a couple of feet away from her. Remaining on his knees, he obeyed her by sliding back the required distance. She crossed her legs and lifted the bottom of her right boot to his face. He could see the blemish grinding out the cigarette had left on the otherwise clean sole of her boot.

"Lick it clean," The Diva said politely.

He hesitated for a second and her exquisite crop landed with dazzling speed and blinding accuracy across his outer upper thigh. The crack of the crop startled him into obedience. Before she could land another vicious blow, his lips and tongue were on the sole of her boot. The blow averted for the time being, he went to work removing the blackened ashes spoiling the perfectly clean beauty of her boots. The new ashes joined the old in his mouth.

She withdrew her foot from him and inspected the sole. Other than the slight burn mark from the cigarette, it was perfectly clean. She pulled both booted feet up onto the chair. Sneaking a look at her through his eyelashes, he saw a small smile playing on her face.

"Lie down beneath my feet, face up," The Diva said beguilingly.

He positioned himself on the floor in front of her chair, his head even with one chairleg, his waist with the other. Stepping onto his chest, using him as the floor, she slid to the edge of the chair revealing to him the top of her thighs. She removed her left foot from his chest, and he felt it tread down on his penis and scrotal sack. The heel of her left boot dug painfully into his tender skin, holding him in place. His mouth opened but his gasp died in his throat. Her right heel was positioned over his face and slowly descended toward his mouth.

"Suck me," she said, purring from the heights above him.

Her five-inch heel played with his lips, pushing them this way and that, using them to move his head around like a puppet on a string. He lay there beneath her like a mindless thing; his universe centered on his groin, suffering under her booted foot. He opened wider, arching his neck back to make his throat longer, deeper. He felt the rubber-encased steel of her lift on his tongue, felt it scrape the roof of his mouth, and he adjusted himself to accommodate her. He wrapped his tongue around her heel and sucked hard, hard as he remembered exhorting the forgotten lovers of another lifetime to suck his penis. Today he sucked her the way he liked being sucked back then. He was a different person now.

Her left foot moved on him, rotating him beneath her sole, digging her heel into his groin, spurring his mouth to greater efforts. She used the ball of her foot to pump on him with no more regard for him than for a gas pedal. The alternating jab of her heel into the soft flesh of his groin made him twitch in pain each time she shifted her weight. All the while she had been working the heel of her right shoe further into his mouth, her eyes never leaving his face. His lips were wrapped around her heel, and he sucked at it passionately, trying to make her feel through the patent leather his devotion to her.

She began to pump her heel in and out of his mouth, stroking his caressing lips and tongue. Her left foot pumped his penis in concert with the right heel in his mouth; a long, low moan of pleasure escaped him.

Suddenly, she removed her left foot from his genitals and brought the crop down sharply on his scrotum, making his body jerk in protest. Her heel almost pierced his throat—but he caught himself in time and settled back on the floor. But it was too late. She withdrew her right foot from his mouth and nudged him away with her toe.

"You still don't understand, do you? You are mine to do with as I wish. Get up. Bend over and put your shoulders on the chair. Instead of the reward you were hoping for, now you will offer me your buttocks for punishment. Display yourself."

Standing, he bent over the chair, his face and shoulders pressed against the leather still warm from her body. He exaggerated the tilt of his hips to present her an enticing target. The crop whistled through the air and landed hotly on his stretched buttocks. She struck him over and over, harder than ever before, each blow landing in a slightly different place. She crisscrossed his buttocks with his gift to her, the crop from Hermes, and he reveled in his punishment. One hundred strokes later she stopped. He would wear the marks from this for a week, a painful, colorful reminder of his failure to submit to her will. She dismissed him without a backward glance.

Covering himself with his hands, lest he offend her, he backed out of her presence into the bathroom that those such as he were allowed to use. Once inside, he fell to his knees, still clutching himself in his hand. He was throbbing with desire and humiliation; she had not given him leave to release himself in her presence, he had not pleased her enough for that. But now, he could release the terrible aching pressure. Wadding up a handful of the paper towels she allotted her slaves, he brought himself to a shuddering climax in the privacy of the cold little bathroom. He cleaned himself up and got dressed. Before he left, he flushed the paper towels soiled with his juices down the toilet. Not once did he think of the consequences of his action.

As he waited nervously in the anteroom, his mind replayed their last session again and again like scenes from a movie. The other mistresses on the premises crossed back and forth in front of the open door, ignoring him, making him feel small, unworthy, invisible. The silence was deafening. A bead of sweat trickled down his forehead to the tip of his nose. He wiped it away impatiently with his sleeve, annoyed at the distraction. When would she send for him?

Finally, after a short lifetime had passed, a petite, dark-haired beauty in black latex came to retrieve him. She looked at him and smiled knowingly, then led him out into the hall and downstairs to one of the dungeons. She ushered him inside and closed the door behind him. A latch fell into place, imprisoning him in the black-walled room. Blinking to adjust his eyes to the darkness, he peered around the room in a vain attempt to unlock its secrets. Was she watching him from a place of concealment? Was there a camera in the room to spy on his every move? The blackness prevailed and he could see nothing. He dropped to the cold stone floor just beneath his feet and settled down to await her pleasure. Suddenly, The Mistress's melted butterscotch voice invaded the silent blackness. He jumped, jittery as a cat in a dog kennel, and strained his eyes to see where her voice came from.

"Your disobedience after your last session has displeased me greatly. You made a mockery of my kindness to you by your actions in the bathroom. And you caused a great deal of damage to my castle by your selfish disregard of my property and of all the time I spent teaching you how to behave properly. I did not grant you permission to relieve yourself, yet you did so anyway. Then, you sought to conceal your duplicity by flushing the soiled evidence down the toilet, clogging it, and causing it to overflow. Think about what you did because tonight you will pay for your careless disregard."

He quailed on the floor, flooded with guilt as the silence enveloped him once more. He thought of the exquisite pleasure of relieving himself into the paper towels and blushed with humiliation that his furtive release had been found out. He wished he could see what else was in the room. But the blackness kept its secrets and told him nothing. The minutes ticked past.

Without warning, the door opened. She was silhouetted in the sliver of light admitted from the hall. At once his eyes were glued to her and he took no further notice of the dark room. She closed the door behind her and the room was plunged into blackness again. He struggled to his knees, ready to demonstrate his submissiveness to her as soon as she gave him the opportunity. He knew she had left him alone all those long minutes to give him time to contemplate his fate at her hands.

"Have you given serious thought to your prior disobedience? Have you recognized the error of your ways or the disrespect you have shown my person? Have you anything to say for yourself, anything at all to explain your willful, unacceptable behavior?"

He hung his head in shame.

"I thought not. No excuse would or could pardon you for what you have done; so, better that you say nothing and accept the punishment you so richly deserve. I have something special planned for you this evening. Pay attention."

With that, The Mistress flicked a switch, but to his surprise, the room was not flooded with light. Instead, one pinpoint of light shone on a bondage table. Long enough to stretch out a man much taller than he, it was encased in black leather with cutouts where his breasts and genitals would be. It stood on eight thick legs and hooks lined the underside of the table.

"Shall it be this? Or shall it be this?"

She simultaneously shut off the first light and turned on another. The second light illuminated an X-shaped spreader bar suspended from the ceiling. At the two ends of the bar hung boots and from the other two dangled two fur-lined handcuffs. Under the spreader bar was a high narrow wooden bench. A closer look at the device revealed that it was an automated suspension device, with a control box like that on an assembly line.

"Or perhaps I should consider this for your punishment?"

Again she flipped the switches, and the spreader bar and suspension system disappeared into the blackness. This time the pinpoint of light fell on a stockade, its three holes gaping and empty without a prisoner. The apparatus hung from the ceiling by sturdy chains and swayed gently in an unfelt draft. The puritanical quality of the stockade was more menacing than the modern equipment he had just seen. He tried to control his terror at being restrained by it; in the past, she had been able to discern what he feared the most and used it against him. He kept his head down in case, like a cat, she was able to see his face clearly in the darkness. He throbbed with terror, anticipation, and desire.

"Or, then again, maybe this would be more fitting."

Again she flipped the switches and the stockade disappeared into the darkness. The tiny spotlight fell on a medieval-looking wooden table, its surface shaped and polished into the form of a man lying on his belly. There were indentations for the breasts, and under the hips the smooth surface rose to elevate the buttocks. Leather straps with buckles, one at each corner for the arms and legs and one in the middle for the waist, guaranteed that the occupant would be kept in position until released by The Mistress. The object was obviously to be used for intense corporal punishment.

He tried to hide his terror. Each of the illuminated objects struck fear into his heart but none more than the stockade. He tried to conceal his thoughts from her, tried to mislead her by thinking of the medieval table, but she saw through him. With two threatening *clicks*, the tiny spotlight on the spanking device disappeared and the tiny spotlight shone on the stockade. A small sound of distress escaped from his lips before he could swallow it back. She laughed a deep, wicked laugh that chilled him to the bone. His member became painfully engorged at the sound.

"Get up. Now strip. Stand before the stockade," The Mistress said in a low growl.

He rose, hampered by the darkness and his own fear, and fought his way out of his clothes, his eyes never leaving the stockade. Once undressed, he forced his feet to take one step after another as he approached the illuminated stockade. He still had not caught a glimpse of The Mistress. When he was in front of the instrument of his punishment, he stood, head down, and awaited her pleasure. He tried not to look at the stockade, but his eyes were drawn to it in spite of himself. His cock pulsed and throbbed at the sight.

He heard her heels click on the stone floor; then suddenly she stepped into the circle of light around the stockade. He was amazed at her manner of dress. Instead of her usual elegant latex attire, she was scantily dressed; a leather teddy with high, French-cut legs and a low-cut bodice barely concealed her beautiful body. Black leather thigh-high boots encased her slender feet and rose up gorgeous legs. Just above the top of her boots, he could see the lacy tops of her thigh-high black stockings. Black leather opera gloves adorned her shapely arms. A black leather hood cloaked her face and head from the nose up, shrouding her in mystery. In her hand, she held a beautiful black fiberglass cane, the cruelest cane in her collection. He whimpered inanely at the sight of her.

The Mistress smiled at him, an icy, cruel smile. She unlatched the top half of the stockade and gestured him into it. So, he was going to be forced into cooperating with his own punishment. Coercion combined with consent was one of her favorite ways of controlling her slaves. But still, he hesitated, humiliated, and very aware of his arousal. Swiftly, her cane came down on his raging organ, biting into him, hurting him, spurring him into obedience. Summoning up his courage, he stepped up to the loathsome, frightening thing, bent over and put his neck into the declivity. Then he put each of his hands in their proper place. The Mistress closed the top down on him and locked him in. Then she quickly moved behind him. Squatting down, she imprisoned his ankles with leather cuffs connected to eye hooks concealed in the floor. In the darkness of his fear, he hadn't noticed

them before. Now he was totally her prisoner in this humiliating position. Recognizing her superiority, he surrendered to it and submitted
his will to her. He awaited his punishment at her hands.

"For transgressions against me, for willful disobedience, for rapa-
cious lust, for thoughtlessly damaging my property, I sentence you to
150 strokes of my cane on the buttocks and thighs. You are to count
out each stroke and thank me after you receive it. Do I make myself
clear?"

"Yes, your majesty."

"Then we shall begin."

She let it fly and the first stroke landed on his tautly stretched buttocks. He knew by the severity of that first stroke that he was in for
the beating of his life. He called out "one." Dutifully, he thanked her.
After the second stroke landed, he called out "two" and again thanked
her. But his number count and thank yous were called too slowly for
her, and she gave him 10 strokes that she did not allow to be included
in the original 150. She flailed her instrument of pain at his quivering flesh harder and faster, again and again. He counted out each
stroke and quickly thanked her after each one as she demanded. After
50 strokes, he was near to tears and his voice was strained from
the effort of holding them back. At 100, the tears were streaming
unchecked down his face. As the count neared 150, he sobbed as he
thanked her for the cruel punishment he was receiving at her hands.
The 10 bonus strokes made him cry aloud. He knew he deserved this,
and his thanks rang with a sincere surrender that was unmistakable.
Finally, the terrible beating was over. The surreal moonscape of his
mind was flooded with the image of himself hanging limply from the
stockade, his buttocks a world of angry red welts.

The Mistress shut the light off on her way out and left him there in
the darkness to dwell on the pain that was a punishment of his own
making. Soon she would send someone to release him from his bonds
and escort him off her premises. She deliberately withheld her permission for release as part of his punishment.

After an unknown length of time, time that he used to focus on the
pain and The Mistress's dominion over him, the same petite, dark-
haired beauty that had brought him to the dungeon entered the room
and unlatched the wooden bar imprisoning him. She stood tapping
her foot impatiently, her arms folded over her breasts as he fumbled

his way into his clothes. Once he was dressed, she led him upstairs, making sure he had no opportunity to get near any of the bathrooms, and showed him out the door into the street. He entered his car, sat gingerly on his swollen red buttocks, and drove away. He was very hard and his erection throbbed painfully, but he dared not do anything so close to her premises.

Once home, he gripped his painful erection in his hand and brought himself to a speedy release. He dared to imagine that perhaps the next time he saw her he would please her enough to be allowed to release himself in her presence. He dreamt of when he would see her again, Her Majesty in her thigh-high leather boots.

Late Again

Adam knew that The Mistress hated it when he was late for one of their sessions. He was terrified of how she would punish him for his tardiness. He awaited her arrival in the front room of her house, filled with trepidation. The Mistress entered the room, closed the door behind her, and leaned against it, glaring at him. He took one quick glance at her before dropping his eyes and looking at the floor. Her black latex catsuit, tightly laced black corset, black latex gloves, and her lace-up over-the-knee boots told him all he needed to know about his punishment tonight; she had dressed for the occasion and looked magnificent. Her eyes flashed fire, and he felt humbled and worthless before her.

"I will not accept any limp excuses from you for your lateness this evening. I will not tolerate being left waiting for you. You should be waiting for me! You have brought this punishment on yourself, and you will suffer for your lateness," The Mistress said in that deceptively cool voice she used when she was extremely angry. The Mistress never raised her voice; indeed, the angrier she was, the softer was her voice. She never used foul language but knew exactly what to say to push Adam's buttons.

"You do wish to get out of the doghouse and back into my good graces, don't you?" The Mistress asked almost sweetly. Adam was not fooled by her sweet tone.

"Yes, Mistress," Adam replied in a voice of surrender.

"Good! Now follow me," The Mistress politely commanded him. Adam knew that a politely phrased command was still a command, and a most serious one at that.

The Mistress led Adam upstairs to her bedroom. Once there, she ordered him to strip; then she cuffed his wrists and put a length of chain between them. She pushed him under the doorframe and attached the chain to an overhead hook. His arms were strained high above his head and Adam's feet barely touched the floor. He was balanced on his toes, and even a small shove would send him spinning.

"Don't you look succulent hanging there naked just awaiting my displeasure! Your body is mine to do with what I wish, especially when you have displeased me. And I can see that you are quite excited by this because your rod is standing out rigidly from your body. This lesson will be very memorable, and you will think twice before making me wait for you again!"

The Mistress turned on her high heels and returned with a wide black plastic hairbrush with bristles protruding from the red rubber on the business side. Adam hated that hairbrush. To tease him, to allay his fears, The Mistress began by brushing his chest hair until it was all nice and fluffy and neatly arranged.

"There. Now that wasn't so bad was it?" Her voice was almost coy, and he knew an answer was not expected.

Standing very close to him, The Mistress ran the hairbrush up and down his chest a few more times; suddenly she stopped at his right nipple and pressed the bristles of the hairbrush into it. It felt like pins were being pushed into his flesh and he winced. She smiled and pressed harder. When he groaned in pain, she turned her attention to the left nipple and gave it the same treatment. Then she stepped back, flipped the brush over to the black plastic side, and used it to slap his breasts over and over. Adam struggled to keep his balance and not to twist and turn with each blow. The Mistress continued to slap his breasts harder and harder until a loud groan of pain escaped him. She gave him a few more slaps across each breast to impress her control over him and her disregard for his pain. Then she stepped away.

The Mistress shoved him aside to walk around behind him. Adam groaned with the strain on his arms and fell to the side when she did this but quickly regained his balance. The next thing he felt was The

Mistress making circles on his buttocks with the cool black plastic of the hairbrush. But this little pleasure did not last long. The Mistress began to beat him with the brush with firm hard cracks across his cheeks, sometimes alternating between one cheek then the other, sometimes beating the bottom of his ass meat, and at yet other times landing the blows evenly between both cheeks. He found himself swaying in rhythm with the blows. And she did not miss one inch of his ass meat. Just when he thought she would show him no mercy, she stepped back to admire her handiwork. The hard blows from the black plastic hairbrush had made his ass meat bright red. The Mistress took off her gloves and first ran her razor-sharp, red-lacquered nails over his hot, red ass and then used her strong but small hands to squeeze and manipulate his cheeks. Adam, his head down, hung there and bore it. He knew he deserved whatever she dished out. The Mistress let Adam hang there for a few minutes, untouched, before she stepped around in front of him. She smiled and forced the handle of the hairbrush into his mouth.

"Lick it!" The Mistress commanded him. "Get it good and wet. You will obey me!"

It suddenly dawned on Adam that he was about to be violated with the same tool that had delivered such a brutal spanking. He gathered up his saliva, opened his mouth, and lubricated the handle of the brush with his own spittle. The Mistress pulled the handle out of his mouth and leaned against his chest, her catsuit cold and slippery next to his skin. She slipped her right arm around his back, and next he felt the handle of the hairbrush searching for his anal opening. She held the bristled side in her hand while she probed between his cheeks. She located his opening and began to force the handle of the brush into him. He felt his opening being stretched, and he made a miserable attempt to twist away from the invading, violating brush.

Infuriated at his attempt to escape, The Mistress commanded, "Hold still! If you fight me, if you clench against my entry, I will punish you with a larger and much bigger tool. Or else I will shove this so far up into you that the bristles will feel like pinpricks around the delicate, puckered skin of your opening! And then there is always the possibility that I would glue a thin strip of sandpaper around the next tool. Do you want to bleed for me? Do you?"

"No, Mistress, please no," begged Adam as he attempted to control the urge to struggle against her invasion.

"Then you are to submit to me and accept the pumping I am going to give you. You are so innocent and so tight! You are never to forget that no part of your body doesn't exist to serve me and entertain me. You are my possession, a toy, an object, to do with what I wish when I wish. You live to please me, your Mistress!"

As The Mistress said that, her left hand moved down to Adam's rigid rod and sack. Alternating between one and the other, she began to squeeze them very hard. She began to stroke his cock and squeeze his balls in time with the thrusts of the hair brush's handle wedged between his cheeks and up his anus. Often the pin-like bristles would poke the tender pink skin around his opening and he would cry out in pain. This delighted The Mistress and spurred her on to greater efforts.

Adam was unbearably excited despite the pain and humiliation of this violation of his body. His arms stretched over his head and the strain of balancing himself on his toes pushed the limits of his endurance. He could feel that the hairbrush handle was imbedded in him as deeply as it would go.

"Clench your cheeks and hold that brush inside of you," The Mistress charged Adam. "And I want to find it just as deeply inside of you when I return."

Adam clenched his cheeks together, which was no easy task considering the uncomfortable and strained position he was in. He had to concentrate very hard on obeying The Mistress's directive. She walked away from him, opened a drawer, and returned with some things balled up in her hand so that he couldn't see what she was holding. She leaned against him, reached around behind him and checked the position of the hairbrush handle with her left hand. She gave it a shove to make sure he hadn't let any of it slip out. As the bristles pricked him, a cry escaped his lips. A smile crossed her face; then she began to laugh, a most wicked laugh. Her laughter hurt him more than the handle up his anus. Then her right hand firmly cupped his hairy sack and gave it a little twist at the base. Adam winced in pain. He barely heard the *snap!* as The Mistress secured a half-inch leather strap around his sack and under his painfully hard rod.

He knew that another part of his body had been captured and put into bondage for The Mistress's pleasure. He felt more and more owned by her, more used and abused by her, and more of an object for her entertainment than he ever had before. Then he felt a soft leather pouch being slipped over his vulnerable round sack, followed by a tight pulling sensation as The Mistress tied and knotted it. Adam didn't know it, but he was soon to find out that the leather pouch had rings on it to which weights could be attached. One by one, The Mistress attached to these rings double-sided clip hooks holding eight-ounce fishing weights, painted a glossy black. When she was done, Adam had six pounds of weights hanging from the leather pouch around his sack. The mean little leather pouch with its six pounds of weights dragged his sack toward the floor.

When The Mistress was satisfied that the pouch was very secure and would not fall off, she quickly and expertly covered his rod with a condom. Standing in front of him to tease him by her proximity, she resumed her insistent rhythm into his anus with the handle. Each of her thrusts caused the weighted pouch to swing and multiply Adam's pain. He could see her face and see that she was very aroused and excited by the control she had over him as Adam hung there so help-lessly and at her mercy. She laughed her low wicked laugh at his misery and continued her relentlessly hard stroking with the handle in his anus. The Mistress grabbed his rod with her free hand and began to stroke it. Adam was so erect that it was painful, and her touch brought a look of exquisite agony to his face.

"I am going to milk you for my amusement. You are familiar with this activity; we have done it before. The condom will ensure that you do not make a mess on my floor. I expect you to perform for me on command, in spite of the distractions that I have attached to your body, like the weighted pouch and hairbrush handle I have inserted inside you. You know that your hot spurts at my command will have to fill up that condom to please me or else I will punish you even more severely."

The Mistress's penetration of Adam's anus had become violent as she sought to force a streaming white fountain from his straining and beleaguered rod. The insistent downward pull of the weighted pouch had stretched Adam so much that he knew his spurts would jet from him in fast pulses.

"When you hear my command, 'do it now, you miserable worm,' you will entertain me with a gusher while I jerk on your rod with one hand and ram the handle into your anus with the other. If I am pleased with the quantity and quality of your show, I'll let you down from that hook. And if I am greatly pleased by your show, I'll cuff you to the foot of my bed for a rest."

Adam's breathing became ragged and uneven as he struggled to maintain his balance and accept his punishment. He didn't know which was worse: her rough milking or the handle up his anus.

"You belong to me and it pleases me to use you like this. I can feel your rod pulsing, I can feel every vein straining with the tension of holding back until I command you that you may release. But not just yet. I wish to torture you a little more!"

The Mistress continued to stroke and ram Adam in that relentless rhythm until he thought he would scream from pain and frustration. Finally, he heard the magic words.

"Do it now, you miserable worm!"

Adam's stream felt white hot as it jetted from his rod into the condom, filling it up more than he thought possible. The Mistress continued to squeeze his rod until she was sure every last drop had been milked from it. Then she carefully removed the condom and inspected the quantity of its contents.

"This is satisfactory," she said in cool acceptance of all he had endured for her.

But instead of releasing Adam from the hook, she lay down on her bed and began rubbing herself between her legs through the latex catsuit.

"Don't you wish your pitiful little tongue could do for me what I can so easily do for myself with just the tips of my fingers?" The Mistress asked teasingly. "And what a good job I do! You could not do half as well or please me half as much no matter what you did or how hard you tried. You will just have to hang there helplessly and watch me satisfy myself! And you should consider yourself honored to be allowed to watch!"

The Mistress came suddenly, a series of moans escaping her lips and her back arching like a cat's as Adam looked on in fascination and desire. When she was finished, she lay there spent, her eyes closed with one arm thrown back over her head. She took her time getting up.

"That was very nice, very nice indeed," The Mistress said in a dreamy voice.

She released Adam from the hook over the doorframe and removed his cuffs and the chain. She pointed to the floor at the foot of the bed, and Adam, weak from his exertions, collapsed onto the spot gratefully. True to her word, The Mistress cuffed one of Adam's ankles to the foot of her bed and allowed him to spend the night sleeping on the floor at her feet.

Sugar Cane

The Mistress restrained the slave's hand in leather wrist cuffs, bent him over the spanking horse, and clipped his wrists to the rings on the front support poles. She knew he was scared and nervous; small drops of perspiration dotted his forehead and his hands clenched the support poles of the horse so tightly that his knuckles were white. His torso was pressed against the black leather of the horse; his legs, straight and slightly apart, fell to either side of the rear support poles. Each ankle wore its own leather restraint with a clip hook to which a chain was attached and entwined around the poles. She had placed the spanking horse directly in front of a full-mirrored wall—all the better for him to see her, as she had her way with him. She liked being looked at and admired. She ordered him to keep his head up, to rest his chin on the bench, and never to look away from the mirror. He never knew what she had in mind for him until it began to happen, but he now understood that this was a night for heavy corporal.

The slave was aroused already. Just the position The Mistress had placed him in made feelings of surrender surge up in him. He put himself deeper into the head space he needed to enjoy fully what was to come and to turn whatever pain she gave him into pleasure. She started by hand spanking him, gentle little slaps at first to bring the blood to the surface of his ass and to sensitize him for what was to come. He relished this part: her hand on his bare flesh was almost a caress as she slapped him again and again. And she gave one hell of a spanking. The Mistress believed that a good spanking should sound good, be rhythmic, and cover the complete ass.

Once, at a very dull spanking demonstration given by a "master," she had gotten up, marched to the stage, and announced that *she* would show "the master" how to give a really good spanking. Using the master's own slave, she proceeded to educate the audience on the different types of slaps, how each slap feels different depending on where one lands it and how to alternate spanks and cheeks to keep the slave excited, among other techniques. When she was finished, she got a resounding round of applause. She was magnificent. The master had the grace to look embarrassed. The slave was so proud to belong to her.

A sudden change in the intensity of her blows caught him by surprise and abruptly brought him back from his reverie. No longer the caressing little slaps of a moment ago, these blows were harder and faster and had his full attention. He watched her carefully in the mirror, delighting in the expressions playing across her face as she hit him, especially when she landed "a good one." Crushed between his body and the leather horse, his warm and full genitals throbbed and surged with each blow. The Mistress then increased the intensity of the blows, causing him to rock forward with each one and further exciting him as his genitals rubbed against the horse. Her hand pounded his buttocks; his ass quivered and shook from each blow. But cuffed to the horse hand and foot, there was nothing he could do but lie there and take his punishment.

The Mistress stopped for a minute daintily to blot the small beads of perspiration on her brow from her exertions with a handkerchief—one of his. As she did this, the slave watched her in the mirror, admiring her beauty, her long straight red hair, her tight black latex minidress, and her over-the-knee patent leather boots. The Mistress had a slender yet full figure and dressed to show it off. While he watched her, he reflected on the hot skin of his ass and knew that the worst was yet to come. He was to be caned this evening. Suddenly, her iron hand landed squarely across the bottom of both cheeks; a small cry of pain and surprise escaped him. Her deep throaty laugh rang out in the silent room, humiliating him. He tried to turn his head away from the mirror so he did not have to see the humiliation on his face, but she barked out a command that he face forward. With great effort he obeyed.

Then she threw her full weight into each blow. As her hand smashed into his beleaguered flesh, he could feel the heat rising from his skin; a sharp contrast to the cool leather of the horse pressed against his chest and pulsating genitals. Harder and faster The Mistress beat him until his ass was hot and red and a little swollen. When she stopped, she leaned over his back and laid her face next to his. She played with his hair, ran her nails down his sides, and gave him an ample drink of water from a bottle with a flexible straw. Then she said she would be back very soon and that he should rest. He heard her leave, her boot heels soundless on the carpet and the squeak of her boots barely perceptible. He knew that she would be back soon because she never left him alone for very long.

Shortly she returned, closing the door behind her. Looking at her in the mirror, he saw that she had something in each hand: a bowl of ice and a jar of Tiger Balm. She placed the Tiger Balm where he could see it, to tease him and terrify him. He knew her uses for Tiger Balm. But first The Mistress rubbed the ice cubes on his red-hot ass, in up and down, left and right, and circular patterns. The freezing cold of the ice cubes felt delightful on his fiery flesh after her very thorough attention to his ass, but under him, trapped between his body and the horse, his erection raged to be free of its imprisonment. As the slave reveled in the cold relief, he felt her spread his cheeks and tease an ice cube in and out of his anus. The feeling was incredible; it cooled his whole body, and he took great pleasure in this unusual sensation. Gently the ice cube was withdrawn from his anus. The Mistress stepped in front of him and pressed the ice cube to his lips until he opened his mouth and accepted it. It tasted faintly of his ass and once again humiliation washed over him. But still he sucked on it thirstily, gratitude in his eyes.

After the slave had swallowed the last chip of the ice cube, he readied himself for the real punishment yet to come. All that had happened prior to this moment was merely a warm-up. But The Mistress had one more surprise for him before the real punishment began. Removing the Tiger Balm from his sight, once again he felt his cheeks being parted. This time instead of the cold ice, he felt the thick, sticky Tiger Balm being applied to his anus. She knew, as he did, that the Tiger Balm generated heat, and once his cheeks were closed and the caning began, the heat would become intense. And the stuff was hard to remove.

The Mistress had done her job well, and the thorough spanking she had given him had prepared him for the caning. She gave the Tiger Balm a minute or two to work its magic while she selected the canes she wished to use. When she was done, she had laid them out in order of severity, a combination of thin, whippy canes, thicker canes that delivered more thud than sting, and a silver-handled cane that she sometimes used as a walking stick. He prepared himself for the pain.

She teased him by whipping each cane through the air so he could hear the whistling sound it made. To him these sounds were as loud as hurricane winds; he gripped the front support pole more tightly to brace himself for the onslaught. But she surprised him by gently rubbing each cane on his red swollen ass, caressing him with them, bouncing them back and forth against his inner thighs, and poking at his genitals with them first. He was panting with delicious fear and anticipation from this unexpected teasing and his erection raged between his body and the spanking horse. The Tiger Balm had set his anus on fire, adding to his agony.

He watched her in the mirror as she selected the first cane she was going to hit him with. As usual, she started out with a thin whippy one, which would sting his already bruised ass. The Mistress let it fly, and he heard the wicked whistle of the cane a split second before it landed on his red swollen ass. Stroke after stroke bit into him. At first he was able to stifle his groans of pain, but as The Mistress continued to beat him, changing from one thin cane to another, he was soon crying out loud as each stroke landed. When she was satisfied with the welts from the thin ones, she moved on to the thick ones, the canes that gave thud rather than sting, and deep muscle pain. After countless strokes of the thicker canes, each followed by a pain that started in his ass and ran up his spine to explode in his brain, he could not stop himself from crying out, but he did not beg for mercy. When he could, he watched The Mistress in the mirror as she beat him, and he loved her for her beauty and intensity. She had a look of single-minded attention on her face as she landed each stroke perfectly.

Tiring of the thick canes, she stopped for a moment to wipe the sweat from her brow with his hanky before picking up the silver-handled cane. He knew this would be the last instrument of his pain and that it would be the most painful of all. The first stroke rocked his world and stars exploded in his eyes. On and on the caning went; he had long ago lost count of the strokes The Mistress had landed. The repeated whistle of the cane followed by the cruel bite when it landed pervaded, invaded, his mind to the exclusion of all else. The only thing he was certain of was that his ass was a world of misery, welted and red, bruised and battered, and just a few strokes away from breaking his skin, drawing blood.

"Just five more strokes, only five," The Mistress whispered in his ear. Her voice was soft and sexy, like a lover's, and her hot breath so close to his ear made his whole body quiver.

For a short time, she showed him some affection. She gave him a long drink of water, ran her nails lightly down his back, ran her fingers through his hair and then, standing in front of the spanking horse, massaged his neck and shoulders. This relaxed him, but his erection still raged, squashed between his own body and the horse. Stepping behind him, she squeezed each of his cheeks in each of her hands, loosening up the skin, making it suppler. He struggled to control the urge to rub his member against the leather. This would make her very angry, and his punishment would be extended for his infraction. He did not want to displease her.

"Ready, my dear?" The Mistress asked him sweetly.

"Yes, my Goddess," he replied sincerely, although his hands gripped the front support poles more firmly and he physically and emotionally braced himself for the final five strokes.

The first stroke of the silver-handled cane was harder than he expected it would be, and he knew that her plan for these final five strokes was to make him bleed. He accepted his punishment, focusing on the pain and turning it into the pleasure only a masochist would appreciate. The second stroke was harder than the first, and he felt his skin break. The third stroke drew more drops of blood, and with the fourth, he felt blood trickle from his ass. The fifth stroke took him totally by surprise. The Mistress came around to stand in front of him and aiming very carefully, landed the final stroke in the crack of his ass.

The pain was agonizing, and even though the beating was over, he screamed, "Mercy, Mistress, mercy, please have mercy on your poor slave!"

As soon as he uttered these words, she dropped the cane and quickly released the leather restraints, hand and foot. After applying salve to his broken flesh, she allowed him to curl up in a ball on the floor at her feet. He clutched her boots and kissed them, thanking her in between kisses for her attention to him and his needs. His erection throbbed painfully between his legs, and he whimpered until her voice called him back to earth.

"You have borne your punishment very well, slave, and I am pleased with you. You will wear my marks for many days, and each time you sit down you will think of me. You deserve to be rewarded for your service to me, your Mistress."

He was thrilled to hear these words; she didn't always reward him. He must have pleased her very much.

"For your service, you will be allowed to release yourself in my presence and on my command. You will have until the count of ten. You are not to release sooner or you will be punished. If you do not come on the count of ten, you will not be allowed to come at all and you will be punished."

He loved it when she spoke to him like that.

"Now get into position and await my count," The Mistress commanded.

He lay flat on the floor, his head between her feet, and clutched his member and eagerly waited for her to start the count. Usually she added descriptive phrases in between each number to tease him further.

"One," she said, tapping the floor with her cane for emphasis. "Two!" Again she tapped the floor with her cane. With each number she called out, she tapped her cane on the floor for emphasis. More quickly than he would have liked, she called out *TEN!*

As soon as he heard ten, he exploded like a volcano, almost screaming with relief at his spurting release. His ropes of pearly jism decorated his belly, and he stroked the last few drops out as The Mistress looked on intently, an enigmatic smile on her face.

After a couple of minutes, The Mistress said to him, "You are released from service. Rest a few more minutes and then you may clean yourself up. When you are dressed and ready to leave, I will be in the living room. You may kiss my feet before you depart."

She left the room and he did as he was told. When he entered the living room, he crawled in on all fours, although she had not commanded him to do this. But he knew it would please her. The Mistress smiled as he crawled in, and she extended her right foot for his homage. Then with a wave of her hand, she dismissed him.

As he rode home, the stiff material of his jeans rubbed against his battered bottom and kept her fresh in his mind. He knew she was right, the marks would last for many, many days. But he didn't really need marks to remind him of her. Her beauty and sadism were always on his mind.

PART THREE

Lovers

Cat's Paw

She sat calmly in the big, comfortable, oversized armchair by the fire, which provided the only light in the sumptuously furnished living room. My Mistress loved thunderstorms; she loved the beauty and violence of nature. During them she became lost in a world of her own, and tonight was no different from other stormy nights. Thunder rumbled across the sky outside, and the clouds boiled in the firmament like foam from the sea. A stab of lightning lit the room, turning it silver with its glow, illuminating her lovely face. She sighed in delight at the joys of nature and looked down at me, smiling. She was dressed in jeans, a low-cut, long-sleeved shirt, and ballet shoes; it was a casual evening around the house. I was curled up at her feet—my own little shelter from the storm. I had no need to fear the storm or anything else; My Mistress was near. Safe and warm, I crouched at her feet, rubbed my long slender body on her leg and meowed.

Absently, she kicked off her shoes and began to stroke and caress me with her feet. I loved having my Mistress's feet on me; her slender, delicate bones were encased in soft pink flesh, and her delectable, suckable, lickable toes were shapely and well formed. There was not one callous, not one bone spur, not one corn on her feet to mar their perfect beauty. Her perfectly applied red nail enamel winked at me conspiratorially in the firelight. I longed to caress her toes with my sandpaper tongue; I hungered for the salty human taste of her in my mouth. Turning onto my back, exposing my belly to her to signal my submission, I purred deeply as she snuggled her toes into my fur.

She sat up suddenly as if called to sentinel duty at the gateway to paradise. My purr died in my throat. All my senses sharpened, and I looked up at her. A questioning little mew escaped me, asking her if something was wrong or if I could be of some service to her, inquiring, perhaps, if I had displeased her in some way. She gazed down at me and smiled, reassuring me that whatever had distracted her had nothing to do with me. Sighing sensuously, she curled back up on her chair, one shapely leg dangling off the edge. I resettled myself on the floor under her foot and felt her toes once again on my belly. I closed my eyes and dreamt of licking her feet, of feeling the pulse of her life on my tongue, rich and deep and sensuous.

Finally, the fireworks of the storm abated and left the steady but musical sound of rain in its place. When the thunder and lightning stopped, they took my Mistress's dreamy frame of mind with them. After a few minutes she shook herself free of the storm's embrace and removed her feet from my belly. She stood up, stretched, and padded into the large kitchen on her lovely bare feet. I heard the water running and then splashing into the kettle, followed by the unmistakable rattle of a teacup on its saucer. I heard her open the tea bag tin, and I heard the clatter of the spoon against the sugar bowl. I rolled over, stretched, and, catlike, got on all fours in one quick movement. I hurried after her, but I did not enter the kitchen. Poking my head around the corner, I peered into the kitchen and spied on my Mistress.

Her back was to me as she opened the refrigerator door and took out a full quart of milk. She opened the cardboard carton, and the sweet aroma of the milk assailed my nostrils. I was overcome with the desire to continue to gaze on her loveliness without her knowledge, the desire to wrap myself around her long, slender legs and beautiful feet, and the overwhelming desire for the milk she held so casually in her hand. The kettle whistled merrily on the stove, demanding her attention. She leisurely poured the boiling water into the teacup, let the tea steep while she put away the sugar, and then added the scrumptious milk. The gentle clatter of the spoon as she stirred her tea went unheard by me as my desire for my Mistress was temporarily forgotten; my whole furry being was overwhelmed by my craving. My obsession for the milk became the whole reason for my existence.

Unable to control myself any longer, I sprang around the corner and hurled myself at her legs. Laughing in surprise, my Mistress gazed down at me. Calling me her favorite names for me, "little bag of bones," and "fluffy hank of fur," she stood on tiptoe and retrieved a wide, shallow bowl from one of the upper cabinets. I quivered with delight at the sight of it. She must be pleased with me indeed; it was a rare treat when my Mistress took out that particular bowl. She placed the carton of milk in the microwave and warmed it up. I waited impatiently, rubbing my body on her legs purring deeply while the seconds ticked by. After a lifetime had passed, the machine gave its clarion call, and my Mistress removed the precious cargo, now pleasantly heated. She put the carton of milk in the bowl and took it in one hand and her cup of tea in the other. Before she padded back into the living room, she looked down at me—her eyes telling me to come with her. I followed her into the living room, purring in deepest gratitude.

She returned to the large soft armchair by the fire and placed the bowl on the floor in front of her. I sat at attention, watching her every move, my tail flicking back and forth with eager anticipation. I meowed softly, the sound I made when I told her I loved her, and she rewarded me with an indulgent smile. Extending her slim, graceful arm, she lifted the carton of milk from the bowl and poured the milk into it. The milk gracefully arched out of its container and whirled and eddied around the bottom of the bowl, mesmerizing me.

Finally, the last drop of the warm, delicious white nectar fell from its cardboard prison. Smiling and calling me her "pretty kitty," my Mistress placed her sublime feet in the bowl and swished them in the scrumptious ambrosia. "Come, my kitty cat, come drink your milk." I plunged my face into the bowl, extended my tongue, and began to lap at the nectar pooling between her shapely toes. The soft skin between her toes was as sweet, as mouthwatering, and as savory as the milk itself. I curled my tongue in between the silky spaces and lapped up her gift to me, eliciting a murmur of sensuous satisfaction from my Mistress. To each toe crevice, I gave the same meticulous attention, licking up the milk as I did so. Then, curling my tongue, I licked underneath her brightly enameled toenails, eagerly slurping up the droplets of tasty milk hiding there. In a welter of passion, I abandoned myself completely, utterly, abjectly to the enterprise of licking her luscious toes clean and lapping up every last drop of milk in the bowl.

While I, her pretty kitty, gave my full attention to her toes and the savory milk, my Mistress luxuriated in her chair, relishing my tender ministrations, her murmurs of pleasure becoming more and more frequent, more and more hedonistic. Her hands moved to her breasts and started to knead them, massaging the pale skin of her voluptuous breasts through her thin shirt with her long, strong fingers. Then she began to pinch and pull her nipples through the material of her shirt. I watched her through half-closed eyes as I glutted myself on the foot-flavored milk and purred contentedly, basking in the glow of her praise. All too soon, I emptied the bowl of its precious liquid.

"All done?" she purred at me, her voice soft and sweet.

She stood and stepped out of the bowl and then unzipped her pants, letting them fall to the floor. I stayed close by, watching, waiting. Wiggling deliciously, she eased her panties down her legs and took them off. Then, clad only in her top, she crossed the room and lay down on the sofa and used a hand signal to tell me that I was to join her. I sprang into her arms and nuzzled her neck. I meowed in eager anticipation of what was to come next. We had played this game before, my Mistress and I. I knew what I was to do. Breaking free of her arms, I settled myself between her parted thighs. She sighed and threw one arm back over her head.

My purr rumbled in my chest as I set to pleasuring my Mistress. Relentlessly my tongue opened her garden gate; relentlessly I licked her secret garden, searching out her button, pressing it at will. My Mistress growled like a lioness each time my rough tongue touched her, each time my caress brought a fresh flow of her own sweet juices. I lapped them up; they were more mouthwatering than the foot-flavored milk. I did not stop until she was limp from coming.

She laughed her deep, throaty laugh and sat up, dislodging me from my place between her legs. "Your turn," she said. I lay down on the floor in front of the sofa. Her soft, milky feet pressed down on my groin, manipulating me, teasing me, torturing me. I was more than ready to climax; we had been playing together for several hours. Her toe work was inspired, heavenly; she used her toes to knead me and separate me, to stroke me and caress me. Guttural moans escaped from me as she used her delicious feet to bring me to a warm gooey finish.

I was her cat now and forever.

Chastity Is a Virtue

"Have you made any attempts to find a way to rid yourself of your chastity belt this week? If you're smart, the answer had better be 'No, Mistress!' Now, get in here quickly and close the door behind you. I want you stripped out of that silly-looking business suit so that I can inspect your chastity belt for any signs of tampering. For your sake, there better not be any! I thought of you several times over the course of the last seven days, slave, and wondered how long it took you to get used to the belt.

The slave replied that he was always aware of the belt and that it never really took on the warmth of his skin.

"Oh, so you never did get used to it? During those seven little days it gave me great pleasure to think of you driving in traffic, attending board meetings, and sleeping with this locked onto you. I went to a great deal of trouble to have this belt custom made for you, slave, so you had better be grateful. A lesser Mistress would have compressed you into a poorly made, badly fitting, medieval iron belt. By this time, your delicate skin would have been scraped and raw from rubbing."

The slave, his head bent down, murmured his appreciation of the time and trouble his Mistress lavished on him.

"I have a penchant for all things beautiful and expensive, as I should. I am worth it! I had this chastity belt custom crafted from thin, lightweight stainless steel. It fits flatly across your body, and even the hinges on the sides where I have the two smallest padlocks I could find are contoured neatly. After all, I don't want any of your office buddies to comment on any unsightly bulges or lumps and give away our little secret, do I? My wish is to keep you restrained all through the day and night in total secrecy. Only you and I are to know what you wear for my pleasure."

In a low respectful voice, the slave thanked The Mistress for her kindness to him.

"I am going to inspect it now for any signs of tampering. This design reminds me of the garter belt with the attached open-crotch thong that I gave to you, which also had sufficient access for proper cleaning and hygienic needs. I refuse to have in my presence any slave who is smelly or unclean. Now, let me just check the front codpiece attachment. So how did the belt feel for these last seven days? Was it very uncomfortable having your genitalia stuffed into a short, hollow cylinder of stainless steel? Once again, I can't help but admire the workmanship. It's so very practical to have just the head peeking out and secured by the metal lip of the cylinder just under that flared ridge. At least you were able to carry on your normal bathroom necessities in spite of the chastity belt!

"But I can also imagine that when you became aroused, that poor pole of yours was tightly compressed, and it throbbed with pain inside that cylinder, didn't it? You poor little baby. That's why I instructed you to spend an hour at a strip club on Thursday night! I knew that you would feel intense frustration along with the throbbing pain. Since you were unable to achieve an erection, let alone stroke yourself, I knew that you would have absolutely no relief. The thought of you suffering like that gave me such pleasure! And of course, you will be getting no immediate relief now that you are here either! I have several plans for you, and I wish to have you in my service."

The slave remained standing, his head down, his whole body in a subservient posture as he awaited his Mistress's pleasure.

"I am going to sit in this big cushiony leather chair and get comfortable. You are to move the ottoman in front of the chair, remove my pumps, and lift my lovely feet onto it. Now, I want you to kneel on the floor at the far side of the ottoman and face me so that each cheek is pressed up against the soft, pink soles of my feet. Your nose and eyes should remain uncovered, and then you can look at me adoringly."

The slave did as he was told, using his hands to position his face as his Mistress had commanded.

"Keep your knees and hands flat on the floor, slave! I did not tell you that you could put your hands on my feet!"

The slave quickly withdrew his hands, cringing and muttering apologies for his improper behavior.

"Adjust your nose so that it is between my insteps so that the soles of my feet are flat against your cheeks and my perfectly polished toes are brushing your forehead. That's very nice! My feet are so cold and your face is so nice and warm. Now, tell me if you can see anything from under my feet. Can you see up above my knees and up between my nicely muscled slender thighs? Do you see the triangle of my black lace thong? Look up just a little higher, just above the waistband of my thong. Can you see my perfect, delicate navel? Don't you long to dive your tongue into its center? Maybe later, slave. I have other things in mind, and I do have plans for that tongue of yours!"

The slave did as he was bid. The sight of his Mistress almost overwhelmed him. From her lovely soft feet, with their delectable red-lacquered toes, to her slim muscled calves, to her well-toned thighs, she was the Goddess he had sought all his life.

"Do I see you shifting uncomfortably? Is that unruly member of yours straining to fill the steel tube that I have imprisoned it in? Is it becoming a little full in there? Are your balls aching? It makes me so happy to hear that—happy enough to want to flog you. Bend over the arm of the sofa."

She left the room and returned with a black moosehide flogger with many lashes and considerable weight. With no warm-up or preparation, she gave him more than fifty of her best, one right after the other so that the pain was constant, giving him no time to enjoy it. This was pain for her pleasure, and he knew it. Tiring of this little amusement, she let the flogger drop to the floor and sat down in her big comfortable chair.

"Come here. Now, listen carefully and follow my instructions. I am in the mood for some serious foot worship, and you had better do it properly or I will punish you most severely."

The slave's organ grew larger as his Mistress uttered these words.

"First, you are never to slobber or to leave drool on my feet! Either one will earn you a swift and severe punishment. Do you understand?" The Mistress emphasized her words by kicking the slave in the face. "I want you to start by brushing your lips gently back and forth across the tips of my toes. Slowly, lovingly, back and forth, with just the faintest touch. You also may blow very gently across them, with small gusts of your warm breath. Make sure you get all ten toes, slave! They get envious if one is given more attention than another. Now I want you to move your face down lower. I want to feel long, slow, paintbrushlike licks with the flat of your tongue up my insteps, over and over. Repeat this technique again and again. Do it slowly. Savor the taste of me and the sensation of licking me with your tongue. Feel the flat of your warm tongue leaving a trail across the soft delicate skin of my insteps."

The slave did as he was directed. The Mistress's feet were indeed delicious, with just the faintest aroma, and not a callous, corn, or bunion marred their perfection. Her insteps were high and curvy.

"Turn your head to the side, slave. I want you to use your teeth firmly on the back of my heel, as if you are massaging me. Bite them firmly but gently, using a slow opening and closing action. Be careful not to bite too hard! That might anger me, and I might just respond with a sharp kick to your lowly face. But actually, I am pleased. Apparently you do not wish to anger me so that you are performing quite well! Get both heels, slave. And press firmly with your teeth into the fleshy part of my heel. Yes, now you are starting to perfect the technique! That does feel so very nice!"

Happy at pleasing his Mistress, the slave redoubled his efforts.

"Now move your face up to my toes. I want to watch you dart just the tip of your greedy little tongue in between each of my perfectly polished toes. Give me several dry, fast flicks of that tongue before you progress on to the next space. That almost tickles and I am finding it to be very erotic. Keep up the good work, slave, and I just may allow you to watch me slip my black lace thong aside and put my fingers into my secret garden. Then I can touch myself while you work wonders with that tongue of yours. You must be doing something right because my fingers have discovered that I am wet from your attention to my feet! It seems that the crotch of my thong is thoroughly soaked!"

With these words, the slave's member became painfully engorged, mercilessly restricted by the chastity belt. But her words spurred him on to greater efforts to please her.

"I require a change in technique now, slave. Use those teeth again by giving delicate nips on the ball of each toe. Then just gently scrape your teeth across the fleshy pad underneath my toes. Now gently bite the ball of my foot. That is the part of my foot that takes all the pressure when I wear my heels, for my pleasure and for yours. Ummm, I find myself very close to gushing into my own hand. I think I shall give you a small reward by reaching down and rubbing my wet, sticky fingers across your face. Do you smell my fragrance?"

Without stopping his duties, the slave responded with a series of moans and groans to indicate his pleasure at being rewarded so richly by The Mistress.

"I love to wipe my sweet nectar over my toes and feel you and watch you as you lick it off. I'm going to dip my hand between my legs one more time and scoop up the hot slickness with my fingers. Then I am going to transfer it to the tips of my toes. I know you are happy sucking my toes and tasting my womanliness while rubbing your face into my feet. Come up here, belted one. I can only imagine how you must feel being compressed by and aching underneath that cold steel. That does please me, little foot slave. Now I want to feel your face between my legs."

When The Mistress said this, the slave's whole body trembled with pleasure and adoration, in anticipation of what was to happen next. In his eager anticipation of his reward, he overstepped his bounds and tried to wiggle his face under her thong.

"No, no, no, no! You do not get the ultimate pleasure of pressing your lips to the gate of my secret garden!" The Mistress slapped his face hard each time she said no.

The slave's disappointment was obvious in his posture.

"However, I will permit you limited use of your oral skills. I want you to lick my pretty and very wet thong. I do so enjoy how you obey immediately! I wish you were so obedient all the time. Now, press your mouth firmly into my crotch so that I can grind myself in slow, rotating circles into your lowly face. That's it. You are certainly my favorite slave when it comes to oral service. What a lovely picture this makes—I wish I had film in my camera! I would love to have pictures of you down on your hands and knees with your head buried between my thighs, licking, sucking, and tugging on my thong while your own sex organs are imprisoned in my chastity belt. I get such pleasure knowing that the head of your squashed and squeezed organ is certainly oozing. I love knowing that you have been utterly controlled by me all week, unable to achieve a rigid state because of the chastity belt and totally forbidden any kind of sexual relief. And now, at my command, you are forced to perform for my sole pleasure with no regard for your discomfort or need for orgasm. My wants are all that we will think of tonight, you little sucking slut."

The thought of denial humiliated the slave, but, as humiliation tends to do, it forced him to greater efforts to please and pleasure her.

"Do what you are told and make me come. Do you feel the tips of my fingernails digging small indentations into the back of your neck as I hold your head in place and grind my crotch into your face? Can you see that my knees are bent and my head is thrown back in pleasure? Do you notice that my eyes are closed and my mouth is slightly open as I hump your face, intent on my own impending orgasm? That's right, slave! My orgasm! Suck on my thong! Drink up my hot nectar right through it. Worship me by offering me your lowly face!

Oh, yes, I am going to come, slave! Suck me harder! Make your Mistress come!"

Using her hands to pull him by the hair, The Mistress guided his tongue to where she would best be served by it. Uncaring about him, his pleasure, or his discomfort, his nose banged painfully against her pudenda over and over until she came. Her back arched as she climaxed and he sucked with all his might to drink down as much of her sweet, sticky nectar as he could. After her release, The Mistress lounged in the chair. She pulled his head away from her crotch and let him rest it on her thigh.

"By the way, maybe tomorrow morning I'll release you from your chastity belt and allow you to stroke yourself while you wear this thong over your head. I will position it so that my dry and encrusted nectar will be over your nose. But for now, after you turn back the covers and fluff up my pillows, I am going to chain you to the foot of my bed. I'm going to sleep very well tonight!"

The slave did as he was commanded and prepared the bed for The Mistress. The *chink!* of the chain as she pulled it to enclose his ankle in the leather restraint reminded him of the sound the padlocks on the belt would make when she removed them tomorrow. Slowly, his member softened inside the cold steel of the chastity belt. He did not fall asleep until he heard that soft little wheeze she made in her sleep. He dreamt of tomorrow when he could please her, The Mistress, his Goddess, again.

The Enema Bandit

He was in bed, more asleep than awake, when he thought he heard a noise. He listened for a moment, did not hear anything else, and put his head back down on the pillow. He drifted off and fell asleep. He began to dream that someone was tempting him to open his mouth by waving choice tidbits in front of it. Bits of steak, shrimp, asparagus tips dripping with hollandaise, cantaloupe rounds, and chocolates, all passed in front of his lips in a slow dance. Unable to resist these temptations any longer, he parted his lips and closed them on the latest morsel offered to him. The sweet chocolates in his dream had become in reality the bland taste of sizing on cotton. He rolled onto his side and snapped his head up. Through his sleepy, sandman eyes, he saw a woman standing over his bed—her face, her hands, her whole body attired in black. She was tall and slim with an athletic build. Through the slits in her face mask, all he could see were her full lips coated with red lipstick and her unearthly eyes. She was wearing contact lenses that were completely black so there were no whites to her eyes at all. The effect almost paralyzed him.

Trying to get a grip on himself, he attempted to scream but his cry was caught in the cotton hanky she had crammed into his mouth. She quickly reached into a small bag and pulled out a role of duct tape. Expertly, she nipped the side with her teeth to make a slit, tore off a piece with her hands, and slapped it over his mouth, ensuring that he could not spit out the hanky. Then she quickly grabbed his arms and crossed his wrists, turning him over onto his belly. In his sleepy state, he was too groggy to fight. Craning his neck to see what she was doing, he saw her reach into her bag and bring out a length of rope. She used this rope to bind his wrists together, not too uncomfortably but still very securely, behind his neck. Once he was face down, bound, and gagged, he realized with humiliation that he was sleeping in the nude, as usual. One of her gloved hands pressed his head down, keeping him still, while the other hand explored his body. Down his slightly muscular upper back, to the two dimples at the small of his back, her hand caressed his skin, raising goose bumps on each place it touched.

Her firm gloved hands cupped his buttocks cheeks, lifted them, and massaged them. To his further surprise, he felt his cheeks being spread wide. He blushed as he felt her eyes on his anus; he knew she was staring at it. Suddenly, he felt a cool gush of air on his opening, and he tried to clench his cheeks. She laughed and let go of him. Expertly, she manhandled him and rolled him over onto his back. One strong arm held him firmly to her bosom, then she put a finger to her lips in a gesture that would have meant silence if he had not been gagged. He understood it to mean that she did not want him to struggle. He nodded timidly to indicate he would not put up a fight. She slid her arm under him and picked him up. He was greatly surprised at her strength. Not that he was a large or heavy man, but he was about five feet eight and 160 pounds. Noiselessly, she pushed the partially opened bedroom door with her foot and half carried, half dragged him down the hall to the bathroom. Once inside, she put him down on the fluffy rug and left. She brought her black bag from the bedroom and closed the door behind her.

She put the bag on the floor and then bent over him. She got him onto his belly and pushed him down into a kneeling position. She pushed his head and shoulders, with his hands still tied behind his neck, down onto the floor. His back was arched and his hips were high. Her booted foot kicked his knees wide apart. In humiliation, the blood rushed to his face. He heard the zipper of the bag whiz along, then something was removed from it. The water in the sink was turned on; he heard her remove a glove and pass her hand underneath the flow. A variety of other noises, unidentifiable, almost squeaky, almost moist, almost rubbery, played on his ears.

He jumped and gasped as her lubricated finger swiped his anus. There for a second, then it was gone. Did he imagine it? No, he could feel the coolness of the lubrication on his anus. Suddenly, he felt something cold, plastic, and formed press against him. He gasped sharply, and at that moment, the cold, formed thing passed into his tight anal muscle. It was slenderer now that the tip of it was further in. She gently pushed it further inside him, occasionally stroking him with it, until the rim of the nozzle was nestled up against the tender, puckered skin of his opening. Then he felt the stream of warm water gently filling him, its flow regulated by her fingers pinching the tube. He felt it flow softly into him, occupying him, probing him in a relentless yet delicate way. He realized she was giving him an enema.

His tension drained all at once, and this communicated itself to her fingertips. His sigh of surrender was content, audible. Her fingers loosened their grip on the tube and the flow of water ran into him faster. His own arms imprisoned him on the floor. Soft moans escaped his lips; his hips rose and fell in spite of themselves. He felt his manhood hardening and was humiliated by his arousal. One drop escaped and ran down his scrotum. He imagined it glistening, changing shape as it traveled his furrows, growing smaller as it neared the end of his penis. He saw it shimmer and tremble for just one second before letting go, falling to the fluffy rug, and disappearing forever.

The water stopped flowing and the nozzle was gently removed. He was absolutely still, hardly breathing, his belly full of water. A gentle, probing, latex-covered finger was inserted into his anus, up to the first knuckle and then withdrawn. Next, two fingers were inserted up to the second knuckle and withdrawn. Finally, the searching fingers were inserted as far as they could go. But he felt strangely relaxed— the fingers felt good and soothing and even the water filling his belly gave him an oddly sensuous feeling of floating. It was as if the water inside him had been externalized, and he was adrift on the sea under a brilliant sky. The finger playing with his anus was gentle and calming; the water made him weightless yet weighed him down. The finger seemed to grow inside of him. He sighed in surprise at the exquisite pleasure he was feeling from the enema and her fingers.

The two fingers played gentle stretching games with each other, chased each other in and out, and nestled comfortably side by side inside him. His moans alternated with sharper cries and deeper groans as the playing fingers loosened him, relaxed him, probed him, and stretched him. He knew the time was near, and from his body language, so did she, his unknown assailant. Her arms were under his shoulders, pulling him up. The floor receded and the water felt heavy inside him. Clenching his buttocks together to hold his cargo, the room became a blur until his buttocks touched the cool plastic of the toilet seat.

He could hold it no longer, the pressure was too great, the promise of release was too sweet. She backed out of the bathroom and closed the door, leaving him alone. He expelled the water, straining to empty himself, to free himself of this extra weight, this pressure, and to float again, to be light and airy, to be weightless and drained. He groaned deeply and emptied himself. When he was finished, she was gone.

When had she been able to unlock the window? he wondered absently. She was just too damn good at planning these little surprises for him.

For Your Pleasure

He saw himself clearly in the mirrored ceiling, as well as everything else in the room, especially The Diva. She was a latex fetishist, and he had never seen her wear anything else. Tonight she was magnificently clad in a black catsuit with a circular cutout above the breasts, topped by a high collar with two buckles, a black latex waist cincher nipped in her waist, and stiletto-heeled, lace-up, black and red platform boots that came just to the top of her knees. The cut of the catsuit showed off her lovely breasts and pushed them up high to make very enticing cleavage. The waist cincher was tightly laced and showed off her small waist and flat stomach. When her back was to him, her gorgeous round derriere encased in the tight black latex and plumped out by the tightly laced waist cincher made his mouth water. Her long, silky auburn hair flowed over her shoulders and down her back. He got hard just looking at her. And he knew how imaginative, sensual, and cruel she could be. The way she combined sensuality with cruelty really excited him.

Instead of painting the walls, The Diva had cleverly decorated the large windowless chamber in shirred midnight purple velvet cloth, which covered two of the walls from ceiling to floor. The soft shirred cloth made the chamber look luxurious and endless. He knew that the draperies hid the bathroom and also a small kitchenette for when she wanted "room service." The deep purple velvet covering the walls matched the thick plush carpeting. Mirrors completely covered two of the walls as well as the ceiling, ensuring that The Diva and the slave could see all of the action. Her wooden-and-purple-velvet throne stood atop a two-step platform in one corner of the chamber and next to it was a tall, narrow cage with a glass top on which was displayed a large exotic bouquet of flowers. He knew how hard it was to squeeze into that cage, but that didn't seem to be his fate tonight.

The chamber also contained a sturdy wooden X-frame, which tilted back slightly, had a padded, adjustable chin rest as well as foot stands and leather restraints for wrists, ankles, waist, and head. There was a spanking horse covered in black leather, and a long, narrow bondage table with eye hooks up and down both sides. The chamber was equipped with automatic suspension. On one of the unmirrored walls, all neatly lined up, were brass cup hooks that held The Diva's collection of whips, paddles, cuffs, nipple toys, cock and ball toys, masks, hoods, and other toys for her amusement and torture. A large vase held an impressive collection of canes and crops of different thicknesses and lengths. A small bureau contained her electrotorture devices as well as surgical gloves, lube, film wrap, condoms, and everything else the multitalented Diva needed.

But he was not occupying any of these things. He was restrained to the focal piece of her equipment collection. His arms and legs were spread out like an X, and she had used the attached leather wrist and ankle restraints to secure him to a large spinning wheel mounted parallel to the floor. Leather thongs held his head and waist in place. The wheel had eight spokes; his head and limbs were restrained to five of them. The Diva called this device the Katherine Wheel.

Right now, she was over near the door, gathering up some things in her hand. But he could not see what. She had left him his sight, sparing him the blindfold—but every favor had its price. It belittled him to look at himself this way, but he couldn't help but let his eyes drift back and forth from her to the image of himself in the mirror. The smell of her pheromones preceded her, and he strained against the leather straps to see her expression. The Diva's look was pleasant but curiously detached. Then he saw what she was holding—Japanese clover clamps connected by a chain, a pair of rather medieval (with the emphasis on "evil") nipple clamps, and a few dozen clothespins, all painted shiny black. Carefully she laid them out on the table next to the wheel that already held a glass of water with a flexible straw. Her long red nails glinted bloodily in the light in sharp contrast to the black wood of the clothespins and the cold shine of the steel. She ran her fingers over his heaving chest, which she herself had shaved for the occasion. It was going to be a night for nipple torture.

She started by playing with his nipples, using her fingers to sensitize and arouse them, making them attain their own little erection. His member responded as well, and although he knew she was aware of it, she chose to ignore it. When his nipples were aroused to The Diva's satisfaction, she stretched out each nipple and firmly attached the Japanese clover clamps to them. Although painful, these clamps were her "start-up" toy because she considered them the mildest of her nipple toys. Leaning over him, The Diva smiled her loveliest smile and began to pull gently on the chain attaching the two clamps. He moaned a little, but this was a pain he could endure and one that he received great pleasure from. When she began to pull the chain harder and pull it up toward his face, his moans of pleasure began to turn into gasps of pain, but still he knew he could endure the pain and turn it into pleasure. Last, she stood up, and pulling the chain all the way up to his mouth, she commanded him to open his mouth and hold the chain in it. He obeyed.

As he held the chain in his mouth, The Diva began to explore his body with her nails, to seek out his sensitive spots and to exploit them by pinching them, tickling them, and even occasionally biting them. Her mouth on his bare skin sent frissons through him, but still he managed to hold the chain in his mouth. Despite her smile and her offhanded expectation of complete obedience, he knew that she was in no mood to be toyed with. He decided he would be as cooperative as he could, be as receptive to her wishes as he could, and do his very best to endure whatever she had planned for him.

After she had tired of the clover clamps, she removed them one at a time, leaving a couple of minutes in between the removal of the first and second clamp. Smiling deeply into his eyes, The Diva tweaked his nipples as the blood flooded back into them, causing him to bite his lips at the new and different pain and at the onset of the pins-and-needles sensation. The distress and pleasure she saw in his eyes pleased her greatly, and her smile became tenderer and more loving because of his suffering. After his nipples recovered from the clover clamps, she gave him a drink of water out of the glass with the flexible straw. He thanked her sincerely for her kindness and awaited her pleasure.

The Diva picked up the medieval-looking clamps and held them in front of his face. They were U-shaped and connected by a chain, with cushions on both sides of where his nipples would be clamped, and a flanged rod. The flanged rod would be used to tighten the clamps as she entertained herself with his nipples. Grasping his right nipple between her thumb and index finger, she pulled it out and applied the clamp; only two clicks at first. Then she gave the same treatment to his left nipple—her eyes never leaving his face. Then, smiling, she gave each clamp another click. She stepped away from his head and began to tease and tickle his belly with her long red hair. He loved it when she used her hair to tease him; it was soft and silky on his skin, and he felt honored that she would share this intimacy with him. He closed his eyes in pleasure and didn't see her hand sneak up and give the medieval clamps another wicked click. He hadn't expected that one click to increase the pressure on his nipples so greatly. The pain became almost too much to bear, but there was her hair, still grazing his belly gently and tantalizingly, increasing his arousal.

The Diva gave the medieval-looking clamps the fifth and final click, and he cried out in pain. She smiled sweetly, enjoying his distress. She let the pain set in as she watched his face, observing carefully each expression of near agony that flitted across it. After a few minutes of watching him, she removed the medieval clamps one at a time. Then she once again started to pinch and tease his nipples as the blood returned to them. He strained against the leather restraints, but they held him firmly in place. When he had settled down, she gave him another drink of water from the glass with the flexible straw. She stood very near him and gently dragged her nails over his arms and chest, then up and down his legs, to give him pleasure and calm him down. When his breathing had become relatively normal she turned to the table.

When she turned back, he saw that she had a handful of the black shiny clothespins. She placed them at the base of his neck and whispered in his ear that he was not to let any of them fall. Then The Diva ran her hands over his chest and belly, caressing him and making him relax and feel pleasure at her touch. He sighed as she petted him and felt himself grow harder. He could see in the mirror that his member was at a hard right angle to his body, and from the small smile on her face, he knew that his hardness for her pleased her. But it also humiliated him that The Diva paid no attention at all to his response. After several delightful minutes of enjoying her caress, she stopped and turned her attention to the black clothespins at the base of his neck. She began to clip them to his chest, carefully spacing them apart until he had a line of biting black clothespins across his chest. Last, she pulled his erect nipples out, one at a time, and clamped a clothespin on each.

As she attached each clothespin, she looked deeply into his eyes, gauging his reaction, testing him, pushing him. He usually could not take this much pain, but he was her toy; more than that, he was her contracted slave, and he consented to this painful way she had chosen to entertain herself. She stepped back to survey her handiwork.

Suddenly, with a smile that contained a hint of wickedness, she gave the wheel a spin and sent him and his senses reeling. He closed his eyes to spare himself the agony of watching himself go round and round in the mirror above. She noticed this immediately and commanded him to open his eyes. Finally, the wheel came to a nerve-wracking, creaking halt. His chest was no longer a world of pain; the circulation had been cut off long enough for the pain to stop. But his head was still spinning, and he was unprepared for what happened next. She took down a bullwhip from the collection of such things hanging on the wall and then walked toward him, carefully considering the distance between them. She stopped, and without warning, without flinching, without any change of expression at all, just that same detached look on her face, she flicked out the whip.

Its tip wrapped around the first clothespin and with a supple flick of her wrist, she removed it from his chest. The pain was excruciating, but to see her wielding the whip excited him further. Then The Diva waited, her arms folded across her chest, one hip slung out to the side, until his expression showed that the pain had subsided and she could begin anew.

Again she flicked her wicked whip at his chest, the other side this time, and in quite the same painful manner removed another clothespin. Then she waited. And try as he might, he just could not keep his pain from showing in his face. Her smile became more satisfied with each flick of her whip. Her pleasure increased with the level of his pain, and there were eight clothespins on his chest. By the sixth removal, his chest was screaming in agonized protest at the repeated onslaught of the whip and at the rush of blood returning in a torrent to his tortured skin. He was whimpering for mercy, even though there were only two left. But he would not word up; he could stand it, he could turn the terrible pain into pleasure if he lost himself in her. The two remaining clothespins were the wickedest ones, on the most sensitive, vulnerable part of his quivering flesh—his nipples.

Her smile was almost evil as she drew her arm back and flicked her wrist at his far nipple. The rush of blood was stunning in the world of pain it brought with it. Without waiting for this fresh anguish to subside, another stroke of her arm and flick of her wrist sent the final clothespin whirling off into space.

"Mercy, Diva Claudia, mercy on your poor toy," he begged in agony, whimpering and tossing his head. His piteous wailing incited her.

"Do you know the difference between pleasure and pain?"

"No, Diva Claudia," he whispered, afraid he was about to find out.

Giving him a pointed look, she flicked the bullwhip at the tip of his member and then lowered her head to him, her breath hot on his flesh. The searing pain and the soaring pleasure intermingled, and his mind exploded from the volatile mix.

She raised her head enough to look into his eyes and asked him again, "Do you know the difference between pain and pleasure, my slave?"

"No, Diva Claudia, this slave is sorry, but no," he whispered, turning his head to one side in humiliation.

This time she flicked the whip at his engorged head and then fell on him with her mouth.

Again she asked him, "Do you know the difference between pleasure and pain?"

"No, Diva, I am sorry."

Again the whip flicked at the tip and her mouth immediately followed. His member was raging, throbbing, as if it had a life of its own.

"Do you know the difference between pleasure and pain?"

"There is no difference, Diva."

She untied one of his hands and told him he deserved a reward for learning his lesson. The Diva was going to crack the whip ten times. By the tenth crack of the whip, he was to ejaculate. He watched their reflection in the overhead mirror as he masturbated himself and silently counted each crack of her whip. He was ready to amuse her before the count of ten, but he controlled himself until the tenth crack. Then, crying out in relief, he pleased The Diva by releasing in a volcanic eruption of semen.

Remote Control Slave

The Mistress's slave Franco, a long-time friend very dear to her heart, was coming over tonight, and The Mistress was donning one of her alternate personas—that of The Diva. Both she and Franco loved her diva persona because they both loved elegance, grace, and an air of unattainability, and as The Diva, The Mistress perfectly exemplified these characteristics. While being The Diva, she would not be playing with him in her chamber right away but instead was going to start in the dimly lit living room, with soft music in the background and the smell of incense in the air. Earlier, she had anointed a male figure candle, inscribed his name into it, placed it on a photo of the two of them, and lit it to ensure the outcome of the evening. This was going to be a very special night. After pretending that Franco was a first time slave and giving him rudimentary training, The Diva would be taking him to a BDSM club, and before they left, he would be especially fitted out for the occasion.

As she dressed, The Diva could barely contain her excitement about this evening, about "training" Franco, and dressing to kill for the event. She selected an electric-blue ball gown with lingerie straps and bra cups trimmed in black that showed off her breasts to best advantage and was very snug on her slim figure. The gown had a very high slit up to the lower hip on the right side, which was also trimmed in black. To give the gown an even sexier look, she wore black, lace-topped, thigh-high stockings; the lace would show when she walked or sat down. Her lovely feet were encased in black patent leather, platform Mary Jane shoes with stiletto heels. Black latex opera gloves (The Diva had a glove fetish) slinked up her arms. Instead of leaving her hair straight, she had braided it wet and then had taken the braids out after they dried to give her hair a full, crinkled look. The Diva knew that full hair made one's hips look bigger, and she wanted to draw attention to the high slit in her skirt and to her stockings as well as to her breasts.

Franco arrived right on time, and The Diva led him into the living room to exchange hugs and civilities. He presented The Diva with a lovely, expensive bouquet of mixed flowers; she knew that this was a good omen for the success of the evening. Franco took in her outfit and complimented her on the perfection of her look while she arranged the bouquet in a tall vase, which she then put on an antique table. Franco himself was quite a find. He had deep-set dark brown eyes and large soft lips, and at five foot nine inches tall, weighing a slim 150 pounds with a small bone structure, he had the perfect slender body for latex. Since Franco was a hairdresser, he paid the same careful attention to his own long, dark, curly hair as he did to that of his clients. He also cut and dyed The Diva's hair and styled it for her at her request. Franco was about ten years younger than The Diva,

and he appreciated older women greatly and knew how they expected
to be treated. And Franco, realizing that this was to be a very special
evening, had worn his best latex to be a credit to his Diva.

Since The Diva had partially discussed this night's scenario with
him, Franco was prepared to be treated like a first-time slave, but he
did not know The Diva's entire plan. She knew he would comply with
her wishes, and she was tickled to death with what she had in store
for him. But now, it was time to begin the scenario. The Diva led
Franco into the chamber and assumed her place on the throne. She
pointed to a spot on the floor, and Franco immediately stood there,
awaiting her command.

As a Superior Female, she said to him, "So, you think you would
like to serve me. What makes you think you are worthy?"

Franco said nothing but hung his head in shame, not meeting her
eyes or looking into her face, playing their little game to the best of
his ability.

"No answer? You have no answer? Then I shall assume that you
are not worthy, and I will put you through a series of tests. But first,
I want to have a look at you to see if you meet my standards. You will
strip for me," The Diva said to him in a condescending tone. "First,
take off your shirt. Now take off your boots and socks. Now I want
you to take off your pants."

Franco complied obediently with this familiar routine, neatly putting his clothes to one side. The Diva very much enjoyed his strip
because she loved the sound that latex made when one put it on or
took it off. And Franco did have a lovely slender body as well as a
very long, lovely organ that she loved playing with. As soon as Franco
had stripped, he tried to cover himself with his hands. This, too, was
part of their game.

"Hands at your sides! Don't you dare try to cover yourself! In my
presence, modesty is forbidden to you. All you are, all of your body is
mine to do with as I please," The Diva commanded sharply. Franco
immediately put his hands on the sides of his thighs, revealing to The
Diva that he already had an impressive erection.

The Diva continued, "The first thing that I will teach you is that I
expect total and immediate obedience to my slightest whim and
desire. This choke collar will be a symbol of your servitude to me.
Each time, after you strip but before we begin, you will kiss the collar

as I hold it out to you; then, I will put in on you. For as long as you wear the collar, you are mine to command and do with as I wish. Now kiss it." Franco kissed the collar. "Bend your neck and hold your hair up and out of the way." He did as he was told, and The Diva buckled the collar around his neck. "Very good, slave. You are starting to get the idea. You may prove worthy after all. Next, I will tell you my rules that you are to commit to memory. You are not to speak unless spoken to, unless it is an emergency. If an answer is required of you, you are to add the phrase 'yes, Diva,' or 'no, Diva' to your reply in a low respectful tone. You are not to look me in the face without my express permission. Your eyes are to remain downcast at all times. Do you understand, slave?"

Although Franco knew the rules full well, The Diva's treatment of him aroused him greatly. He said, "Yes, Diva," in the tone he knew she liked best just to please her.

Indeed pleased with his respectful reply, The Diva softened her voice before continuing, "When you aren't performing some errand or service for me, your place will be kneeling at my feet, quietly and patiently awaiting my next command. And, of course, each command given to you will be executed cheerfully and to the best of your ability. If you commit any infraction of my rules, or displease me in any way, you will be disciplined in any way I see fit. The punishment shall fit the crime, which means I may chose not to beat you but to punish you in some other way. I may choose to make you kneel in the corner and ignore you. I may put you in the cage or the closet for a few hours. Or maybe I may put you in tight bondage, stop up your ears, blindfold you, gag you, and leave you alone to contemplate the error of your ways. Do you understand me?"

"Yes, Diva, I understand," Franco answered in a very submissive tone.

The Diva lifted Franco's chin and smiled at him. Still holding his head up, she said, "You may look into my eyes for now, slave Franco." Which he did. Then she went on, "I expect your arousal to be visible to me at all times when we are alone and you are naked before me. Your arousal and devotion to me please me greatly, and you should endeavor to please me at all times. And remember, I employ the punishment-and-reward system: punishment for bad behavior and reward for good behavior. But that decision is mine and mine alone. Do we understand each other?"

"Yes we do, Diva," was Franco's devout response.

Pleased with his answer and demeanor, The Diva continued, "Now I will teach you three of the positions I prefer my slaves to assume. The first position is on your knees is front of me"—The Diva pointed to a spot on the floor—"with your buttocks resting on your heels and your hands clasped behind the small of your back. Your knees are to be open wide so I can have free access to your genitals. This is a casual position that you may be required to assume either facing me or facing out. The facing-out position is one you would be most likely to assume in a social setting." Because of long practice, Franco gracefully fell to his knees and perfectly assumed the position just as The Diva had instructed.

Then she continued, "The second position is similar to the first, but instead, you are to raise your buttocks up off your heels so that you are 'standing up on your knees.' I will tell you to assume this position when I want to put nipple clamps on you, or gag you, or slap your face. When you are in position two, your arms will be either clasped behind your neck or outstretched at shoulder level. This is a punishment position. When you are in the arms-out position, you will contemplate the error of your ways as the pain numbs your legs and burns your shoulders. Sometimes I may elect to put glasses of water on your upturned palms to increase the intensity of the punishment. Of course, if you drop the glasses, you will be severely caned or whipped. Have I made myself clear?"

"Yes, Diva, I understand and accept," Franco said, knowing just what answer she expected and the tone she expected it in.

"Good, now I will proceed to the third, and for the time being, final position. You are to be on your knees, with your head and shoulders on the floor and your hips held high. Your legs are to be spread as wide as possible. Do it!" The Diva commanded, and Franco immediately obeyed her. "Now you are to reach back, and with your hands spread your cheeks apart." Franco did so.

The Diva rose from her throne and returned with some lube, two large beads, and a remote-controlled rheostat. But from his position on the floor, Franco could not see this. This was the part of the scenario that The Diva had not discussed with him; this was her *surprise*. As he held position three, she generously lubed the beads and his anus. When he felt the cold lube on his anus, Franco inhaled audibly but held the position. He gasped loudly when The Diva inserted the two beads into his anus one at a time, but he didn't move. With the beads deep inside him, she ordered him to rise and walk to the opposite end of the room. When he was in the corner, The Diva turned one of the knobs on the rheostat. The vibrating anal beads were electrified and The Diva delivered to him a low-voltage shock. Franco's reaction was instantaneous; he moaned and smiled at the mild electric charge that had just been sent to his rectum. Then The Diva pressed the other button, and the second bead joined its partner in a vibrating but mild anal electrotorture. This was going to be an interesting evening for sure!

The Diva then told Franco to get dressed; they had a club to go to, friends to see, socializing to do. She gave him enough time to body glide his latex and get into the tight sexy outfit he had worn before she had inspected his appearance. Franco's appearance was always more than acceptable, but protocol demanded that she find a minor thing or two wrong with it. This time, she ordered Franco to tend to his hair, which had indeed become a little disarrayed while he was in position three. Then he helped her put her coat on, adding the pleasant little touch of lifting her hair so that it didn't get caught under the coat. After that, she ordered him to bring the car around so that she did not have to walk to it. Franco left and returned very quickly with the car; he must have found a spot very close to the house as she barely had time to pick up her purse, which now contained the rheostat. As soon as the car was in front of her door, Franco opened the passenger-side door for her and then, walking back to the front door, he stood beside her while she locked up the house. Giving her his arm for support against the uneven sidewalk, he escorted her to the car, helped her in, and closed the door for her. Off they went to the party.

While in the car, The Diva explained to Franco that she would allow him some free time in the club—time to explore on his own, dance, meet new people, and so on—but when she wanted him back, she would use the rheostat to call him to her. When he was not on free time, he was to stand behind her chair, a cigarette lighter at the ready, and as soon as her drink was empty, he was to inquire if she wanted another and quickly return with it if she did. If his attention wandered, he would be zapped. The more his attention wandered, the higher the voltage would become. Franco smiled and responded that he understood and would do his best to please her. Then he thanked her for giving him free time and for thinking of such a clever way to call him to her. They smiled at each other; they were old friends and knew each other well. She leaned over and gently kissed his cheek, leaving a slight imprint of her lipstick on his skin. She knew he would wear this "badge of honor" with pride and try very hard not to inadvertently wipe it off.

Franco pulled the car up in front of the club, opened the door for The Diva, and helped her out of the car. She would wait in the foyer while he parked the car, and they would enter the club together. Once inside, Franco checked The Diva's coat and then rejoined her as she greeted friends and introduced them to Franco. While he went to the bar to get The Diva a drink, her Mistress friends admired him. They were very impressed with Franco, his appearance, his demeanor, and his attentiveness to The Diva. When he returned, she allowed them to run their hands over him, play with his long curly hair, and spank his latex-clad bottom, and she allowed him to kiss their hands or their boots in homage. Franco behaved splendidly and, of course, loved all the attention he was getting. The Diva could see the beginnings of an erection in his pants, so she reached inside her purse and gave him a little jolt with the rheostat—not a long one, just a moderate spike that she could see register on his face. Her Mistress friends, thinking that this was a sign of his arousal by them, redoubled their attentions. They searched out his nipples and pinched them, they noticed the start of his hard-on and teased him, and they bent him over the table and spanked him some more, sometimes reaching between his legs and playing with his cock through his latex pants. The Diva was amused by this and let her friends play with him for as long as they liked, as long as they did so in front of her. After all, Franco was The Diva's property, and it was her responsibility to shield him and pro- tect him from unwanted use.

Soon some of the Mistresses went off on their own concerns while a few remained at the table with The Diva. Franco stood almost vigi- lantly behind her chair and was unobtrusively attentive. He was quick on the draw with the cigarette lighter and was quite the waiter when it came to getting drinks and emptying ashtrays. Sometimes when he went to the bar, The Diva would give him a zap, causing him to turn around and smile at her. During one trip to the bar The Diva handed the rheostat to one of her friends and told her to give him a moderate zap. Franco immediately turned around to smile at The Diva, but she held up her hands in an "I don't have it" gesture and shrugged. He began to search the faces of the Mistresses to discern who had it, but all of them dissembled very well, and he couldn't tell who was presently in possession of the rheostat. Soon The Mistresses were passing the rheostat to each other surreptitiously under the table, and little zaps would shoot up Franco's ass without him knowing who had zapped him. Since they all laughed each time he reacted to the voltage being shot into him, the Mistress in possession of the rheostat remained a mystery to him.

This went on for about an hour before The Diva decided that she and Franco would go check out the rest of the club. After regaining possession of the rheostat, he held her arm as they went downstairs to the dance floor, dungeon, and other bar/lounge areas. They progressed through all the rooms, greeting friends and having a few dances, during which The Diva gave him the occasional zap when she wanted to see a little more hip action from him. She herself took great pleasure in twirling and spinning so that the high slit of her dress opened and exposed her leg and its sexy stocking. Finally, they sat together at the bar for a drink after their exertions on the dance floor. The Diva saw an ex-lover she wished to speak with privately so she gave Franco the free time she had promised him. She told him she would give him a good long zap when she wanted him to return. Then she went off to speak with her ex.

The Diva and her ex, Nigel, embraced warmly and exchanged kisses on each cheek. They found seats together and caught up on what had been happening with each of them since the last time they had spoken. He was doing well with his computer business and worked on Saturday afternoons in a famous local fetish shop. She told him about her book contracts, her slaves, her funnier happenings that had gone on in the sessions, and her slave/escort for the evening, Franco. She showed Nigel the rheostat and told him about the beads, which he found to be very amusing. A song came on that they both liked, so they had a dance and then another, working up a thirst. A bottle of water appeared and they shared it. The brutally handsome Nigel (who could have portrayed the Marquis de Sade in a movie) still possessed what had attracted her to him when they first met: a strong, sexual smell of pheromones. That smell still had its effect on her after all these years, and she was beginning to get aroused. Time for Franco!

The Diva took the rheostat out of her purse and turned both knobs up high, unsure of their range. Well, either the range was very long or Franco wasn't very far off because he appeared at her side in a matter of seconds. After she had turned the rheostat down to a low but constant voltage and stowed it back in her purse, she introduced Franco to Nigel without telling Franco about her old relationship with Nigel. Between her power over Franco and her arousal from Nigel's pheromones, she was ready to leave the club, go home, and play privately and more intimately with slender and sexy Franco. The thought of inviting Nigel along to play with them temptingly crossed her mind, but she hurriedly dismissed it as something she would have to discuss with Franco beforehand. Thinking that the discussion would distract her from her original purpose and most likely put her out of the very sexual play mood she was in, she kept it to herself. After all, there would be other nights!

After they had made their final good-byes, The Diva and Franco left for home—The Diva giving him zaps along the way to make sure he kept up a good speed. Every time she zapped him, he put the pedal to the metal and off they went. This also helped to keep them both aroused and in a state of eager anticipation. They were home in considerably less time than it had taken them to get to the club.

The Diva shut off the rheostat while Franco parked the car and went into the house to prepare for the rest of the night. She had told Franco that she would leave the front door unlocked so that he could just come in, lock up behind him, and meet her in the bedroom. Unfortunately, Franco's parking karma, due to the late hour, was not as good as it was earlier. By the time he returned, The Diva was ready and waiting for him.

As Franco entered her bedroom, the first thing he noticed, of course, was The Diva. In the room many mirrors hung from the walls and her image was reflected in most of them, as was the light from more than a dozen tall, thick white candles. The Diva, still clad in her electric blue gown, was lying on her side on the bed; she appeared to be floating on the black satin duvet cover like an exotic lake on a black sand beach. He noticed that the only thing she had taken off were her gloves. Then his eyes took in the entire scene. The bouquet he had brought her earlier graced her dressing table, the fragrant smell of the flowers pervaded the room, and their favorite music was playing in the background. No toys were in sight except for the rheostat on the bed near her hand and a barely concealed bottle of body glide.

"Undress for me, Franco. Do it nice and slowly and to the music," The Diva said in a tone that showed her arousal.

Although tight latex isn't the easiest of garments to remove sexily, Franco did quite well by just slowing down the regular actions one would do to get out of latex clothing and stopping when, for example, he reached his nipples so that The Diva could eat them up with her eyes. When he pulled the shirt over his head, he paused so that his shirt covered his face; he then became just a body for The Diva's desires, a faceless slave to be used for her pleasure. When removing his pants, he pulled them down to the top of his groin without exposing his erection and used his slender body to snake dance. The Diva was increasingly pleased by his performance and very excited by it too. As Franco continued to remove his pants, he turned around and rolled them down, exposing his small tight buttocks. Instead of the silly butt wiggling most slaves would do at this juncture, he bent slightly at the waist, stood still, and looked over his shoulder into her eyes. The Diva found this to be much sexier than butt wiggling. Slowly turning to face her again, he slipped his hands down his pants and rolled them down just a little more—his eyes never leaving her face.

As for The Diva, Franco's sexy body, the creativity, the grace and slowness of his strip, and the look in his eyes were making her creamy. A dreamy look came over her face that she knew he was not only aware of but also knew the meaning of.

Before Franco could get his pants off, he had to remove his boots. To someone else this could be a clumsy process, but not for Franco. Facing the nearest wall, he put both hands on it in an "up against the wall and spread 'em" position and used one boot to take off the other and then remove the other boot with his socked foot. The "spread 'em" position seen in so many cop shows was a very submissive one in The Diva's eyes, and her excitement grew. Casually pushing his boots to the side, Franco walked toward her and began to roll down his pants a little more with each step. His slow sinuous movement as he walked and the languid way he continued to roll down his pants made The Diva breathe heavier with each step he took. Sliding his hand down the side of his pants, Franco used his wrists in an outward motion to roll them down far enough so that his beautiful cock sprang free. The Diva gasped her approval and motioned for him to continue.

Franco complied happily, feeling the electricity emanating from The Diva and filling the whole room. He was very aware of the beads still in his ass, although they were not being used at this time. His erection was impressive, and from The Diva's pleasure with him tonight, he knew he would be richly rewarded. As his pants cleared his hips and his sack sprang free to join his erection, he now had to get the latex pants down the rest of his legs. Not an easy thing to do and something that required some thought before attempting. Continuing his sinuous walk toward the bed, he lay down on it on his back, pulled his legs up to his chest, and using one hand for each leg, he rolled them off inside out, taking his socks off along with the pants. Then, with a graceful, catlike motion, he slinked off the bed. The Diva rolled over onto her side, luxuriating in the feel of her latex against the satin duvet cover, never taking her eyes off Franco for even a second, and letting her sexuality mount unchecked. Finally, standing naked before her, Franco moved and swayed gently to the music, turning slowly so she could see all of him but without making any of those clownish motions he knew she did not like.

"Come here, Franco. Join me on the bed," The Diva said softly. It was the most seductive command he had ever heard.

He walked slowly to the bed, not wanting to appear too eager or in any way entitled, and stretched out next to her, face to face. Moving closer to him, The Diva ran her hands over Franco's body. His black-on-black bedroom eyes, deep liquid pools of sensuality, held hers as she touched, caressed, and fondled him. His skin was smooth, soft, and hairless, except for his groin; even the skin of his circumcised cock was silky soft and without blemish. His sack was high, tight, and close to his body. He moaned in ecstasy as she caressed his genitals and moved her body closer to his. Her latex was cool against his warm skin, but the coolness excited him further. He threw his arm around her and hugged her as she fondled him. She began to kiss his face, light gentle kisses on his forehead, cheeks, eyelids, nose, and, finally, on his large soft lips.

When Franco felt The Diva's tongue gently tease and probe his lips, he opened his mouth and responded to her. They began to kiss slowly and sensually, taking their time, letting their passion build but in a controlled manner to prolong their enjoyment. There would be no rooting around like pigs but rather The Diva leisurely pleasuring herself while rewarding her slave.

In time, their kisses became more passionate, their bodies pressed closer together and soft sexual moans could be heard coming from The Diva while Franco's passion expressed itself in deeper, masculine, growling sounds. The Diva's thighs were creamy from Franco's kisses and his lovely erection pressed against her, occasionally rubbing across her swollen cunt and making her groan with pleasure and desire. She wanted to come, and she wanted Franco, her dear friend and slave for the night, to come too. She reached for the body glide and liberally applied it to his gorgeous hard-on, rubbing him sensually as she did so.

Then, gently turning in his arms so that her back was to him, she rolled them both onto their stomachs on the bed; his naked body pressed against her back, covered in the now-warm latex. While his head was buried under her hair, kissing her neck, she reached for the rheostat.

She spread her legs and said, "Wrap your arms around me, Franco, and hold me close."

Franco's arm encircled her, and one arm reached down far enough to hold her hips up off the bed. She creamed when he did this, it was one of her favorite positions. She worked her own hand underneath herself and buried it between her legs, greatly aided by the high slit in her ball gown.

"Now, Franco, my dear Franco, pretend you are taking me from behind; pretend that we are lovers. I shall use my hand, and you will go through the motions of penetration against my dress. We shall come together, you and I; you on the outside of my dress and me on the inside of it." The passion in her voice was unmistakable; her arousal could not be denied, and neither could his, and the room already smelled of sex.

He began to stroke himself against her dress as she had so seductively commanded, slowly and gently in rhythm with the motion of her hand and hips. Her well-conditioned latex was somewhat slippery and the generous amount of body glide she had so lovingly applied to his cock felt wonderful as he stroked. As his strokes got a little faster and harder, The Diva used her free hand to turn on both beads with the rheostat, setting a low constant voltage with the occasional sharp spike to egg Franco on. As the intensity of his strokes increased, The Diva edged up the voltage with the rheostat and the occasional spikes she gave him became more intense. There was no denying that the electricity from the rheostat spurred Franco on and increased her passion and pleasure as her hand moved between her creamy, sticky thighs.

Finally, The Diva could wait no more, and she knew that Franco was as ready as she was. "Let's come, Franco, let's come together."

She needed no verbal response from him, she felt him go into his come stroke and held on until she felt his body jerk. At that very instant, she pressed her button and had the most smashing orgasm. Spent, they lay there wrapped up in each other until their passionate intensity turned into the afterglow of appetites satisfied and needs met, the rheostat no longer emitting its charge.

Quite a long time passed before Franco rolled off her and lay flat on his back. She was still on her stomach, not yet ready to move, relishing the stickiness between her thighs and the looseness of her limbs. Quietly, so as not to disturb her, Franco got up and came back into the bedroom with their cigarettes and a selection of beverages. Over his arm was a warm wet towel that he used to clean his pearl jam off her dress. He lit a cigarette, gave it to her, and then poured her a glass of sweet lemony iced tea. Before she accepted either, she reached out her arm and pulled him to her for a deep kiss. Then she took both the cigarette and glass with a smile.

"You may go into the bathroom and remove the beads now, Franco. Bathe if you want to, and then return to me as quickly as possible," The Diva said gently.

Franco thanked her and hurried down the hall to obey. She could hear that he was taking what she called a "birdbath," not a full shower, but kneeling in the tub and using the removable showerhead to thoroughly wet and wash himself. She had taught him how to take the quick yet effective birdbath herself; it was especially good if one wanted to be clean without getting one's hair wet.

Franco returned to the bedroom in the freshly washed nude to find that The Diva had taken off her dress and shoes but left her sexy black thigh highs on. The duvet cover had been pulled back, and only one candle remained lit. The music was softer and sexier than before and the volume was lower. The Diva was already ensconced in the large bed and patted the place next to her. Franco was to stay the night, and they would cuddle while they slept. His deep dark eyes looked into hers as he climbed into the bed. She immediately turned onto her side next to him and put her head on his chest, a position familiar and comfortable to both of them. His arm curled around her and held her close. She fell asleep in no time at all.

Franco, on the other hand, lay there for a long time thinking about the wonderful experience they had shared. He loved her, he loved her when she was The Mistress, he loved her when she was The Diva, but most of all he loved her when she was just herself. Finally, he fell into a light sleep, constantly aware of her body pressed so close, so trustingly to his.

She-Wolf in Sheep's Clothing

Right up until the moment the slave first came into my presence and I imposed my will on him, he had fancied himself a dominant male. Many "masters" had come to me to explore their submissive sides, but they had no true understanding of submission, of how to surrender to their inner desires and of what to do to become my slave. So they had remained "tops" and played the top game, all the while waiting for the one woman whose caress would awaken them from their long sleep.

I knew him to be my slave before he knew me to be his Mistress. We saw each other at a party, I was there with friends—he, alone. He was tall, with long, straight dark hair pulled back in a ponytail, deep-set bedroom eyes, and a swimmer's well-toned body. He was well dressed; his black leather pants clung tightly to his ass and hugged his thighs. His white Lord Byron shirt was a perfect contrast to his good looks, and his green eyes glowed with sexuality. This man was a very romantic figure indeed, and I could just bet that any number of female slaves were his for the taking. All through the evening I felt him watching me, and whenever I turned, wherever I was, he was just a few feet away. Still believing himself to be dominant, this handsome man with a whip hanging from his belt made me curious, so I got a slave to give me a foot massage so that I could observe this master. I was quite cruel to the slave serving me just to show this man that I was a top and not for him unless he was ready to submit to me and become my slave.

A month later we ran into each other at another party. Dropping our dominant personas like coats checked for convenience, we sat and talked for a couple of hours and found we had a few important "outside" things in common—a love of the beach and a penchant for bookstores and antique and secondhand shops. When I said I was tired and wanted to leave, he offered to drive me home. We exchanged numbers at my front door and after a sweet, almost chaste kiss, we parted company. He promised to call me, I promised myself not to hold my breath. The next day he called and we made a date for Monday.

It was a work holiday, and he came over around three, empty-handed, not even a cheap bouquet of flowers in hand. Handsome as he was, this man needed to be taught the manners of a gentleman before he could be taught how to be a proper slave. We went out for a bite to eat and had the restaurant all to ourselves. We spent a couple of hours talking over our meal. At least he paid for the meal. Maybe it was because that was his intention all along, or maybe it was because I looked away when the check arrived and made no move to reach for my purse. Then at my suggestion, we went back to my place. We hadn't been on the black leather sofa for five minutes when he tried to pull me onto his lap. I slapped him hard across the face and asked him what he thought he was doing. He looked absolutely astonished that I had slapped him. Then I told him that a *gentleman* didn't behave in that manner and that I was not his for the taking. He had to prove himself to me before I would accept him into my service. He looked utterly stunned when I said *service*. I laughed in his face, but gently and with girlish humor, because I didn't want to appear cruel and scare him away. Besides, the smell of his pheromones drove me wild.

"Haven't you realized yet that you are here to explore your secret desire to be submissive? Haven't you recognized that you want to surrender your control to a powerful woman who knows what to do with the power you have given her? I saw it written all over your face in the club while the slave was giving me a foot massage. You spent more time looking at the slave than you did looking at me. Your whole stance told me that you wanted to be in his place or in a position of submission to The Mistress," I said in a sweet voice.

He sat in silence for a few seconds, pondering my statement and wondering how to answer it. Would he admit to his secret desires? Was I pushing him too far too soon? I asked myself. Would he continue to play his little top game?

"Well," he said, pausing before he went on. "I have always had fantasies about being a certain type of slave and of being used and under control of a powerful woman. But I have always been embarrassed to admit to these fantasies out loud. I am afraid of speaking about them, and even more afraid of what enacting them and releasing them would unleash in me. I would be terrified of what people would think about me if they knew."

"What goes on in the dungeon stays in the dungeon," I replied in a level voice, looking him directly in the face. "That is part of the creed of the sensual female dominant. Unlike male creatures who fancy themselves dominant, the female dominant does not need to brag of what she did with whom or make herself seem more important by telling tales out of the play space. Nor do we use our male submissives to procure for us. I have often wondered how the poor female submissive feels when she is sent off on a quest to find another girl for her master to play with."

Knowing what I said to be true, he at least had the grace to look embarrassed. After all, I had been in the scene long enough and in enough different cities and countries to have heard these male-told tales firsthand. They stood around exchanging these stories, laughing. I found this extremely distasteful and disrespectful to the poor female submissive who expected her sexual exploits with her master to be held in confidence. And I had often wondered how the woman felt to be commanded to procure another female for him. Did it make her feel inadequate, unable to fulfill her master's desires? Was it plain greed on the master's part? Was it a very good excuse for him to fool around with another woman? Or was it just to bolster his fragile male ego? I suspected it was all those things.

To set him at ease, I offered him tea. I served it in my silver tea set, on a silver tray but my manner was that of a good hostess, not that of a female slave. Over tea, I turned the conversation to more casual subjects, feeling that I had pushed him enough for one evening. I knew he would be back. After tea, I said that it was getting late. He took the hint and thanked me for the lovely afternoon and evening. As he stood in the doorway, he asked if he could call me again later on in the week. I smiled and said yes. Deep inside of me, I knew I had won the battle, if not the war. After all, he must like me before he could become submissive to me; if not, all he would be was rebellious. And to me, dominance and submission is not a contest of wills.

Luckily for him, he called on Thursday night. If he had called on the day itself, I would have been "busy." We ladies have a saying that if a man calls you after eight o'clock on the same night he wants to see you, there is nothing but a hard-on on the other end of the line. But he asked if he could see me on Sunday. Although a Thursday call was plenty of time for a Sunday date, I told him no, that Sunday was not a good day for me. Actually my Sundays are sacrosanct; on Sundays I visit with my girlfriends or go out with them to brunch or early dinner, wander off on my own little adventures to occult shops, antique shops, fetish shops, and the like, or just stay at home and spend the day in my pajamas reading, listening to music, or talking on the phone. I didn't feel that at this point he was worth wasting a perfectly good Sunday on. I suggested Saturday at six o'clock in the evening instead, and he said yes.

"Please call me at four to confirm that you are still coming. We will have dinner together. And remember, a gentleman never appears at a lady's door bringing nothing but his attitude and his appetite. A gentleman brings the lady flowers or chocolates or cigarettes or some other token of his appreciation to show the lady that he knows proper manners and that he is a gentleman," I said with a smile in my voice to take the edge off my words before hanging up. Only his arrival on Saturday would tell if he had caught on. Men, especially masters, can be so dense.

At four o'clock sharp on Saturday, the phone rang. I let it ring four times before picking it up. "Let him think I forgot," I thought to myself. When I picked it up, I said "hello" in a deep sleepy voice, although I was not sleeping. I could hear the relief in his voice that I had answered, and he asked courteously if he had woken me up. My little ploy had worked; the four rings and the sleepy voice did make him think I had forgotten. But would he show up with at least one of the aforementioned "gifts?" We exchanged pleasantries, confirmed his six o'clock arrival, and said that we should have dinner together. I didn't say that I wanted to "order in." Although he didn't know it, "dinner in" was one of my little tests for potential submissives. I would place the order; he would answer the door and pay for the delivery, then under my instruction and supervision, serve the dinner, clear the table, and place the dirty dishes and cutlery in the dishwasher. He was lucky that I had a dishwasher; otherwise, he would have to wash the dishes by hand!

At one minute to six, my doorbell rang. Before answering it, I peeked out the front window. There he was, freshly showered and shaved, with a rather nice bouquet of flowers in hand. Good! At least he could be taught how to treat a lady properly and that would make him easier to train as a submissive. I hated a man, even in a vanilla situation, who was too cheap or too boorish to behave like a gentleman. After all, was a ten-dollar bouquet or a box of chocolates too extravagant an expenditure for an evening with a lady? I think not. I straightened my sleek black dress, checked my coiffure and makeup, and answered the door with a welcoming smile. I gestured him in, and he gave me the bouquet as we exchanged European-style kisses, one on each check. I thanked him graciously for the flowers, took his coat, and escorted him to the living room and asked him to wait while I tended to the flowers.

I returned to the living room with his bouquet in a vase and placed it in a "position of honor" on the mantel over the fireplace. The mirror over the fireplace reflected the flowers, making the bouquet look much larger than it was. The bouquet was flanked by tall taper candles in brass candlesticks that I had found in an antique shop, as well as framed photos and other decorative items from people and places around the world that were close to my heart. I turned to him, smiled, and asked him if he would like some wine. He said yes. In the kitchen, I put the wine, a glass, and corkscrew, plus a tall glass of iced tea with four ice cubes and a good squeeze of lemon for myself on the same silver tray I had used to serve tea on his first visit and entered the living room smiling. I placed the tray on the coffee table in front of the sofa and sat down about a foot away from him. I told him I wasn't very good at uncorking wine and asked him to do the honors. He complied quite graciously; he even poured the wine himself, just as I had expected him to do. Then we toasted to our health and happiness.

We sat conversing and sipping our drinks. As darkness fell and the room grew cooler and dimmer, I lit several candles and turned on two lamps that were at opposite ends of the room and that had 25-watt pink lightbulbs in them. Then I asked him if he knew how to make a fire. I just love the crackle and glow of a fire. Who doesn't? But as it turned out, he didn't know how, so I offered to show him. What I actually meant was that I was going to tell him what to do and he would do it. On our knees together in front of the fireplace, I told him how to place the kindling, handed him the Duralog to put over it, and told him how to place the firewood over it all. Then, I handed him the long fireplace matches and pointed out where to insert the match so that the kindling would catch and ignite the Duralog, which would in turn light the firewood. I told him he had done well for a "first timer." He didn't even notice that I hadn't done anything other than hand him the matches. So far, so good.

The crackle and roar of the fire, its warm, flickering glow, and the soft candlelight made the living room very intimate, very sexy. Indeed, the fire made it seem like there was nowhere else in the world but the living room; that the rest of the world had somehow disappeared and taken all its occupants with it. It was quite lovely, and I could tell he was enjoying it as much as I was. We sat on the sofa, sometimes speaking, sometimes just sitting quietly and staring into the fire. The primal and mesmerizing force of fire unfailingly had that effect on everyone; beautiful yet dangerous, accessible yet mysterious, fire was an uncontrollable force of nature that humankind, with some success, tried to control. I related to the fire. I, too, was beautiful yet dangerous, accessible but mysterious, and a force of nature that could and could not be controlled. Yes, I was fire. And I was also ice.

I suggested that we order dinner in and he agreed. I rose, went to the kitchen, and returned with several menus offering a variety of cuisines. He seemed confused with all the choices, so I asked him if he liked Indian cuisine. He replied that he had never eaten it but would be interested in trying it. I told him he was in the hands of an expert, and all he need do was tell me if he liked hot dishes or mild ones. Before he could reply, I said that we would order one of each, lamb korma as the mild dish and butter chicken as our hot-and-spicy selection, plus the mixed appetizers for two, poori bread, nan, kasundi (a chopped onion dip made with lemon, paprika, and cayenne pepper), basmati rice, and two mango lassis. Of course, he agreed to everything I suggested, so I called and placed the order. It would arrive in half an hour. Perfect! Just the amount of time I needed to instruct him in setting the table for dinner.

I didn't have a dining room, but my living room was very large and I had placed an antique cherry drop leaf table and two matching chairs in the front of the bay window. I directed him how to open the leaves of the table and to make sure they sat correctly against the support molding so the table didn't collapse on us while we ate. I pointed out two candles that I wanted placed on the table and he hurried to get them. Things were going well, quite well. He was learning how to be a gentleman and a submissive at the same time. He was completely relaxed in my company, and after dinner I would broach the subject of his submissive fantasies. I already had an idea of what they were, and I would be extremely surprised if my instincts were wrong. I am hardly ever wrong about these things.

I took him into the kitchen where I sat on a high stool as I pointed out where the plates were, which ones and how many we would need, which glasses I wanted, and where the cutlery and linen napkins were. He pleasantly set about retrieving everything from its appointed place, put it all on a tray, and happily followed me back into the living room to set the table. I told him the proper places for the cutlery; I instructed him how to fold the napkins into pleats and place them in the glasses so the napkins overflowed the sides like flowers. He was most cooperative; I was very pleased with not only his acceptance of my instructions and his willingness to perform these actions but his potential as a submissive. I smiled to myself that he was acting like a slave and didn't even realize it. The iron hand in the velvet glove usually worked better than the iron hand alone, especially with a man who fancied himself dominant. These things had to be done slowly and in their proper order.

Once the table was set, we sat on the sofa, again mesmerized by the fire until the doorbell rang a few minutes later. Like a good little boy, like a proper gentleman, and like a good slave, he hurried to the door to pay for the delivery. I heard him tell the delivery person to keep the change. Good, very good. He returned to the living room, bag in hand, and asked where I would like it. I "suggested" that he clear the coffee table of the tray and lay out the dishes there, buffet style. When he was in the kitchen, I called out to him to bring several large serving spoons from the cutlery drawer, which he did. Then he unpacked the bag and placed the tin take-out dishes on the table; entrees with entrees, appetizers with appetizers, and bread with bread. I told him to leave the entrees covered so they wouldn't get cold while we enjoyed the bread and appetizers. When he came to the table to get his own dish, I handed him mine. He didn't seem the least bit surprised. He divided the appetizers in half, and at my suggestion, he served half of the bread with them, leaving the other half for dipping in the sauces of the entrees.

We talked when our mouths were not full of the delicious spicy appetizers. I explained to him what each one was—which ones were finger foods versus fork foods, which dipping sauces were aromatic, and which ones were hot. I laughed kindly when he took too much of the hot sauce, and tears ran from his eyes and his nose started to run. I excused him from the table to go clean himself up and to drink some milk; then, I graciously gestured him back into his chair on his return. He was laughing at his misadventure and I laughed with him. I like a sense of humor in a man, vanilla or submissive, especially when he has the ability to laugh at himself.

The appetizers finished, I asked him to clear the table of the used dishes. On his return from the kitchen, he automatically brought both of our plates to the buffet. He was a fast learner too, all the better; I hated to repeat myself. I told him I liked a line of rice down the

middle of my plate with the entrées on either side of the rice. He
served me first, then filled his own plate, bringing the last half of the
bread to the table along with his own dish. But he had forgotten
about the mango lassi, so I let him sit down before I politely asked
him to go get a bowl of ice, fill the glasses with it, and pour the lassi
over the ice. He apologized for his oversight and didn't spill one drop
of the rich thick liquid as he poured it over the ice. Then we dug in.
The delicious aroma of the highly spiced food pervaded the living
room as we dined by candlelight near a glowing fire. After we finished
gorging ourselves, he cleared the table, gathered up the remains of
the buffet, and brought everything into the kitchen. I could hear the
rattle of cutlery and the clink of dishes being loaded into the dishwasher. I smiled.

When he returned to the living room, I was seated on the sofa; I
patted the cushion right next to me and he sat down, our thighs just
touching. The time was right to try to get him to speak about his fantasies. He was relaxed and comfortable in my presence, and I knew he
did not feel threatened by me or anything else. He was enchantingly
enmeshed in the world I had made for us, and nothing would shatter
or dispel that feeling. My body language said that I was relaxed and
receptive and that I was someone in whom he could confide, but
inside, the predator in me was closing in for the kill. He was mine; I
knew it.

"So," I said in a low conspiratorial voice, "I'll tell you my pleasures
as a domina if you tell me yours as a master. But you have to go first."
Then I smiled and moved a little closer to him. I looked directly into
his beautiful green eyes and held his gaze; my eyes were warm and
inviting, conveying that he could trust me. I knew that often a top does
to the bottom what the top secretly desires to have done to them.

He hesitated for the briefest second before he said, "I like to control my slaves by taking away their control over their most intimate
and taboo opening." My heart jumped for joy; I was right! Then he
continued, "After I teach them the way I want to be served, I use anal
penetration as reward and punishment, enforced with humiliation and
the occasional beating." He cleared his throat and went on, "I use
dildos, butt plugs, my fingers, and anal balls, all with the intention of
one day getting my hand up their asses. I make them reach back and
feel my hand in them up to my wrist, walking them to a mirror so

that they can have a good look at my wrist buried in their opening and their hole stretched to accommodate me. I wiggle my fingers inside of them and make them tell me which finger that one was. If their answer is incorrect, I punish them by making a fist and pulling it out of them, instead of my hand. I like to crupper large plugs or dildos into them while they serve me. I love watching them insert large objects up their anuses at my command and making them push their own fingers and hand into themselves. I love the way their holes gape open after I have used them, and to humiliate them, I look up their rectum."

I said nothing but moved in closer to him as he confided more and more of what were actually his own desires to me. As he spoke, my desire for him increased and his pheromones assaulted me. I knew why he was reluctant to say that these were the things he wanted done to him; these things he had dreamed about as he put himself in the slave's place. Fear of being called a homosexual, fear of confronting that he would enjoy surrendering his own most intimate, most taboo opening to a woman, fear that once his demon was released he would not be able to control it. Thus, he took control of it in his female slaves. I waited for him to go on.

"When they need to be disciplined, I do not beat them with a whip, I make them get on their knees, shoulders to the floor. Then I order them to spread their cheeks, and I punch or slap their anuses, depending on the severity of the infraction committed. When I want oral sex, I face fuck them or use my hands to hold their heads and push their mouth down on my cock until they gag. Sometimes, with the proper coaching, one of them will be able to swallow my length, and I count out how many strokes I can get in before she retches for air. Not often enough, I can make one throw up from my deep thrusting into her mouth." He took a deep breath and looked into the fire. I took his hand and said nothing. Inside I was thrilled; my instinct had been right, I could almost read his mind and see that he was putting himself into the slave's place. He didn't even think to ask me what I liked to do as a domina.

It was getting late and he had had enough for one evening. We sat until I felt his mood change, and then I passed a surprised comment on the time. He took the hint and prepared to go. I escorted him to the door and gave him a soft lingering kiss on the lips on his way out.

Stopping in the threshold, he asked if he could call me again. I agreed at once; after all, he had told me all I needed to know and plenty more. On his next visit, I would begin granting him his desires.

The She-Wolf Pursues Her Prey

He called Tuesday evening. He thanked me for the lovely, intimate evening we had shared the previous Saturday and asked politely if he could see me on Friday. Although I knew I was free, I told him I had to check my schedule, wanting to keep him in suspense for a little while. Yes, I was free on Friday evening. Would eight o'clock be convenient for him? He said yes right away. I said I was in the mood for some chocolate truffles.

At eight sharp he arrived at my door, a box of expensive truffles in hand. Instead of a slinky black dress, I wore a pair of white latex jodhpurs, shiny black stiletto boots, a white ruffled latex shirt, and a black latex waist cincher, laced as tightly as I could get it. I wore dark eye makeup and very red lipstick. When he first saw me, his eyes opened wide, and as he handed me the truffles, he said I looked really sexy. I thanked him most graciously, accepted the truffles, and gestured that he follow me into the living room. I had already set the coffee table with fruit, wine, glasses, and a glass pitcher of ice tea afloat with lemons. A silver ice holder was off to the side. I had started the fire myself, the candles were lit, the incense was burning, and soft sexy music played in the background. I played the role of the perfect hostess, putting him at ease in these new yet familiar surroundings by pouring his wine and making sure of his comfort. We chatted amiably while he drank his wine and I opened the truffles. I made a big deal eating them, licking out the soft delicious centers with my tongue, teasing him, and playing with him until his body language told me it was time to begin.

What he did not know was that one of the table drawers contained black latex above-the-wrist gloves and an assortment of toys I planned to use on him tonight, as well as the lube if things got that far. This evening was to be very different from the first.

Smiling and making a sexy noise in my throat, I moved closer to

him and unbuttoned the top two buttons of his shirt. He looked
pleased at my attentions as I ran my hand up and down his almost
hairless chest inside of his shirt. I tweaked his nipples and he sighed;
they were very sensitive but actually had nothing to do with my plan.
This was just his warm-up time—the time he needed to get used to
me slowly but surely taking control. I continued to run my hands over
his chest, lightly dragging my nails on his skin and using my fingertips
to offset their sharp square-filed edges. I did this until he finished his
wine; he downed it so fast that he got a little tipsy right away. Then I
asked him to stand up and take off his shirt; I said I wanted a good
look at what felt so beautiful under my hands. Highly pleased by my
compliment, he stood and stripped off his shirt, proudly showing me
his well-toned, nicely muscled chest and arms. Then I opened my
knees and asked him to kneel between them at the edge of the sofa.
In a sexy voice, I told him I wanted to run my hands over his chest
and arms without the encumbrance of his shirt. He did not hesitate
for one second, and I made a most feminine show of appreciation as
I touched him.

After a few minutes of this, I patted the sofa next to me to invite
him to sit and poured him another glass of wine. He sat and accepted
the wine, making a small toast to me before drinking. Now I wanted
him to take off his pants, but I continued to play my coy little game to
lure him in. I sat very close to him, curled my legs up onto the sofa,
and leaned against his shoulder as he drank his wine. I watched him
carefully, looking for any signs that he thought he was falling into the
role of the master. There were none; he was just a man enjoying the
attentions of a playful woman. I was playing a dangerous game, and I
had to plan each move carefully to make him mine. But so far things
were progressing according to my plan, and I expected no difficulties
in getting him to disrobe entirely at my gentle, politely phrased commands. After I stripped him of his clothes, I would tenderly begin to
strip him of his inhibitions.

As he sat drinking his wine, I ran a hand up and down his thigh.
With the other, I played with his long, straight dark hair. He luxuriated under my touch as I pulled his hair firmly and raked my nails like
a comb over his scalp and then massaged his head. All this time, the
other hand was busy touching his thigh and drifting closer and closer
to the hard bulge that had appeared in his pants. Occasionally, I

would "accidentally" go up too far and brush the back of my hand against his bulge, then withdraw it as if embarrassed at having touched him there. When he finished his wine, I took the glass from him and placed it on the table, telling him to stay comfortable and relaxed. Then I suggested that he let me remove his shoes—he would be so much more comfortable without them. I knelt before him and efficiently removed his shoes and then positioned myself between his legs, which had spread while I had played with his hair and rubbed his thigh. One hand on each knee, I smiled up at him and gave a throaty laugh at our "sudden" intimacy.

He leaned forward to pour himself another glass of wine, quite aware that his handsome chest would come very close to my face. Although I did not accept his obvious invitation to kiss and rub my face on his chest or give in to my own desire to do so, I purred and wiggled my hips in appreciation of his proximity. Again, I smelled his pheromones and became very aroused. I knew my spell was working, on both of us. After he sat back, I knelt up and put one hand on either side of his shoulders and teased his chest with my long, straight auburn hair. His third glass of wine was beginning to have the desired effect. He chuckled at the new sensation, and I laughed from under-neath my veil of hair. Then, I flung my hair back from my face. I knew I looked lovely when I did this, and from the look on his face, he thought so too. I ran my hands down his chest, my eyes cast down, although I could see from beneath my lashes that his eyes never left me. I knelt down between his legs. My hands played over his belt, and I coyly pretended to grow bolder. Slowly, I unbuckled his belt. He made no move to stop me; after all, weren't all men greedy pigs when it came to the possibility of having their cocks touched?

After I had unbuckled his belt, I remained on the floor between his open legs and massaged his thighs and calves; I even spent a short amount of time massaging his feet through his socks. I felt the tension flow out of him and continued with my plan, massaging him and touching him until he was completely at ease. Except for my latex outfit, this could have been a vanilla date. I gave him a finishing caress and curled up on the sofa very close to him. He put his arm around me and I laid my head on his chest, my fingertips making gentle circles on his chest. I noticed he wasn't sipping his wine as quickly now and thought to myself "good." I didn't want him drunk, just relaxed. I didn't want him to claim that I had taken advantage of him while he was too intoxicated to know what was happening and consent to it.

His head was resting on the back of the sofa, his eyes were closed, and every inch of his body told me he was thoroughly enjoying my attentions—the night's entertainment—only who was being entertained? I moved my hand from his chest down to the top of his unbuckled belt and gently unbuttoned his black jeans, dipping my hand in them only as far as the extra space would allow. I would not push or importune; I had the entire night to accomplish my goal and begin to give him some of his secret desires. I continued to play with his chest, only occasionally "dipping" my hand into the top of his jeans. Very shortly, he reached down and unzipped his jeans; I helped him by holding the waistband up to make the unzipping easier. Since this was obviously an invitation to touch him more intimately, I did take him up on it, but not immediately. No sudden plunging, no sudden reaching for his cock, which was now an all-out pole in his jeans, just the same gentle caressing that only now included touching his cock through his black jockey shorts. He moaned softly each time my silken touch moved over his cock, and I was greatly satisfied by this. All the better to bend you to my will, my dear, I thought.

Soon he gently disengaged me from his encircling arm and stood up. Without asking, he removed his socks and jeans. As he took off his jeans, I took in every inch of his body. He had long, lean almost hairless legs and a great ass with nice tight cheeks. Finishing, he reseated himself on the sofa, wrapping his arm around my shoulders and drawing me close. I was very pleased with the toy I had chosen to play with and silently congratulated myself on having made such a fine choice. In just a few moments, I suggested that we would be more comfortable on the floor in front of the fire. I gestured for him to remain seated while I went to get a large, faux fur throw from the bedroom. Then I added another couple of logs to the fire and tossed the throw onto the floor in front of it. I smilingly gestured that he take up a position on it. He stretched out on his stomach full length, almost catlike, and I couldn't help but admire his good looks and lean physique. What a great catch this one was!

I stretched out on my stomach next to him and together we gazed into the fire, relaxing into our new positions, our bodies very close.

He didn't seem to find it at all odd that he was wearing only his jockey shorts while I was fully dressed in latex. I rolled over onto my side and again began to play with his beautiful, long hair. Then I ran my nails up and down his back. Since he obviously enjoyed this, I suggested that I give him a real massage. He agreed immediately, and I got up to get the lube that I was going to use as a massage lotion. He wouldn't know the difference because I had bought the water-based kind made for women, which didn't cake or get sticky. It would feel like regular lotion to him. Although he didn't know it, I also took out the black latex gloves. I straddled him and sat on his lovely ass. Then I squeezed a large dollop of the lube/lotion into my hands, rubbed them together to make the lube warm, and set my hands on his back, spreading the lube all around in large circular motions. He moaned in pleasure under my tender ministration. Then I set myself to giving him a real massage.

Moving his long, dark hair out of the way, I started at his neck and shoulders, gently at first, and then I used my strong thumbs and fingers to find the knots and stress spots and worked them out. I massaged his shoulders, digging my fingers into the declivities of his muscles front and back and eliciting moans from him. I continued down his arms, one at a time, and finished each arm by giving him a hand massage. Then I returned to his back, briefly massaging his shoulders again before moving down his back to his shoulder blades and trapezoid muscles. His traps were so tight I used my elbows to work out the kinks, and then I gently folded one arm at a time behind his back and attended to the muscles under his shoulder blades. Next, I worked both hands up and down each of his sides in a combination thumb and finger action. By this time he was very relaxed beneath my hands. His body was almost hairless; he was firm with hardly any body fat, and his skin was smooth and supple and a joy to my fingers. I dislike hairy bodies and usually shave them.

I massaged up and down the sides of his spine and then massaged his lower back. Moving on to his legs and thighs, I kneaded his firm flesh between my fingers and thumbs. I made certain that after I was finished with his legs, my hands were at his lovely tight ass. There was no tension at all left in his body: I had kneaded it all away, even his fingers were loose and curled in a natural position. I leaned forward and lightly lay against his back. I whispered in his ear, asking him if he would mind if I took off his underwear to massage his ass. He murmured that he didn't mind at all and helped me by raising his hips as I pulled his shorts down and off. I relubed my hands and set to work on the object of my desire, and of his. He moaned as I dug my fingers into his glutes, seeking out knots and tight spots. I knew a special spot that never failed to elicit groans of pleasure; it was on either side of the sweet spot just below the anus. I drove my thumbs into it, increasing the pressure slowly until he was groaning with pleasure.

As quietly as I could, I slipped on the black latex gloves that had been beside me for the entire massage. I lubed them well and gently began to spread his cheeks. He didn't tense up or try to clench his cheeks closed; he lay there as if he had been expecting this all along. In a psychic flash, I read in his mind that he was not only expecting it but desiring of it, too. I caressed his anus, making sure that he didn't clench or change his mind and letting him know that I wasn't going to hurt him. Actually, I did plan on hurting him, but not tonight; tonight would be a gentle introduction to his deepest desires, and when he was ready for more, I would give it to him.

His opening was very tight; it was clear he was a "virgin," and I was thoroughly going to enjoy deflowering him. Slowly I worked my index finger into his anus, and when he started to tense up, I said to him in the most hypnotic voice I had at my command that he was to take ten deep breaths and to push down when I penetrated him with my finger. To help him further, I began to breathe loudly and slowly so that he could match his breathing to mine. After the ten deep breaths, I told him to keep breathing deeply. Then I began to penetrate him further with my index finger. He was pushing down as well as breathing deeply, and in no time at all, my finger was as far up his anus as it could go. I began to stroke in and out of him, slowly and gently, giving him much pleasure and making him ache for more. I played with his opening, stretching the muscle until it had loosened up enough to take two fingers at once. Lubing my middle finger, I prepared to enter him with both fingers.

Withdrawing my index finger, I gently worked both fingers back inside him. When he felt the extra finger entering him, he moaned and tried to tense up again, but I told him to continue his deep breathing and to push down. He obeyed me, and I gently worked both fingers into him. His muscles were tight around my fingers, and I worked them to loosen him up more, a wonderful sensation I totally enjoyed. Soon his muscles had loosened up enough, and I began to work him just a little harder. He did not resist; indeed, he raised his hips, which spread his cheeks open more, and soon he was thrusting rhythmically against my fingers. I cannot describe how happy I was at my conquest of him and his surrender to me. What a beautiful picture we made: this tall, handsome man with the long, dark hair lying naked on his stomach in front of the fire and me in my white latex outfit offset by the black accessories and my auburn hair kneeling between his open legs, two of my fingers deeply buried in his anus. His moans made the music sound more exotic, and the completely erotic atmosphere in the room and my power over him was very exciting to me.

The more aroused I became, the more intensely I played with his opening, putting my fingers into different positions from time to time to keep him wanting more and more. Sometimes I was gentle with him, and sometimes I caused him some slight pain. He raised his hips more, balled his fists up, and placed them under his hips to keep them elevated. I lay down on his back, kept my fingers inside him, and by rocking against him with my hips, I pretended that my fingers were a penis thrusting into him. With my free arm, I pulled his head back by his long, thick hair and kissed his face and throat. His response thrilled me. He turned his glowing face to me and eagerly returned my kisses; moving his hips to meet mine, he moaned and sighed and begged me not to stop. Then he said the word I had so wanted to hear: *more*. Now he was ready for the small silicone beginner's dildo I planned to penetrate him with that had remained hidden in the drawer all this time, awaiting its moment. The predator in me, the She-Wolf, howled silently and shivered with delight. But the other part of me, the human part, was starting to like this man.

Leaving my fingers inside him, I leaned back and got the dildo from the drawer. I was not going to use a harness with it this time; I felt that a harness would be too intimidating for a virgin. That would happen on another night, and I knew there would be many more nights and many more things to introduce to him and into him. I lubed the dildo really well, and as I began to withdraw my fingers, I began to penetrate him with the dildo. He groaned very loudly as the slightly larger object entered him, but I reminded him to breathe and to push down. I laid my face on his lower back and kissed it, not only to control him, but to calm him. I spoke to him in a low seductive tone of voice, not even thinking about what I was saying, only caring that my words soothed him as I pushed the dildo farther into him. When his upper muscle tensed up, I stretched out next to him, my cool latex-encased body right up against his hot naked one, and threw one leg over his legs, holding the dildo in place as I did this.

Kissing him on his face and lips, nuzzling his neck, and whispering into his ear, I felt the upper muscle relax and I pushed the dildo past it. His cry was one of pain and then of pleasure as the exquisite sensation overcame him. He lay there panting and moaning as I continued to kiss and caress his face and neck and hold the dildo inside him. He grabbed me with the arm closest to me and held me to him; he hugged me tightly and kissed my face with great passion. When his lips met mine, I parted them and felt his tongue enter my mouth. He was a gifted kisser, and I was surprised to feel myself getting wet from sexual arousal, not from the power I had over him. I lay next to him and relished his kisses for several more minutes as I gently worked the dildo inside him until his sweet anus had taken all of it.

Disengaging myself from his deliciously passionate kisses and encircling arm, I held the dildo in him while I slowly moved onto his back. The hand holding the dildo was underneath me, but now I would use my body to hold the dildo inside him. Withdrawing my hand and replacing it with my pudendum, I wrapped my arms around him in a combination of an embrace and control of his movements. I buried my face in his long hair, nibbled his shoulders, and whispered filthy words in his ear as I started to move my hips gently against the broad base of the dildo. His arms grabbed mine and held on to me; he arched his neck back so that his face could be closer to mine as I penetrated him with my silicone penis. My legs wrapped themselves around his of their own accord as I rocked and thrust into him. His ultimate act of submission to me, the complete surrender of his most intimate opening, was transcendental, and at that moment, nothing else existed in the world except the two of us and our mutual pleasure. The She-Wolf threw her head back and howled while the heart of the human woman rejoiced.

As our mutual pleasure and arousal increased, I began to pump against him harder and harder. He met my hips, helping me to penetrate and probe him, consenting to his own surrender. I used my encircling arms and legs as levers to give my thrusts more power and soon we were like two animals in a mating ritual. I was moaning and groaning as loudly as he was because I had positioned my clitoris on the base of the dildo, using my penetration of him to make myself come. I could feel my sticky wetness inside my latex pants, and I relished the warm gooey feel. Spurred on to great efforts, I withdrew my right arm, wiggled it under me, and used it to push the dildo farther into him than my hips could. I began to stroke it in and out of him, driving him into a frenzy. As his thrusts against me became harder and more urgent, he tossed his head, flinging his beautiful shiny hair around his face and against mine. I asked him in a soft voice if his cock was hard, and I was electrified when he answered yes. This was very unusual because most straight men could not attain an erection during anal penetration.

I told him that he could reach one hand under his body and stroke his cock while I pumped him. We both lifted ourselves up, mostly using his strength to push us up off the fur throw so that his hand could slide underneath him. My own hand was positioned on the dildo so that I could make myself come anytime and as often as I wished. As he stroked himself, I stroked myself and his welcoming opening with the dildo, all at the same time. I was on fire, overwhelmed by the passionate intensity of the experience and on the verge of having an exploding orgasm, but I held back until I felt him go into what I call the "come stroke." I wanted us to come together—a reward for him and an ecstatic experience for me. When I felt his stroke tempo change and felt his body convulse under me, I pressed my enlarged button, my very own little penis, and had the most smashing orgasm at the same time as he did.

Spent, we lay there panting from our very gratifying exertions, our bodies almost one. I withdrew my arm as did he, and once again, we embraced and kissed but made no move to disengage ourselves or get up. The moment had been too intense to part so soon, and I knew that he wished to savor it as much as I did. So we lay in front of the fire for countless minutes, our bodies and minds molded together and awash in the afterglow.

When both of us were breathing normally again, I reached under my hips and slowly and gently withdrew the dildo from him. I had to move my lower body off him to withdraw the dildo completely, but I kept my upper body on top of his back. He groaned as I did so; I knew the feeling of being vacated after such an impassioned experience, so I kissed his back and shoulders to lessen as well as intensify the feeling. After I had pulled the dildo out of him, I lay down on my back next to him. He put his head on my shoulder and threw one arm across my chest. I hugged him to me and kissed the top of his head. His thick hair was a little damp and clung to his neck and shoulders in errant strands, but our proximity to the fire would soon dry it. My human side found this endearing. The She-Wolf howled in joy and victory at her conquest. I smiled and held him closer. I was already planning our next encounter.

The She-Wolf Rules the Night

The insistent jangle of the phone intruded on the sublime space I was in, a place I didn't want to leave. I was deep in fantasy-world thinking about the very successful and erotic encounter I had had with my new toy just a few nights before. Since I have not yet mentioned his name, I will tell it to you now. His name was Jean Luc, and saying it was like music to my ears. Perhaps that is why I didn't wish to share it with you sooner. But the phone was still ringing. Should I let the machine pick up or should I answer? The machine, of course, that is what machines are for—to keep out the unwanted. I listened to my own voice and then the caller spoke. I let him speak for a few seconds before I picked up the receiver. It was Jean Luc, his voice like sweet melted butterscotch, saying that he was disappointed that I was not home and that I could call him or that he would call another time.

"Hello?" I said, pretending that he had awakened me and that I didn't recognize his voice. "Who is it?"

"Lovely one, it is Jean Luc. Did I wake you? Shall I call you back another time?" he asked solicitously.

"No, no, I must have dozed off for a little while. We can speak now." I pretended to shake myself awake as I thought of his beautiful, long, dark hair, his wonderful physique, and hairless body, and most of all, how he had surrendered to me. I knew from his voice that he had been thinking of his surrender too.

"How are you, Claudia?"

"I was a bit bored, which is probably why I dozed off. I am glad that you called and broke the monotony. It has been such a dull day and dozing off at seven in the evening is so very—*normal*," I replied in a lazy but sexy voice.

He laughed, and then there was a pause. "Would it be possible to break the dullness of your evening by coming over for a visit? I mean, of course, if it is not too little notice and you feel like having company . . ." Jean Luc trailed off hesitantly.

I pretended to think about it for a minute, just to hear him hold his breath as he awaited my decision. After all, I would be breaking my own rule of no same-night dates. In spite of my rule, I heard myself saying, "Yes, I think that would be nice. How about eight thirty?"

Eighty thirty would be just fine, lovely lady," he said. "I will see you then."

I knew from the way he spoke, the way that he called me "lady," and his general demeanor that he was hoping for a repeat of our last encounter. Since I was reliving it in my mind when he called, he was going to get exactly what he had hoped for and then some. It was time to take him one step further down the golden path of anal dominance and submission. I got up, stretched, and went off to dress for the evening's encounter.

I chose a black latex sleeveless top that laced up the front so that I could tease him with my lovely breasts and a floor-length black latex skirt with a high slit on the left leg. To take away from the severity of the outfit, I wore black lace-top, thigh-high stockings, the tops of which would show when I walked, and regular black patent-leather pumps with five-inch heels. I left my arms bare and pulled my hair up in a loose French twist with curled strands left loose to soften my face and show off my small square shoulders. I would let my hair down later for added effect at the proper moment. My eye makeup was medium dark, but my lipstick was a very dark and shiny red. I had just enough time to load the CD player, light the fire and candles, throw the faux fur rug on the floor in front of the fireplace, and start

the incense burning before the doorbell rang. The bathroom prepa-
rations would be done in front of him; a way to obtain his silent consent by allowing him to witness them.

I took my time answering the door—I didn't want him to think I
was waiting for him—and to his credit, he didn't ring the bell more
than once. I went through the motion of looking out the little window
set into the door to make sure it was Jean Luc before I opened it.
There he stood; his long dark hair shiningly clean was flowing loosely
down his back and over his shoulders, and he was wearing black
jeans and a well-fitting black turtleneck covered by an expensive
black leather jacket. In his arms, he had two bottles of wine and two
dozen long-stemmed red roses. I opened the door and with a smiling
gesture invited him over the threshold. As I did this I said to myself,
"'Come into my parlor,' said the spider to the fly." He lavishly complimented me on my outfit and appearance as he handed me the
roses, his eyes lingering on my breasts then moving down to take in
the leg I had put forward out of the slit to show off my stockings. The
heart of the Lady in me beat faster, but I had to restrain the She-Wolf;
it wasn't time for her to come out and play just yet.

I led him into the kitchen first so that I could arrange the beautiful
roses in a tall vase while he opened the wine. Then I directed him to
put the glasses on a tray, along with the wine and a pitcher of iced
tea for me, and to follow me into the parlor. I placed the vase on the
mantel over the fireplace, in front of the mirror, so that the flowers
and their flanking candles would be reflected there. He placed the tray
on the table in front of the sofa. He waited for me to sit before he sat
down and then he poured me an iced tea and wine for himself. He was
a fast learner and seemed to know instinctively that pleasing me and
not having to be told the same thing repeatedly before it sank in was
one way to do it. Another way was his newly acquired gentlemanly
manners. He had told me how he rewarded and punished his female
submissives, but I wondered absently about his demeanor with them.
Was he the iron hand in the velvet glove, or was he the cruel demanding type, quick to punish even the smallest infraction severely? Not
that it really mattered; I knew his needs, and I knew how to fulfill them.
When he was here, he was mine. Now I allowed the She-Wolf her silent
howl of joy.

We sat on the sofa sipping our drinks, becoming closer and closer.

I could feel the desire in him rising as we spoke. I could see it in the way he sat and leaned toward me, his eyes on my face, his attentiveness to each word I said, and his quickness to light my cigarette and refill my glass. Putting my glass down, I turned toward him and ran my hands over his chest. The turtleneck was thin and tight fitting and clung to him like a second skin; even his protruding nipples were prominent through the silky thin material. I played with his hair and caressed his neck, planting little kisses on his face and letting him put his arms around me while allowing him to run his hands over my bare skin and latex-clad body. When our excitement began to mount, I suggested that we would be more comfortable if we moved to the fur on the floor in front of the fire. Jean Luc immediately agreed. He stood and offered me his hand and helped me up off the sofa and down onto the throw. I lay on my side and patted the floor next to me, inviting him to join me. He gracefully lowered himself and stretched out catlike on his side facing me.

We moved closer to each other and began to run our fingers over each other, with light, teasing touches meant to arouse by their very delicateness. The firelight flickered on our faces, and the fire's warmth engulfed our bodies, heightening our excitement. We teased each other until I knew he was ready. On seeing the hard-on in his jeans, I moved in closer and rolled him over onto his back, holding him down with my upper body while I fondled his penis through his jeans. He groaned as I touched him and unleashed a small bit of the She-Wolf to increase our pleasure. His groans spurred the She-Wolf on to handle him harder, more dominantly. Through his pants, the She-Wolf wrapped her hand around his hard penis and gripped it firmly, making a small up and down stroking motion. Then she cupped his balls in her hand and squeezed them. His response to this rougher handling was very encouraging; unresistingly he lay splayed on his back, his legs open, loudly and uninhibitedly groaning with pleasure at the hard touch of the barely held-in-check She-Wolf. A low growl came from her as his groans of pleasure grew louder and more abandoned with her touch. I let a little more of the She-Wolf rise to the surface.

The She-Wolf straddled him and unbuttoned and unzipped his pants. Of his own accord, he partially sat up, and in one quick movement pulled his turtleneck off over his head and tossed it aside. When she started to pull down his pants, he raised his hips and helped her. Positioning herself at his feet, she pulled off his shoes and socks and freed his legs of his underpants. Now he was naked before her, looking into her eyes as if awaiting her next action. In a catlike motion, she crawled up his body and lay down on top of him, imprisoning his legs by wrapping her own around them. When she was stretched out full length atop him, she gripped his hair firmly at the scalp and gazed down at him with the eyes of a predator. He was breathing heavily, his eyes half closed, his hard-on raging beneath her. There was no fight in Jean Luc at all, as if he knew that an alternate, more savage part of Claudia's personality was now in control. She used his hair to pull his head to one side and bent close to his ear.

"I know why you keep coming back to see me, Jean Luc. Do you know why? Have you admitted it to yourself yet? I know you have been thinking about what I did to you the last time you were here; I know you have been fantasizing about it happening again. That is why you are here tonight—hoping for it, wanting it, craving it—and you will have it, Jean Luc, you will have it. But first you will have to submit to me completely. Are you ready to do that? Are you ready to give up your power to me so that I will give you what you want?"

"Yes, yes, I am ready. But who are you? You are not the lady I know as Claudia. You are her, yet you are different."

"Yes, you are right I am her yet I am not her. You may call me Lupia." As she said this, she took her hair out of the loose French twist it was in and shook it over her shoulders. From being in the twist it had become slightly wavy and full.

"Yes, Lupia. What do you wish me to do?"

"I want you to obey me and to surrender to me, and I will fulfill your deepest desires. If you do not obey me, I will hurt you in places that even your female slaves will not think to look." The She-Wolf had taken over, and Claudia was waiting in the background, holding the She-Wolf's leash loosely just in case, but watching and anticipating the outcome of the plan the She-Wolf was about to put into action.

Lupia climbed off Jean Luc and ordered him onto his hands and knees. Taking hold of his hair, she used it as a leash to pull him down the hallway on all fours into the bathroom. Once inside, Lupia pulled up her skirt and sat down on the toilet bowl. Using his hair, she pulled his head as far in between her legs as she could get it and began to urinate. Some of the drops splashed on his face, but her firm grip on his hair held him in place. When she was finished, she ordered him to lick her clean and then blow on her lips until they were dry. When she was satisfied with his performance, she used her knees to kick him a few steps back from the toilet bowl. She got up, opened the vanity cabinet under the sink, and removed a two-quart red rubber enema bag. After making sure the clip was secure, she ordered him to watch her as she filled up the red rubber bag with warm water. In front of his eyes, she lubricated the douching nozzle and then hung the full bag from the towel rod.

She pushed his head and shoulders onto the floor and commanded him to spread his knees. She stepped behind him and waited a couple of minutes to see his reaction to this humiliating position and its effect on him. After a minute, he began to tremble, but Jean Luc made no move to get up or escape, nor did he say anything, although low incoherent sounds escaped him. She used the lubricant directly from its bottle, running it down his crack in a stream to lubricate his opening. Then she took the long nozzle and worked it into his anus and up his rectum. Taking the hose in her hand, she partially loosened the clip and let the water flow into him. His moans as the water filled his belly made her want to howl aloud, but Claudia restrained her, and Lupia's howls remained in her head. Before the bag was half empty, he begged her for a pause and she allowed it. He needed time to take in all she was to give him. For the way she was going to play with him tonight, she wanted no brown matter to distract her from her goal. In just a few seconds, Jean Luc begged her to continue, and it was with great pleasure that she released the clip and emptied the rest of the bag into him.

Lupia stripped off her skirt and stepped in the harness Claudia had placed in the vanity. There was a small dildo there as well, one that fitted nicely into the harness. All of Claudia/Lupia's dildos fitted that harness; it was their favorite one. First, she put a surgical glove on one hand and checked his rectum to make sure there was no water in his passage. Then, after lubricating the dildo, she piled several towels on the floor behind Jean Luc and knelt on them. She worked the small dildo into him, commanding him to breathe but not to press down as she entered him. Grabbing hold of his hips, she rocked into him while his belly was full of water. Jean Luc moaned mindlessly at this invasion and, to increase his torment, Lupia let go of one hip and reached her hand around in front of him to play with his penis while she penetrated him. Although most males did not maintain their erection during this kind of play, Claudia/Lupia was delighted to find that Jean Luc did. Her hand pumped his penis in rhythm to the strokes of her hips, and she abandoned herself to her pleasure.

When she had made herself come with the flanged base of the dildo, she pulled out of him and told Jean Luc to insert his thumb into his anus and climb onto the toilet bowl to release himself. She watched in fascination as he pushed his thumb inside and struggled to his feet. This was the first time he had seen her since she had stripped off her skirt and stepped into the harness. He was enthralled by the contrast between the harness and dildo and her lovely lace-topped thigh highs and lace-up latex top, which showed off her beautiful breasts. As soon as he had seated himself, she gave him permission to unplug himself and rid himself of the water. She listened closely to determine if one enema would be enough or if he would need another. Jean Luc was humiliated that Lupia stayed in the bathroom and watched him as the water exploded from his bottom, but he could not take his eyes off her, and he said not a word. If this was what he needed to do for her to fulfill his fantasies, no humiliation was too great to endure.

When he had emptied himself, she ordered him into the bathtub and told him to wash thoroughly. After he was finished washing, she ordered him to stay in the tub, get on his knees, and put his head on the bottom of the tub. Using soap on her index finger, she rubbed it on his anus, knowing that the soap would cause a spasm that would rid him of any drops left behind. Lupia didn't feel like waiting for those drops to come out on their own, and she didn't want him fouling Claudia/Lupia's linen. The soap did its nasty stinging work, and the last few drops squirted from his bottom. For a moment, Claudia pushed Lupia aside, and she herself took a fresh washcloth and gently washed Jean Luc, speaking to him tenderly, telling him how proud she was of him, how happy she was with him, and that tonight, yes, tonight, she would give him his heart's deepest desire. Then she bid him to rise, and she dried him and brushed his long dark hair for him. He greatly appreciated this sudden and unexpected demonstration of tenderness from her, and it showed in his eyes and posture. He grabbed one of her hands and kissed it and pressed it to his cheek before letting it go. She returned his gesture of appreciation with a sweet smile and held Lupia in check.

It was Claudia who removed the small dildo from the harness and blindfolded Jean Luc with a towel. She then put his hands on her waist and softly said "right, left, right, left" to keep him in step with her, as she led him to the bedroom. It was Lupia who waited eagerly because she knew that soon she would be in control again and have her way with him, guided by Claudia. When Claudia removed the blindfold, Jean Luc was facing the bed. Fur-lined leather wrist and ankle restraints on chains that were attached to the metal legs of the bed were lying on the luxurious purple silk coverlet. A mountain of matching pillows lay against the headboard. The heavily mirrored room reflected the light of dozens of tall, thick, white candles, and the bouquet of flowers that Jean Luc had brought her at their last meeting had been moved to the vanity table. Sexy but dark music was playing in the background. On the nightstand next to the bed were another harness and a collection of dildos, placed in order of their size. Jean Luc felt himself grow stiffer as he looked around the room.

Bidding him to "stay," Claudia walked over to the nightstand and gestured to the dildos. "I want you to see what I am going to use on you and in the order in which I will use them, so that you will know what is inside you, opening you, stretching you, penetrating you. I want you to memorize each one so that when I use it on you, you can envision what the dildo looks like entering your anus." Her voice was low and seductive, and Jean Luc stood there, completely under her spell, and he did as he was told. Then he watched as Claudia stepped into the harness and buckled both sides around her waist.

She climbed onto the bed and settled herself back against the mountain of silk-covered pillows, but it was Lupia who reached for the first dildo, a flesh-colored silicone one, and placed it in the harness. Jean Luc could see the change in attitude and demeanor as Claudia released the She-Wolf from her bonds. Her eyes darkened and her body appeared more lean and muscular as the elegant grace of Claudia was replaced by the savage grace of Lupia. He bowed his head in submission and awaited the pleasure of the She-Wolf.

Lupia opened her legs and bent them at the knees, then sexily growled for Jean Luc to climb onto the bed in between them. As she said this, Lupia stroked the dildo as if it were a real penis that she wanted to make hard. To Lupia, the dildo was a penis, one of her many penises, and tonight Jean Luc would experience them the way his female slaves had experienced his own male member.

"Come up—closer—position your mouth over my cock," Lupia rumbled throatily. "First you will suck me. I love having my cock sucked. Open your mouth and take the head inside."

Jean Luc moistened his lips and lowered his open mouth onto Lupia's cock. He was highly aware of his closeness to her vagina and could smell the delicious aroma of the juices from the orgasm she had given herself while she used him while holding the enema inside him. Her hand with its red-lacquered nails held the base of her cock, keeping it steady as his mouth closed on its head. He slid his mouth up and down over her head, using his tongue to make circles around it and alternating between sucking it gently and sucking it hard. As he did this, he managed to turn his head to the side a few times as part of the sucking and was able to see their reflection in a couple of the many mirrors. The visual of himself between her legs, her slender body with her full breasts pushed up by her top, the lace-topped stockings on her open thighs, her high-heeled pumps still gracing her feet, and his mouth encircling and caressing her cock were tremendously exciting to him. Crushed between his body and the silk coverlet, his penis grew harder and harder, egged on by the slight rubbing caused by the up-and-down movement of his head.

He felt Lupia's hand on the back of his head, then she growled, her arousal evident in her voice. "Now I want you to take more of me into your mouth. I am going to move my hand down my cock and I want to feel your lips against it. Once you have accommodated me that far, I will move my hand down and you will take that much more of me into your mouth."

Even as Lupia commanded him to do this, neither she nor Claudia could ignore his great physical beauty, his quietly enthusiastic obedience, his surrender to his deepest desires, and his trust in his captors and tormentors, the elegant Claudia and the wolflike Lupia. Claudia used one hand to hold his hair back out of his face and exerted slight pressure to force his head farther down on her cock. As

Lupia kept lowering her hand on her cock and Jean Luc took more and more of "their" cock into his mouth, their hips began to thrust in rhythm to meet his mouth. Lupia threw her head back against the pillows and let loose a low howling moan. In her excitement, she pushed his head down on her cock and made him gag. This made her wild.

She did it again and again, out of control like the animal she was, exhorting him, "Yes, suck it, gag on it, suck it like you make your female slaves suck *your* cock." She forced Jean Luc's head farther down on her cock, making snot run out of his nose and his eyes tear, until Claudia stopped her.

Lifting Jean Luc's head off her cock, Claudia gently cleaned his face with a wad of tissues, then held some fresh ones to his nose, and bade him to "blow" as if he were a child too small to manage this little task for himself. She stroked his hair and let him lean on his side and rest his head on her belly between her open legs. They wrapped their arms around each other and Claudia spoke tenderly to him, aware that the instrument of his recent torture was pressed against his body. She noticed his gorgeous penis, throbbing and erect and completely ignored. She trailed her fingertips over it gently and elicited moans of pained delight from him as he cuddled in closer and held her more tightly. Lupia was watching intently, gathering her strength, and planning her next move; let Claudia have him for now, he deserved this little respite if he was to take what she was going to give him.

Deciding that Jean Luc had been given enough attention and was feeling sufficiently cared for to continue, Claudia stepped back and let Lupia come to the fore. Immediately, Jean Luc felt the change in personas, and without being told, he lifted himself up from Claudia-now-Lupia and knelt between her legs to await the She-Wolf's next command. Leisurely, she took out the dildo he had been sucking and replaced it with the next somewhat larger one, also made of silicone, but this one was red. Lupia stroked it for a minute or two, a wolfish expression on her face as she watched him watching her from under the lashes of his downcast eyes. He was mesmerized by her hand as she stroked the red dildo.

"Stand at the end of the bed and bend over," the She-Wolf said. "Spread your legs for me."

She took her time getting up, allowing him to appreciate the vulnerable position he was in. She rose from the bed and seemed to slink around behind him like a predator would slink up on its prey. From the vanity drawer she took out surgical gloves; he heard the unmistakable snap as she pulled them on. A second later he felt the cold lubricant on his anus followed by the insertion of her two prime fingers into his opening. After working them into him as far as she could, she ordered him to stand up straight. To his humiliation, she led him around the room and then up and down the hallway by the fingers she had implanted in his anus before leading him back into the bedroom. Her action left no doubt in his mind as to who was in control. And it was not him. He was overcome by the feeling that the penetration of his mouth and anus by Claudia/Lupia was his ultimate act of submission. His heart pounded in his chest in fearful, yet in eager anticipation, of what humiliation she would impose on him next.

Once she had led him back into the bedroom, she abruptly removed her fingers, causing him some small pain that was over almost as soon as it began, but the removal of her fingers left him feeling alone and vacated. Leaving him to face the bed, Lupia made a show of making her red cock bob up and down as she walked to the nightstand and took out a thick sheet of latex. Then she climbed on the bed and began to arrange the mountain of pillows in a particular order in the center of the bed. When she was done, she covered it with the latex sheet. Wolf or not, she knew how to make the most of her body and her grace; her pointed toes, her arched back, her arm muscles as she arranged the pillows, and her way of tossing back her hair when it was falling into her face were reflected over and over in the mirrors. He was greatly excited to see all of the reflections, which made it look like there were many Lupias in the room with him, all ready and eager to take him and fulfill his most secret desires.

Once it was arranged to her satisfaction, Lupia used a commanding gesture to order Jean Luc onto the bed. With another gesture from her, he placed his hips over the mound of latex-covered pillows. Then she reinforced her control over him with the fur-lined wrist and ankle restraints by pulling the chains tight, adjusting their length by using the clip hooks attached to the metal legs of the bed frame. Small almost sobbing sounds came from Jean Luc as he realized and reveled in his helplessness—freed from guilt over his desires by the bonds holding him firmly in place. Turning his head sideways, he looked at himself in the mirror, saw Lupia's reflection as well, and was overwhelmed by the absolute beauty and eroticism of their image. He watched as she walked to the end of the bed, and with wolflike grace climbed onto it and then on her hands and knees crawled between his spread and bound legs.

When her hands spread his cheeks, he gasped loudly but didn't flinch or resist. He knew that in his position, resistance was futile and a voice in his head asked him why he would even try to resist what he wanted so badly. He relaxed into his restraints and let all tension flow out and away from him. This gave him great peace, and for the first time, Jean Luc knew what it truly meant to submit. He heard the wet noises of the lubricant Lupia was using on her red dildo before penetrating him. He did not know, he could not know, how beautiful, how sexy, how desirable he looked to Claudia/Lupia, and how much she wanted him as he lay there on their silken bed, his surrender to them obvious in his recumbent posture and deep even breathing. Gently he felt the head of the dildo probe for his opening, not know-ing that both Claudia and Lupia were about to enter him. He felt the head slip past his anus and up into his rectum. He groaned loudly and tossed his head, his hair flowing around him like a dark cloud.

She let him enjoy for a moment the feeling of exquisite pain that anal entry, no matter how gentle, always caused. Kneeling between his open thighs, Claudia/Lupia ate him up with her eyes, looking at his anus with part of the dildo still protruding from it, his well-toned body spread-eagled before her, and his hands lightly holding on to the chains that held his restraints to the bed. Forcing Lupia inside, Claudia lay down on top of him, pushing the dildo deeper into him as she did so, and wrapped her arms around him. She wanted to break him in gently and tenderly and give him the pleasure he deserved because he had submitted to her so completely and with such trust. When he turned his head to the side, she swept his hair away from his face and whispered sweet things to him and kissed his neck, his ear, his face. As he responded to her caresses, she slowly began to work the red dildo deeper and deeper into him. His soft incoherent moans, mingled with hoarse, lust-filled, whispered "yeses," thrilled her, and she felt her own little penis grow hard.

When Jean Luc's hips began to thrust up to meet her own, she plunged into him harder and faster; in her head, she heard Lupia growling to be let out but Claudia commanded her to be silent. She would have her turn soon, when Jean Luc was ready to take what Lupia had to give him. But not now. Now was Claudia's time, and she would have it without the demands and howl of the She-Wolf in her head. Lupia slunk away, equally distressed that she had upset Claudia and that she could not have Jean Luc now.

Although Claudia took Jean Luc with more and more abandon, she was careful not to cause him any more pain than necessary and to show him a lot of affection. She was also very careful to make sure that the flanged base of the red dildo massaged her own little penis. As she pumped into Jean Luc, she also pumped her own button. Her whole engorged vagina was throbbing with desire, and she had many little orgasms as she took him from behind. She wiggled one hand under Jean Luc's hips and began to play with his penis. He raised his hips up from the pillows in an endearingly obliging way; she changed her position to accommodate both of them by raising herself off his back and bracing herself up with her arms. This gave her new leverage, and soon she was working herself up to a smashing orgasm. After that she would allow Lupia, the She-Wolf-in-waiting, to take over and have *her* way with Jean Luc. In the new position, it was harder for Claudia to control herself, and soon she felt an earth-shaking orgasm rock her from head to toe. She collapsed on Jean Luc, spent, sweaty, and sticky. Withdrawing from him gently, she lay next to him on her side and cuddled and kissed him.

Lupia, the She-Wolf, was howling to be free, and in just a few moments she would have her wish and her way. Claudia, deeply satisfied and tired from her exertions and multiple orgasms, finally let Lupia loose, and Lupia's unmistakable howl of joy was audible to Jean Luc. He began to tremble with anticipation and pleasure; even without Lupia's vocalizations, by now he knew the difference between Claudia and her alter ego, the She-Wolf. He loved and feared them both, but he knew not which one he favored more.

Lupia rose from the bed, and as she walked over to the nightstand, she casually removed the red dildo from the harness and let it drop to the floor. Passing over one dildo, she chose the last and largest one instead. Jean Luc had never seen a dildo like this before; it had a button on the side of it and a plug on the flanged base that Lupia had removed. She was now filling the shaft with lubricant. She smiled wolfishly at him as she did this. When he quailed at the sight of it and moaned in fear, she threw her head back and laughed, delighted at his distress. She inserted the dildo into the harness and climbed onto the bed in a slow and threatening way by bracing both arms on the bed first and then using her legs like pistons to land both of them on the bed at the same time. The motion reminded Jean Luc of the way an animal might spring up onto a bed. The wolfish grin on her face strongly enforced this impression. Despite his fear, he felt his penis grow harder, and unconsciously he began to rub it into the pillows.

Lupia grabbed him by his long dark hair and turned his face toward her. On all fours she crouched over him, positioned herself so that her cock was over his face, and began to bounce her hips up and down so that her cock beat him in the face. Lupia was grunting and growling with each thrust, obviously aroused and greatly enjoy-ing humiliating him. After a few minutes, she collapsed on him, her cock thrust in his face and his head imprisoned under her body; she just lay there panting. But another thought occurred to her as she caught her breath. She got up and uncuffed his wrists and bade him to kneel as far down as he could with his buttocks on the bed. Jean Luc quickly obeyed her, although with his ankles still cuffed spread-eagle, it was an awkward position for him to hold. Lupia knelt up in front of him, her cock directly in front of his face.

"I am going to face fuck you," she rumbled. "You will open your mouth and hold it open, your tongue covering your bottom teeth. You will not try to suck me or use your tongue on me. I am going to use your mouth as a hole for my pleasure. There will be little or no pleas-ure in it for you. The only pleasure you may receive from it is know-ing that you are pleasing me. Open your mouth."

As he opened his mouth, Lupia grabbed Jean Luc's head, one hand on either side. She held his head firmly in place, exactly where she wanted it. Then she maneuvered her cock into his mouth and began to pump. She started somewhat gently, considering her persona, but soon her thrusts became deeper and harder. He could smell the odor of her previous orgasms, and even through this humiliation, this out-right use of him as a receptacle for her pleasure, it excited him more. As she hit the back of his throat, his eyes teared up and his nose started to run. Soon he was gagging as she pumped into his face more cruelly. Once in a while Claudia would tell him to relax his throat and not to fight so that it would not be so rough on him. He tried to listen to her, to follow her instructions, but with Lupia holding his head in place and pumping into his mouth so violently, he was having trouble doing so. As Lupia pumped harder and harder, occasionally the harness would hit him in the lips, increasing his discomfort and the inflammation building to a crescendo inside him.

After making him dry heave, Lupia wore herself out and lay back on the bed, stroking her cock using his saliva as her lubricant. Jean Luc stayed in his awkward kneeling position because he had not been told he could move and watched her from under hooded eyes. Her legs were splayed open, and the middle of her back had landed on the pile of pillows, thrusting her cock upward while her neck arched back over the pillows. Her right nipple had worked itself entirely out of the top of her blouse, and both breasts were on the verge of escaping completely. Her long hair was tangled and messy. By the way she was stroking her cock, Jean Luc knew that she was maneuvering it to rub her clitoris to orgasm. Shortly, her breathing became heavier and her strokes became harder as she held the dildo close to its base for maximum effect on her button. A few seconds later, a growl followed by her cry of pleasure as her body spasmed let Jean Luc know that she had come. Lupia lay prone, one arm thrown back over her head, her eyes closed, as she floated back down to earth.

Lupia sat up and looked at Jean Luc as if she didn't know who he was or how he had gotten there. This lack of recognition frightened him more than anything else that had happened that night. His whole body tensed, and quite irrationally he thought that she would spring on him and rip him to pieces with her sharp wolf teeth. But slowly her blank look disappeared and was replaced by a smile that was Claudia and Lupia, and she became herself once more. Jean Luc's relief was enormous, and the tension flowed out of his body in a great rush. He continued to kneel while Claudia/Lupia rearranged the pile of pillows. When she was done, more Claudia now than Lupia, she gestured to him that he should spread himself over them. Once he was in position, she re-cuffed his wrists to the leather restraints. As she crawled down his body on her way to his spread legs, she rubbed her body against his, bit his neck, and dragged her long sharp nails down his back, sending frissons up and down his spine. He moaned in pleasure at her attention to him and prepared himself for what he knew was to come.

When Claudia had situated herself between his legs, she let Lupia have a little more presence. Lupia ran her nails up and down his thighs and then kneaded his firm shapely cheeks in her hands. She used her tangled hair to tickle and whip his buttocks and then she bit one cheek after the other. She stretched out on top of him, gripped his hands in hers, wrapped her legs around his, and crushed her breasts into his back. More little bites on his neck, more nibbles on his earlobes, more hot breath blown into his ear, and more nails once again dragging across his flesh, this time up and down his sides. She moaned and writhed as she took total possession of him: his mind, his soul, his body. Jean Luc was quickly getting to the place they both wanted him to be—complete surrender to her will. Then she would give him his heart's deepest most secret desire.

Jean Luc moaned under her, and through his moaning could be heard just coherent words. Lupia, too lost in her animal nature, could not hear these words, but Claudia could. Jean Luc was begging her to sodomize him, pleading with her to penetrate him, saying over and over that he wanted her to sodomize him, to sodomize and grant him his heart's deepest desire. Claudia's heart melted at these words; these were the words she was waiting to hear. Everything that she had done to him before this had been with his wordless consent, but wordless consent and begging were as different to her as day was from night. Before he had submitted to her, but he had not surrendered to her; to her his verbal surrender signified that his mind and soul had admitted to his desires and could now accept them without guilt but with joy and pleasure. She brought Lupia under control, telling her that they had what they wanted and could grant him his desires without leaving him feeling coerced, guilty, or damaged.

"My darling, my dear Jean Luc, your words mean so much to me. Without them, we would have gone no further; tonight would have been the end. But because of them, I will give you what you want, my sweet Jean Luc, I will give you what you want because you have asked me to. And after this, we will be lovers if that is your wish, as it is mine," Claudia, still lying on his back, whispered tenderly in his ear in between soft kisses.

"Yes, Claudia, yes. Tonight will not be the end. I give myself to you . . ." Jean Luc's voice trailed off, choked with passion.

Claudia reluctantly lifted herself off his back, missing the feel of his strong, sweaty body under hers. She lubricated the dildo and positioned herself to enter him. Because this was the largest dildo, she entered him slowly and gently, making sure that each sound she heard from him was one of pleasure not of pain. She told him to push down to help her in and he did. Soon he was working the dildo in himself, moaning wildly as he stretched and penetrated himself deeper and deeper. Claudia wrapped her arms around him, under his hips, and let him have his way with her dildo. His rhythmic thrusting was rubbing his penis against the latex covered pillow and the dildo against her engorged clitoris. They were to climax at the same time, and to this end, Claudia wrapped one of her hands around his penis and began to stroke it, grabbing it firmly in the center and bringing her hand up and down over its head. She was holding back, ready to come at any time with just one thrust of the dildo against her body.

Jean Luc began to groan and begged for permission to come. She said nothing for a second as she kept working his penis, keeping him on the edge while she pulled one hand out from under his body and placed her finger on the button of the dildo. She was on fire, as was Jean Luc, and this was going to be the most exciting, most pleasurable moment of his life. She wanted it to be perfect. When neither of them could hold back for another second, she gave him permission to come. With her hand around his penis, she would know the exact moment of his orgasm. When she felt his penis begin to jerk and felt the first hot drops of his pearl jam, she pressed the button on the dildo and the now-warm lubricant shot up inside him. When Jean Luc felt the warm lubricant shoot up into him as he came, his cries and moans filled the room, and he called out her name over and over. When she had pressed the button to release into him, she made sure the base of the dildo smashed into her clitoris, and she herself had another head-to-toe orgasm. Lupia howled with relief and pleasure as she and Claudia shared this earth-moving experience.

Lupia receded deep into the recesses of Claudia's erotic mind, sated and exhausted. She had no interest in the gentleness and tenderness Claudia and Jean Luc would now share. Claudia stayed inside of Jean Luc, caressing him and speaking sweet words into his ear, kissing him and cuddling him, and enjoying the feel of their sweaty bodies still pressed together in their passionate embrace until the afterglow had begun to wear off. Then she gently withdrew from him, removed the harness and dildo, and in one motion dropped them to the floor, out of sight. Then she released him from his restraints. Jean Luc sat up and caught her in his arms and kissed her passionately. Breaking the kiss, she tossed the latex sheet aside and pushed the pillows back to the head of the bed. Stretching out on her side, she invited Jean Luc to lie next to her. He was quick to oblige, and within an instant they were in each other's arm, legs entwined, kissing passionately, the way lovers do.

Before long, Jean Luc had an erection and Claudia was wet with desire for him. She opened herself to him, and he entered her. His lovemaking was a perfect mixture of rough and gentle, and he had great self-control. It was a long time before he gave her another body-wracking orgasm. Once again, in a lovers' afterembrace, they whispered to each other that this was just the beginning; that they would continue to explore each other, enjoy each other, and become closer. That they had each found who they were looking for.

PART FOUR

Multiples

Cissy Maid

One night The Mistress decided to host a party and have Cissy, her French maid, serve her and six of her Mistress friends. Knowing that she was a great cook, Cissy was also to make the hors d'oeuvres as well as perform other duties for the Mistresses. These were to include bringing the floral arrangement, helping the Mistresses in and out of their coats and hanging them up, remembering which coat belonged to each, serving drinks, setting and clearing the table, washing up after dinner, emptying the ashtrays, massaging feet, and generally making herself useful to The Mistress's guests. The Mistress ordered Cissy to arrive three hours early so that Cissy would have plenty of time to cook and to be properly dressed by The Mistress in Cissy's French Maid outfit before the guests arrived. Cissy would be totally transformed into a woman complete with makeup, wig, and, most important, tying that pesky appendage back up between her legs! Cissy realized the great honor The Mistress was bestowing on her and promised to be on her very best behavior.

When Cissy arrived, the first thing The Mistress required her to do was make the hors d'oeuvres and snack platters so that they would be artfully arranged on the table with the flowers when The Mistress's guests arrived. The Mistress had a very specific way she liked to have the food arranged: not flat on the table, but making the offerings more appealing by cleverly using upside bowls and other things under the tablecloth so that the food was on various levels—a pretty sight, and it made the food look even more appetizing. The floral arrangement was in the center, and some of the leaves and flowers were used to decorate the empty areas. Tall tapered candles were in highly polished brass candlesticks at each end of the table. When The Mistress was pleased with the look of the buffet, she took Cissy in hand to get her into her maid's outfit.

The Mistress made Cissy strip and gave her a woman's robe to put on. Then she commanded Cissy to give herself a very close shave before she started to apply Cissy's makeup. Cissy was a blond, so The Mistress's job of making her up was not hindered by a dark beard and complexion. The first thing The Mistress did was to apply blush to where Cissy's beard grew in. This evened out Cissy's complexion and made it ready for the next step, the foundation and undereye concealer. Next, The Mistress applied loose face powder to Cissy's eyelids and under her eyes. Carefully she picked out the eye shadow, dark colors because she wanted Cissy to look a little sluttish tonight. The Mistress had a treat in mind for Cissy at the end of the evening, a treat that the other Mistresses were in on, and the dark colors would make a statement about The Mistress's plan.

After the eye shadow was applied, The Mistress applied a thin stripe of black eyeliner to Cissy's upper lids. Then she used the eyelash curler, to the count of twelve Mississippi, and applied two thick coats of mascara, one a volumizer and the second coat, a lengthener. A coat of slightly dark blush was brushed onto Cissy's cheeks, right along the line of her high cheekbones. The dark red lipstick would be applied last, but Cissy was starting to look like a girl.

The next action The Mistress performed on Cissy was to insert a small-to-medium size butt plug in Cissy's anus. The Mistress had taught Cissy how to accept the plug without any time-wasting fingering and unearned pleasure for Cissy. Cissy pushed down hard, so the plug slipped right in. The next step was to tie back Cissy's appendage so that Cissy would have a nice smooth front, a pudendum, just like a real girl. The Mistress often used castration as a threat when Cissy was a bad girl. This was a very effective means of control. The Mistress tied back Cissy's cock by using a version of the crupper. Using slender rope for cock-and-ball bondage, The Mistress folded the rope in half, attached the looped end to the head of Cissy's cock, and tied it off. She pulled Cissy's cock back between her legs, right down the middle of Cissy's balls, and pulled the rope tightly back and up Cissy's crack to her waist. Then The Mistress proceeded with the crupper as usual, wrapping it around Cissy's waist, looping it through itself in the front, then pulling it around Cissy's back, and tying it off.

If Cissy got an erection while she was tied up like this it would be very painful, and both The Mistress and Cissy knew it. They also knew that Cissy could not help but get a hard-on. The butt plug, although not that large, was to be kept in for several hours, and that would work its magic on Cissy too. It was part of the fun.

After Cissy's cock was securely out of the way and would not offend any of The Mistress's guests by its proximity to their faces when they were seated, The Mistress selected Cissy's undergarments. She handed Cissy a pair of nude control-top panty hose. The Mistress had long ago taught Cissy how to gather the hose up in her hands before putting her legs in them, how to work them up her legs, and how to settle them in place between her legs and around her waist. A wide black garter belt with four garters for each leg was handed to Cissy and she put that on. Then The Mistress gave Cissy a pair of black fishnet stockings with lace tops to put on over the pantyhose. The Mistress did not require Cissy to shave her legs because Cissy's hair was fine and very blond, but the double layer of pantyhose and fishnets concealed all of it.

Next was Cissy's bra and the lifelike silicone breasts, size D, to fill the cups out properly. The bra was black and lacy; The Mistress liked everything to match, and she picked out this lingerie set for Cissy herself one day when they had gone shopping. After Cissy had put her bra on and adjusted the straps under the ever-watchful eye of The Mistress, The Mistress pushed up Cissy's own small "man-boobs" and put the fake breasts under them to make Cissy's cleavage look natural. Now Cissy was ready for the pièce de résistance, the black satin corset. Cissy's natural waistline was thirty-one, so The Mistress had picked out a corset for Cissy that was a size twenty-six.

First, The Mistress loosened the laces so that Cissy could close the busk in front. Then The Mistress set to work lacing the corset as tightly as she could. The Mistress loved having Cissy tied back and plugged up when she was corseted. She knew it gave Cissy a tight and full feeling, constantly reminding her of The Mistress's dominion over her. The Mistress told Cissy to hold on to the doorjamb while she worked the laces. The Mistress's nimble fingers, combined with the use of her knee in the small of Cissy's back, was just the first step in The Mistress's tight-lacing regime. The second step was to have Cissy hold her arms over her head while The Mistress, her knee still in the small of Cissy's back, pulled the laces tighter. The third step was to have Cissy lie on her stomach on the bed while The Mistress gave the laces their final tug. Then Cissy elevated her hips and waist so that The Mistress could loop the excess laces around the front and then bring them around the back to be tied off. Only then was Cissy allowed to get up for inspection by The Mistress.

The Mistress ordered Cissy to stand in the middle of the floor. The Mistress walked around Cissy, straightened out her fishnets, readjusted the fake breasts as well as Cissy's own, gave the butt plug a little punch just to remind Cissy it was there, and made sure the corset was properly snug. Cissy loved being in her corset; it was as if The Mistress was giving her a hug every time she moved. The Mistress liked corseting Cissy because of the bondage and control aspect of wearing a corset and the way Cissy's nipped-in waist made her look more feminine. Satisfied with Cissy's appearance, it was time to pick out a wig for her. The Mistress kept all of her cross-dresser's and sissy maid's wigs in her possession, because once she had made a mistake of letting Cissy take a wig home. When Cissy returned it, the wig looked like Cissy had slept in it for a week and never once brushed it. Cissy was severely caned for this, and the wig was taken away from her.

Because Cissy was a blue-eyed blond with a fair complexion, The Mistress could keep her blond or make her raven haired. Tonight The Mistress passed over the blond wigs. She also passed over the long, flowing black ones because she did not want hair in the food. Instead, The Mistress chose a black wig cut into a neat pageboy with bangs. She combed the wig neatly, styling it just so. The black hair, combined with the dark eye makeup and Cissy's blue eyes, made Cissy look slightly slutty, just perfect for The Mistress's little surprise later on in the evening. Now it was time to pick out a maid's outfit for Cissy for the night.

Opening the closet doors, The Mistress looked at each possibility with a discerning eye. She looked at the black latex maid's outfit but passed it by because she did not want the latex polish near the food, nor did she want Cissy to get ugly dull spots on her dress. Finally, she pulled out a black satin uniform with a low-cut neckline trimmed in white lace, short sleeves edged in the same white lace, as well as the hem. This uniform had been tailored to fit Cissy perfectly. Cissy was thrilled with The Mistress's choice and stepped into the dress carefully so that she wouldn't mess up her hair or makeup. Black patent leather pumps with a comfortable three-and-a-half-inch heel were produced for Cissy's feet. Cissy slipped into them and stood up for The Mistress's inspection. After smoothing down an errant hair or two, readjusting Cissy's cleavage, and puffing up the short sleeves on Cissy's dress, The Mistress applied what Cissy thought to be the finishing touch: dark red lipstick.

But The Mistress was full of surprises and handed Cissy a pair of snowy white cotton wrist-length gloves, which Cissy was to wear while she served The Mistress's guests. Although the gloves looked lovely and really completed the outfit, both The Mistress and Cissy knew that the gloves would make certain aspects of serving the Mistresses more difficult. Cissy was only allowed to remove the gloves when giving a foot massage. After the foot massage, she was to wash her hands and put the gloves back on.

Just a few minutes after The Mistress had finished dressing Cissy, the first Mistress, Alexis, arrived. Cissy opened the door, welcomed her, hung up the Mistress's coat, and offered her a drink. Cissy had been taught how to carry a tray correctly by holding it with only one hand on the underside and to serve the drinks from the far end of the tray first. Cissy had earned many beatings before she had become proficient at this, but now the white cotton gloves added an additional challenge: they made the tray slippery, and Cissy had to be more careful than usual. Punishment would be swift and severe if she embarrassed her Mistress by dropping the tray or spilling drinks or both.

No sooner had Mistress Alexis been served her drink than the doorbell rang again and Mistresses Brianna and Claire arrived. Again Cissy performed her welcoming duties but had to hurry to serve the latest arrivals their drinks because the bell rang again. Another two Mistresses, Mistress Elaine and Mistress Meris had taken a cab downtown together. Coats and drink orders were taken, and Cissy hurried to get the drinks to the Mistresses before the bell rang again. The last Mistress had arrived, Mistress Francesca.

After Cissy took Mistress Francesca's coat and served her drink, she had a moment to look at the Mistresses as a group. Each one was beautiful in her own way, and Cissy was proud that her Mistress had given her the honor of serving at such a lovely and eclectic gathering. Although Cissy was trained to keep her eyes downcast and never to look any Mistress in the face without her express permission, Cissy stood a little taller at being so honored.

The Mistresses kept Cissy busy refilling drinks, emptying ashtrays and frequently making her eat the ashes, serving plates full of the hors d'oeuvres she had made earlier, and giving foot massages when none of those other tasks were required of her. Because no one corrected her throughout the evening, Cissy was deliberately deceived into thinking she was doing a wonderful job. She knew nothing of The Mistresses' secret plan for her.

The secret plan was that no Mistress was to say anything about any part of Cissy's performance that displeased her. About an hour before the Mistresses were due to leave, the secret plan would be put into execution. At last, the time had arrived. The Mistresses formed a seated circle and Cissy's Mistress ordered Cissy to stand in the middle of it. Then she told Cissy of the secret plan.

"Do you think you have done a good job serving us this evening, Cissy?" asked The Mistress.

"Yes, ma'am!" Cissy replied somewhat cockily because no one had corrected her over the course of the evening.

"Well, before we hear what the Mistresses have to say, I wish to tell them about what you are wearing tonight," her Mistress said coolly. "Cissy has had her cock tied back between her legs and nestled in between her balls to give her a pudendumlike front. I used the rope from that to hold in the butt plug Cissy has had up her anus all night."

Cissy blushed with shame, just as her Mistress knew she would and hung her head, her chin on her breastplate and her eyes firmly glued to the floor.

"Now let's hear what my Mistress friends have to say about your performance! Let's hear Mistress Alexis's thoughts first," The Mistress said, pleased by Cissy's humiliation.

Mistress Alexis complained that it took Cissy a very long time to bring her a fresh drink, and then it was too strong and another one had to be made, keeping her waiting even longer. Mistress Alexis ordered Cissy to bring her her coat. From an inside pocket she removed a leather flogger and ordered Cissy to bend over the arm of the sofa and lift her skirt for twenty-five lashes. Each lash was to be counted out, and Mistress Alexis was to be thanked at the end. Cissy accepted her punishment, thanked Mistress Alexis, and, at her Mistress's command, returned to the middle of the floor.

Next was Mistress Brianna. Although Mistress Brianna found Cissy to be an acceptable ashtray, she was unhappy that her crystal ashtray had been full to overflowing, and Cissy repeatedly forgot to empty it. Mistress Brianna removed the leather belt she was wearing, doubled it, and pointed to the arm of the sofa. Cissy's skirt went up once again, and she received twenty-five strokes of the belt in silence from Mistress Brianna. After the twenty-five strokes, Cissy was commanded to kneel and kiss Mistress Brianna's boot. Cissy complied and returned to the middle of the floor to receive her next criticism and punishment.

Mistress Claire was next, and she chided Cissy for her mannish walk, "clumping around the room like a truck driver" were her exact words. She removed one of her own pumps with which to discipline Cissy, but instead of bending Cissy over the arm of the sofa, she made Cissy bend at the waist and grip her ankles. This position naturally made Cissy's skirt fall forward, revealing buttocks that even through the pantyhose could be seen to be reddening. The twenty-five strokes from the sole of Mistress Claire's shoe deliberately landed right on the end of the butt plug and was the most painful punishment Cissy had yet to receive. Humbly, Cissy thanked Mistress Claire for her correction and punishment and returned to the center of the floor.

Now it was Mistress Elaine's turn. Mistress Elaine complained that Cissy's lipstick was smeared. Mistress Elaine found this to be very offensive and quite unladylike. Cissy's punishment was to be slapped in the face, forehand and backhand, five times each. Commanding Cissy to kneel, Mistress Elaine administered her chosen punishment with gusto, leaving Cissy's lipstick even more smeared. When Mistress Elaine stepped away from Cissy, all the other Mistresses laughed at Cissy, and Cissy's shame was clearly visible to all.

Mistress Meris, a chef herself, complained that Cissy did not tend to the buffet properly, allowed platters to become empty before refilling them, and did not take sufficient care that everything remained neat, clean, and appetizing. All the Mistresses agreed that this was a very good point and waited to see how Mistress Meris would punish Cissy. Mistress Meris decreed that Cissy open her mouth and swallow Mistress Meris's spit. They all knew that Mistress Meris had sinus problems, so some very good goobers were expected. Mistress Meris did not disappoint them, and Cissy was forced to swallow many gooey mouthfuls. The Mistresses were laughing so hard that the last Mistress, Mistress Francesca, had to wait until they calmed down before stating her complaint and exacting her punishment. All this while, Cissy was forced to stand in the center of the floor, the object of their laughter.

Mistress Francesca complained that the foot massage she received from Cissy was not very good, not very good at all. As Mistress Francesca ordered Cissy to bend over the arm of the sofa once again, she laughingly remarked to the other Mistresses that Cissy must have the pattern of the sofa memorized by now and perhaps that would be a good place to put the book on foot reflexology she thinks Cissy should buy! Once again the Mistresses laughed, and Mistress Francesca did a little curtsy in acceptance of their enjoyment. Mistress Francesca's punishment was befitting of the crime: she lifted Cissy's skirt and gave Cissy twenty-five kicks in the ass, being quite careful to land some of the kicks squarely on the end of the butt plug.

To Cissy's surprise, her own Mistress did not join in the group punishment, but that had never been part of her secret plan. Her punishment of Cissy was to be administered privately and not in any expected way.

"Now, Cissy, I want you to get on your knees, crawl to each Mistress and apologize to her individually, state your infraction, and thank her once again for correcting you and punishing you. Then I want to you to kiss her shoe," Cissy's Mistress commanded her. Humbled and honored, Cissy did as she was told.

The party was now officially over, and it was Cissy's job to help each Mistress into her coat and see her out the door. After all the Mistresses had left, The Mistress gave Cissy permission to shower and change back into her manclothes. Cissy's punishment from The Mistress was to be that he/she was not allowed to release in her presence this evening. Instead, Cissy was to call The Mistress at eleven o'clock the next morning and maybe then Cissy would be allowed to release on The Mistress's command.

In spite of this disappointment, Cissy left The Mistress's house with a big silly grin on her face, knowing that she had been very privileged indeed to have been chosen to share in such a wonderful and rare time with the Mistresses.

Daisy Chain

Being a Mistress has its pleasures and, accordingly, its annoyances. One of the worst annoyances is receiving a phone call or e-mail from a male submissive who wants me to "teach" his wife or girlfriend how to dominate him. Why, you ask, is this an annoyance? Because after questioning the male in detail, it becomes apparent that this "training session" is going to be a "surprise" for the wife or girlfriend. What a surprise if she has no knowledge, or worse yet no interest, in his plans for her, and has not consented to the training session—which is usually the case. To solve this problem and dispose of these males quickly and easily, I tell them I love to train couples but that I will only set up the appointment with the woman involved. I ask him to have his significant other call me so that we can chat to see whether we hit it off and then discuss what she wants from the session. As you can imagine, only one out of one hundred women actually call.

But fortunately this was not the case with Mistress Sonya and her husband/slave Joel. Joel e-mailed me, followed the proper protocols, and stated that Sonya had enjoyed reading *The Art of Sensual Female Dominance*, which had started them off on their sexual adventures. I replied with a request for Sonya to call me. Much to my surprise, she did. We hit it off immediately. Sonya and I spoke for more than an hour, not only getting to know each other, but discussing in detail Joel's interests. That was the start of a lovely and satisfying, not to mention, fun, relationship.

Joel's interests were diverse: bondage, nipple torture with weights, flogging, caning, paddling, giving foot massage, eyesight deprivation, oral dildo service, and anal penetration. And most interestingly, he was curious about being in session with a male switch who would start out as his co-slave and then later on dominate him. With so many interests, how could one ever be bored in a session with Joel? Especially that last one. But Sonya and I understood that the three of us would have to become very comfortable together before bringing in the fourth person. Whether you are in the straight world or the kinky one, the more people involved, the more complicated the scenario becomes.

After several successful and satisfying threesome sessions, Sonya called and asked whether I knew a straight male switch who would be available and willing to do a session. The session was to include the other male being Joel's co-slave, and then he would turn into a dominant and allow Joel to give him head. For some, this would not be an easy request to fulfill: most straight men do not become erect when another man gives them head. There is that ugly homophobia problem. But I have a treasure, and the treasure's name is Wyatt. Wyatt is all male and very easy on the eyes. He is medium tall with a slightly muscular build, bright blue eyes, clean-shaven head, and an accomplished switch who couldn't care less who is giving him head as long as a condom is used. It is because of this particular talent that many Mistresses keep Wyatt busy. Sonya was delighted when I described Wyatt, and she agreed to have him in the session immediately. Now we needed a way to turn Wyatt from Joel's co-slave into Joel's master.

I came up with a great scenario that would be fun for all of us and get us from point A to point B. I ran it by Sonya to get her approval and to hear whether she had any suggestions. First, we would start with a simultaneous strip and inspection of both slaves by each of us; this was something from my book that Sonya really liked. Then, there would be a foot massage for each lady. A courtesy pouch in the business-class section of an airplane contained a little booklet on foot reflexology. The different areas of the foot were numbered, and the number corresponded to a description of the effect massaging that area of the foot would produce. I would copy it and all four of us would have a copy. Wyatt would start on me, and Joel would start on Sonya; then we would switch, and at the end rate their performances. The rating would be followed by the appropriate reward or punishment. After that we would hold a "contest," best out of three, to determine the winner. Of course, this was a setup so that Wyatt would win two of the three contests and turn into a master. Joel, as the loser, would have to obey Wyatt.

The appointed evening arrived, and Wyatt and I met outside the very elegant New York hotel where Sonya and Joel were staying. With both of our "bags of tricks" in hand, which contained all the toys we would need for the session, we went up to the forty-seventh floor to Sonya and Joel's suite. After introductions all around, Wyatt and I went into the luxurious bathroom so that I could don my outfit with his assistance. Since the grand finale required that I wear a harness and dildo, I had chosen a long black latex skirt with a high slit up the left leg that would slip off easily and a leopard corset, furry to the touch, that I would leave on while wearing the harness. I emerged from the bathroom, the still-dressed Wyatt respectfully walking three steps behind me and carrying our combined toys. Sonya and Joel had prepared the room while I changed: shawls had been draped over the lamps to dim the lights and a sexy CD was playing in the background. Beverages, glasses, and a bucket of ice were on a tray to slake our thirst, and the foot massage oils were arranged on the desk.

Sonya and I sat and chatted while Joel helped Wyatt lay out the toys Wyatt and I had brought. I could see in Sonya's eyes that she was very pleased with Wyatt; after all, he was quite a good-looking man. After finishing their chores, each slave stood in front of his mistress, and the ritual strip and inspection was performed. Sonya and I inspected our own slave as well as the other's slave and found them fit for service. Then they were given the foot reflexology instructions, and the massaging began. Sonya and I instructed our slaves to massage the points each of us needed most. Then we switched slaves. Both Wyatt and Joel had very good, if different, techniques, and at the end, Sonya and I decided that the massage test was a "tie," and both slaves were to be rewarded. We rewarded them by allowing them to worship our feet with their lips and tongues, but made it clear that we did not appreciate "schluggy" on our toes. Schluggy is the word I use to describe too much saliva left on the toes, and we commanded them that a drier form of worship was what Sonya and I desired.

The slaves' performance was more than satisfactory, and soon Sonya and I decided that it was time for the contests to begin. The first one was the "pantyhose contest." Each slave was given a pair of pantyhose that he was to get on as quickly as possible while lying on the floor. The first one to finish was to stand up. We both knew Wyatt would win this contest, not only because he occasionally cross-dressed, but because he was much thinner than Joel was; hence, it would be easier for him to get the hosiery on. We were very amused as both men squirmed around on the floor like landed whales. Joel was still struggling to get his foot in the second leg when Wyatt finished and stood up to indicate victory.

The second contest was the "nipple clamp" contest, and it was the only one Sonya and I knew Joel would win. Joel's nipples were huge, but Wyatt's were very small and shy. After adequate manual stimulation of each slave's nipples by Sonya and me had been accomplished, we applied Japanese clover clamps simultaneously to each slave's nipples, and then one at a time, circular magnetized weights were attached to each clamp. Wyatt was groaning in real pain after just two light weights had been attached to each clamp, while Joel's moans were of genuine pleasure. After the third weight was attached, both of Wyatt's clamps fell off, and Joel, with his huge nipples, was declared the winner. Now the contest was tied: each slave had one win to his credit. The final contest would decide the winner.

The final contest was humiliating in a humorous way. I had brought two very large dildos that Sonya and I were to throw to the farthest end of the large room and that the slaves were to "fetch." The rules were that each slave had to remain on all fours and bring his dildo back in his mouth to his mistress, without the use of his hands. Although the room was very large, the passageway to the farthest point of the room was very narrow; it was the aisle between the king-size bed and the dresser, and only one slave at a time would fit through. But once again Wyatt had the advantage. Being smaller and quicker than Joel, Wyatt leapt onto the bed and quickly scrambled across and sprung off, far out in front of the slower Joel. Sonya and I were in hysterics; Wyatt's antics were totally unexpected and pleased us greatly. In a flash Wyatt had his dildo in his mouth and was ready to return to me, except the larger Joel was lumbering along and was in Wyatt's way. But the creative and enthusiastic Wyatt literally leapfrogged over Joel, dildo still in his mouth, and quickly made his way back to me. Laughing so hard that my sides hurt, I took the dildo from his mouth, and Sonya and I declared Wyatt the winner of the contests. Joel, pretending to be sad at losing, awaited the announcement of his punishment with his head down.

After "due consideration," Sonya and I declared that Joel's punishment was to be taken from behind first by me and then by Sonya. After we had our way with him, he was to suck Wyatt's condom-covered cock until Wyatt came. If Sonya, Wyatt, and I were pleased by Joel's performance, Joel would be allowed to come on a dish and lap it up. While Wyatt went into the bathroom and donned his leather pants and got into his master persona, I made a big show of removing my skirt and strapping on my harness and fitting in the dildo. Sonya did not have a harness; her method was to hold the dildo in her hand and then use her pudendum to thrust in and out of Joel. Joel was moaning and pleading for mercy most eloquently, but Sonya and I knew it was just part of his act. "Mercy" was not his word, so his repetition of it became music to our ears.

Wyatt emerged from the bathroom an entirely different person. Gone was the submissive attitude and posture, and in its place were the power, strength, and height of a dominant male. Joel was sufficiently cowed and awaited our invasion of his orifices. Bending Joel over the bed, I got behind him and easily penetrated him. He and Sonya played this game all the time, and Joel needed no instruction or loosening before full penetration with a dildo. It was a real pleasure to slide my well-lubricated dildo up his ass in one long, smooth motion and to begin pumping him. Sonya positioned herself on the bed so that Joel could eat her pussy while I penetrated him deeply. While Joel was eating her, Wyatt positioned himself next to Sonya so she could use one hand to pleasure Wyatt and make him ready for Joel. Joel was not to be allowed the pleasure of Wyatt's cock until both Sonya and I had had our way with him.

Sonya had trained Joel to pleasure her in the way she liked best, and after a few minutes, Sonya had a wonderful, and quite loud, orgasm. While she recovered, I continued to penetrate Joel until Sonya got up and said to me that now it was her turn to penetrate Joel. I withdrew from him and Sonya took my place, using a larger dildo. I tossed my dildo and harness aside, climbed onto the bed and motioned Wyatt to join me. I unzipped Wyatt's pants and removed only his cock. As a slave Joel had no right to see Wyatt's body; that pleasure was to be denied him. I covered Wyatt's member with a condom, and Wyatt placed himself in the position similar to the one Sonya was in. Then I sat behind Wyatt and held him in my arms, his head pressed between my breasts. After all, just because he could get a hard-on with a man didn't mean that the man was the cause of his arousal. I played with Wyatt's nipples, kissed him, and rubbed my body against his until he was fully erect. Then Sonya ordered Joel to open his mouth and suck Wyatt.

Joel fell on Wyatt like a starving man. His tongue action was excellent, and he worked his head down on Wyatt's cock with unabashed enthusiasm. The harder and deeper Sonya pumped into Joel, the deeper Joel's head went down on Wyatt's cock. In no time at all, Joel was deep-throating Wyatt, and Joel's saliva was so abundant that no lubricant was needed. I unzipped the front of my leopard corset and crushed Wyatt's head between my breasts. I had wrapped my legs around Wyatt's stomach and was rubbing my pudendum on his back in such a way that I soon had a little orgasm of my own. The jerking of my body as I came excited Wyatt, and his cock grew harder. His hands found their way to the back of Joel's head and forced it farther down on his cock; Sonya pumped into Joel harder and faster until both of Joel's orifices were completely filled.

I pumped against Wyatt, Wyatt pumped into Joel, and Sonya filled Joel from behind. Wyatt's cock was so far down Joel's throat that Joel began to gag, and Sonya told me that Joel's asshole was so loose that she could fist him if she wished to. This was the signal that Joel was to make Wyatt come, and Joel redoubled his efforts. In just a few seconds, I felt Wyatt's body spasm as he discharged into the condom. Sonya moved away from Joel and pulled the dildo out with her hand in one long motion. Quickly, she reached for the tray and pulled Joel off Wyatt's cock by the hair. Sonya, Wyatt, and I stood around in a circle as Joel assumed the position and began to masturbate himself while we three looked on. It didn't take Joel very long to come onto the tray, and in our combined kindness, we gave Joel a minute to catch his breath before the grand finale. Making Joel get on all fours, Sonya gave the order that Joel was to lick up every last drop of come he had ejaculated onto the tray. Joel lapped up his own juices lovingly and made sure the entire tray was spotless before he lifted his head for our approval. We carefully inspected the tray just to keep Joel in suspense before we praised and petted him for his performance and obedience.

Spent from our exertions, Sonya dropped into a chair while Wyatt and I flopped down onto the bed. Joel just collapsed onto the floor, his head next to the tray. In silence, the four of us thought of what an intense experience we had just shared and what it meant to us.

After we had recovered, we changed our clothes and decided to go out to dinner. We laughingly agreed that playing made one very hungry afterward. Sonya and Joel ordered a bottle of wine called "Claudia's Choice." I took the empty bottle home with me as a souvenir!

The Dance of the Threesome

After folding his clothes into a tidy pile in the foyer, Kevin padded softly on his bare feet into the living room. I lounged on the divan, my soda and cigarettes on the long glass coffee table in front of it. I was dressed in a black-beaded evening gown, black opera gloves, and suede pumps, and as I lolled around, I thought of my plan for the evening. It was difficult to keep the wickedness from showing in my manner and my eyes. Kevin only knew part of what was in store for him: that this night he was to arrive completely shaved of hair, except for his long, beautiful, straight, brown locks. When he entered the room, I pointed to a round Oriental rug in front of the window. I enjoyed making him stand naked in front of the huge picture window, risking possible observation by the residents of the high-rise apartment building across the street.

I ordered Kevin into position two and performed the visual and physical inspection for worthiness. He was just under six feet tall, slender yet muscular with a nice flat stomach, a great ass, amazing sea green eyes, and long lovely hair. Although Kevin was something over forty years old, he looked years younger than he was and was always deemed fit for service. After all, we had been lovers in the past, and no unfit person ever got to be my lover. The strong musky smell of his pheromones still had an amazing effect on me. I trailed my ungloved fingers all over his body to detect even one recalcitrant strand of hair. But Kevin had taken my command very seriously: his face was smooth and his armpits were hairless. He had shaved the small patches of hair that decorated the middle of his chest, and the stragglers around his nipples were gone too. Even Kevin's legs were bare and devoid of those hard curly hairs.

But what especially pleased me was that Kevin had taken extra time and care shaving his groin; it was so cleanly shaved that I had visions of him pulling his sack this way and that, getting around and underneath his entire package so as not to miss even one hair. Kevin could see from the lascivious grin on my face that I was pleased.

"Turn around. Bend over." I took a cheek in each hand and spread them open. I felt him tense, and then he let go.

"How nice! You even shaved the crack of your ass and around that puckered pink opening. I like attention to detail. You are as smooth as a baby's butt. And you know, shaving off all your hair makes your cock look longer," I said sweetly, thinking to myself that Kevin had a beautiful cock and was quite well endowed and didn't really need that extra inch exposed by shaving.

When Kevin's cheeks relaxed in my hands, I blew hard on his anus. Such a small thing, almost like a caress, but Kevin jumped as if a cane had landed squarely between his cheeks. I gave him several hard spanks to show my displeasure and then had the pleasure of seeing my red hand marks appear on his pale, hairless butt.

"Stand up. Put your hands behind your neck, put your elbows out, and then turn around and face me," I commanded him. He did as I said, his eyes cast down, but I knew he was enjoying the view *down* provided: my cleavage and long hair.

"I'm so glad you did such a good job on yourself, Kev, because that was just a practice run. You have another shaving chore to perform. Look up and turn around."

From the dark hallway behind him, which led to the private quarters of the house, emerged my beautiful Renee. I had met Renee when her husband mistook me for her; we looked that much alike, and then he introduced us. Soon all three of us became friends and very intimate ones at that. Renee was wearing a long, sheer black robe, which floated open with each step she took, and black platform lace-up corsetlike shoes. Under the robe, Renee wore nothing but her beauty. Kevin's eyes flew open in shock; then I saw his appreciation of Renee's great beauty register on his face. Her beauty was so great that it utterly humbled him. And of course, Renee, my darling exhibitionist, especially in front of a good-looking male, any male, just had to flirt with him, although she kept her eyes cast down. Renee had the most beautiful green eyes and was the best flirt I have ever known.

When people saw Renee and me together, they always asked if we were sisters, aunt and niece, or related in some way, perhaps half sisters or first cousins. The answers to all the questions were actually no, but men get turned on when they think they're "with" women who are related to each other. Because I look so much like Renee, what you saw when you looked at us together was this: when you looked at me you saw *her* fifteen years from *now*, and when you looked at Renee, you saw *me fifteen years ago*. Our whole crowd joked about it. So when we were asked any of those "related to each other" questions, we said yes to the first one they suggested. We thought this was hilarious.

Kevin had never met Renee, but he had heard me speak of her many times and saw her pass by briefly, offering preplanned tantalizing glimpses. I knew a second woman was one of his fantasies; what man does not have that fantasy? All those times I spoke to Kevin about Renee, when added to those fleeting glimpses of her, had primed him for this interlude. The seed had been planted and taken root! And I was in the mood for a little fun with my friends. Renee still had him paralyzed and under her spell, and he continued to look at her while I told him his next chore. And a terrible chore it was to be too; I knew he would utterly hate it.

"You are to shave her, Kevin," I said in a "sentencing" tone of voice. "You are to collect all the materials you need: several large towels, the big soft sponge, a large basin of warm water, a small one for dipping the razor in to clear it of hair, the massage oil, the razors I left for you in the bathroom, the new bar of mild soap, and the two pairs of leather wrist restraints, one for a man's wrists and the other for a woman's wrists. Return here with everything, and I mean everything. And do it quickly."

Delighted with this sentence, he went off in search of his equipment. Renee and I hugged each other and kissed passionately until we heard Kevin returning. We kissed just long enough for him to see us before we broke apart and then resumed our roles. I knew that seeing Renee and I French kiss would drive Kevin wild. Assuming my role as The Mistress, I inspected the items he had brought and found everything I required, so I gave him a nod of appreciation. His face glowed; I brushed my lips across his as a reward—some of Renee's saliva was still on my lips and I passed it along to him. Then, I motioned to Renee to stand at the end of the glass table with her back to it. When she was in position, I ordered Kevin to face Renee. Although her robe was sheer, it still did conceal some of Renee's natural grace and lines.

I stood next to Renee, facing Kevin, so that I could observe and absorb Kevin's every move, every nuance, every quiver, and every movement of the hardening of his lovely cock. Then, I gently took the long sheer robe off the beautiful Renee, letting it fall to the floor in a filmy puddle at her feet.

Kevin gasped and just stood there, again in a state of shock. Renee had a very beautiful body. Her round breasts stood out above a flat stomach; she had delicate hips and a heart-shaped ass. At five foot seven inches, she was just tall enough to have the legginess everyone admired and envied. I am sure Kevin was thinking to himself, "Some chore *this* is going to be!" Just when he thought things couldn't get any better, they did. I stood next to Renee while Kevin, at my signal, spread one of the towels out and then helped her lie on her back on the glass table, with her knees up and braced against the finials of the table. She moved down so that her ass was slightly over the edge of the table and her knees and thighs were gloriously spread open. She looked like something out of a dream. Feeling our eyes on her, her green eyes closed and her chest rose softly and fell with her breathing, with the familiar little whimper of excitement escaping from her lips every now and again.

"Begin your assignment, my dear. What are you waiting for?" I asked Kevin with a hint of puzzlement in my voice, as if I couldn't understand his hesitation.

At that, Kevin fell to his knees and was face to face with Renee's downy auburn triangle. Greatly surprised, Kevin noticed for the first time that Renee was pierced. She had two rings in each of her four labia and a barbell at the top of her cleft. Those areas were roughly shaven but here was Kevin, all ready, eager, and willing to perform his task to utter perfection. Kevin dipped the sponge into the water, made it very sudsy, and began to work up a rich lather on Renee's pussy. I watched him, making sure his mind was on his task, and it certainly was. His eyes were glued to Renee's pussy, and he definitely was giving his task his full attention. I saw him stiffening and then surreptitiously trying to stimulate himself by rubbing his member on his own thighs or between them.

"Don't bother trying to hide your excitement, dear Kevin. I've given you this assignment specifically so that you will be rock hard. I have plans for you, my pole dancer. Now back to shaving Renee," I said.

He soaped, shaved, and dipped, over and over until the basin was floating with the red ringlets he had denuded her of to expose her sweet cleft.

"Did you get them all? Don't be afraid to spread her lips apart and shave off any stray hairs, especially around her piercings. I want to see nothing but pink." When I said this, Renee moaned and arched her back, vocalizing wordless noises as Kevin's fingers touched her.

God! She was gorgeous! Kevin fell to his task with renewed enthusiasm, and in no time at all, Renee was thrashing her head back and forth as his fingers searched her labia for stray hairs. He found two or three and removed them carefully. Then I commanded him to refill the large bowl with clean water so that he could wash away any hairs clinging to her moist pink cleft. After that, I directed him to use the remaining towel to pat Renee dry.

"Now, I want you to smooth a few drops of this raspberry kiss oil onto her nether lips, Kevin. I want you to do it gently, and I want Renee begging when you are done."

He took the bottle from me, poured a generous amount on Renee's cleft, and gently began to stroke oil onto and into Renee. Not only did this particular oil taste of raspberries, but it got warmer and warmer with friction. However, I was the only one who knew that! I thought it would be a nice surprise for both of them when the real fun began. Renee quivered from head to toe as soon as he touched her. Kevin dutifully reported to me that his fingers were met with a sweet and sticky gush the moment he began to apply the fragrant oil. Kevin did not completely control himself either concerning Renee. Several times as he was applying the oil, when he thought I wasn't looking, he slid two fingers into Renee's pussy and, once, his thumb up her ass.

But Renee loved this. She was beginning to grind her hips and starting to moan in that mindless way she had. Her nipples were erect, and she was panting with excitement and begging for more. I knew that the raspberry massage oil was warming up and that it was increasing her pleasure. My dear Renee! I wanted her to have her fun, too, so I decided that Kevin would be punished for his "unauthorized" penetration of Renee—at another time—and very severely too. But not tonight, that would spoil my plan.

As for Renee, well, her nipples were just begging for some tender torture, sticking out as pertly as they were. I played with her beautiful breasts and then reached for two pairs of Japanese clover clamps. I made sure Kevin saw me attach only one clamp from each pair on her. Her moan turned into a short sharp shriek at the placement of each one. Kevin's eye peered up her belly hungrily, his face just above her freshly shaven pussy.

"Get up. You have done well." I ordered Kevin to his feet.

I ordered Kevin to bend over Renee, and I attached the free ends of the two pairs of clamps to each of his nipples. He gritted his teeth and bore the pain, but I could see how excited he was to be attached to Renee in this new way. As I attached the clamps to his nipples, I said, "Here, these are for you," a superfluous statement I was fond of making after a gesture like that. But I couldn't keep Renee waiting too long, so I reached for the two pairs of leather wrist restraints.

I commanded Kevin to lie on top of Renee but not to put his full weight on her by bracing his arms on the table, near her wrists. When he was in position, I told them to hold hands; then I cuffed their hands together, using the larger men's restraints for Kevin and the smaller women's pair for Renee. Kevin's arms were long enough to keep himself suspended over the prone Renee, who was getting more excited as I secured the restraints and clip hooked them together. In this position, the chains between the two sets of clamps were fully extended, and any move by either one of them would affect the other. I left them there like that so that either they could watch me as I readied for the next step or they could become involved with each other. They chose each other. Good! All was going according to plan.

While they were doing the midair bump and grind, I let my dress drop to the floor, took off my bra and G-string then stepped into my harness and slid a sweet slender dildo through the opening. Taking some condoms in my hand, I approached Renee and Kevin, who were moaning and groaning from the occasional bumps to their genital areas and pulls on the dual nipple clamps that they were able to accomplish during their mad gyrations. I smacked Kevin several times with the dildo, not only to get his attention, but to make sure he noticed it.

"Enough, my hot and heavy darlings." At least I didn't need a hose to separate them.

Kevin lifted himself off Renee as far as the restraints and clamps would allow and tried to stand straight. Renee had quieted down but was still writhing on her towel on the table, her nipples stretched taut. Quickly I ripped out two of the condoms, and snap snap, rolled one down onto Kevin's pole and the other onto my dildo. I had the lube in one hand, for Kevin as well as Renee, but Renee didn't need it. My dildo, the one I intended to use on Kevin, got a generous application.

I got behind Kevin, grabbed him by the hips, and then began a playful little external pounding. Suddenly I stopped pounding him but continued to grip him firmly by the hips. In his excitement, I didn't want him going too far with Renee until he had my permission.

"Penetrate her." Kevin stood stock still in pleasure and surprise at my command. "But I want only your head inside of her."

Renee moaned loudly and then started to beg, "Yes, oh please, yes, do me, please put it in me," over and over; her arousal was so great it increased my own desire as well as Kevin's. She really wanted it and Kevin did a great pole dance. She lifted her legs to her chest to invite him in, to show her willingness and consent, and continued her litany of begging. Kevin bent over her and gently probed his head into her dripping pussy. She was wiggling around and begging to have more cock inside of her, my sweet hot little bitch, and she'd get it too. But not just yet.

"You'll get more, my beautiful little slut Renee, as soon as Kevin takes his."

Quickly relubing my own silicone cock, I searched out Kevin's nether opening with my fingers, stretched him a little, and got just enough of the head inside of him to make him try to rise up, straining against the restraints and clamps and taking Renee's entwined arms and legs with him. "When I am done with you, for every inch you have taken of me, that will be another inch you will be allowed to enter Renee. But *not* until I am done with you. Do you hear me?" I grabbed his long hair, pulled his head back, and kissed him hard.

Kevin's excitement and gratitude was evident in his voice when he said, "Yes, Mistress," and began to prepare himself for me. As he began to inhale and then exhale slowly, I could feel his muscles relaxing and could feel him pushing down as he made himself ready to take me. Every time he exhaled, I pushed into him a little farther and generously applied more lube. Slowly but surely he was taking more and more with each thrust, not only because of his eagerness to get his cock into Renee, but because he loved being penetrated anally. Renee was luscious chocolate icing on his cake.

While I was invading Kevin, Renee was doing her best to keep him excited by pulling on the nipple clamps, grabbing the base of his cock and squeezing it, and manipulating whatever bits of his balls she could reach. And just the sight of her on her back with her legs up and partially wrapped around Kevin, her red hair framing her face with her gorgeous green eyes looking up at Kevin, should have been enough to keep any man hard—and "testosterone Kevin" was no exception. His pheromones had gotten so strong, the whole room smelled of them. With one final thrust, I had my dildo as far into Kevin as it would go. He clenched and unclenched his cheeks as I rode him. I had my way with him, thrusting deep and hard, enjoying myself a little while longer and amused by my frantic yet oh-so-thrilling penetration of Kevin, until I was breathless and my legs ached. Then I stood still, my cock still in him, and let him dance around on it and pleasure himself. Renee and I knew exactly how he was feeling at that moment, and I gently trailed my fingertips up Renee's thigh, to impart and to include her in my joy and extreme pleasure.

After a short while, Kevin had worn himself out, squirming and dancing up and down on the dildo. He hung from it panting, nearly forgetting about the beautiful, and very hot, very wet, Renee right underneath him with his head inside of her. I pulled out of him just up to the head—leaving myself no farther into him than he had been allowed into Renee.

I pulled his head back by the hair and whispered in his ear, "I am in control here, I say what happens and how. As I penetrate you again, you will penetrate Renee. For each inch I drill into you, that is how far you may enter Renee. How I fuck you is how you will fuck Renee."

I knew that as the rear person, I would be the real mover and shaker of the whole undertaking, with Kevin having to follow my lead. I started gently, so that Renee could enjoy the pleasure of slow pene-tration until Kevin was as far into her as he could go and I was into Kevin as far as I could go. Then we began our slow dance. Renee was fully enjoying the well-endowed Kevin as well as the raspberry oil that was very warm by this time. I was enjoying myself enormously as I rammed into him from behind. From Renee's cries, I knew he was hitting Renee's hot spot regularly as he was being penetrated by me while penetrating Renee. My dildo base had just worked its way down to make direct contact with my clit, which was standing at attention like a good soldier. It crossed my mind to buy one of those squirt cocks that shoots lubricant; I would enjoy it if Kevin knew what it felt like to have someone come inside of him.

"Give her one more orgasm," I panted out to Kevin.

He complied eagerly and changed his stroke. Renee unloosened her legs from around his back and let them dangle spread wide open and unresisting. Soon I heard the familiar moan/scream that Renee made when she had a smashing orgasm. As soon as I heard that sweet sound, I stopped stroking into Kevin but did not pull out of him. He would pull out of Renee at the same time I pulled out of him. For a few moments, we all just stood, hung, or lay there, catching our collective breaths. My clit was dripping from the friction caused by the base of the dildo as I had pumped Kevin. But in the end we all would be satisfied. Kevin was able to come many times over and still retain a wondrous hard-on. Kevin: the pole dancer, the sex machine, the testosterone factory. And I knew he would thoroughly enjoy his reward for the servicing of Renee.

"Kevin, start to pull out of Renee, but slowly, slowly," I commanded but my voice still reflected how aroused I was.

He did as I ordered, and I began to pull out of him at the same slow speed, milking the mutual withdrawal for all it was worth. When my dildo cleared Kevin's anus, I was gratified by the fact that it was gaping open. I bent over and spread his cheeks apart so that I could look up his rectum; a place even he had never seen. It looked so smooth and silky, just as it felt when my naked fingers were inside of him. I stepped to his side and commanded him to spread Renee's lips; I wanted to see how big her opening had gotten from Kevin's pole dance. As he spread her, she moaned again. I knew how small her hole was and was more than satisfied with the amount that he had stretched her. And although Kevin had come, his cock was still rock hard. Perfect!

I removed Renee's and Kevin's mutual nipple clamps and the restraints, my harness and dildo, and condoms from all of us accordingly and casually announced that we would have a "break" before continuing. They both looked surprised at that statement. There was more to come? they were asking themselves.

"But of course there is, my dears. The night is only half finished!" I said with a big smile.

Kevin helped Renee up from the table, and she and I lounged on the sofa in each other's arms. Kevin got cigarettes, lit them for all of us, and then Kevin went into the kitchen returning with an assortment of beverages and chilled fruit. We fell on the platter as if we hadn't eaten for days. But sex does work up an appetite, and all that panting and heavy breathing definitely leaves one's mouth dry. Even the cigarettes tasted delicious.

But since there was more to come, there were also a few more chores for Kevin to perform. I languidly commanded him to clear away the bowls, sponge, soap, and towels; dispose of the condoms; wash my dildo and harness, and stow away the restraints and nipple clamps. I added that he should bring more condoms. He obeyed enthusiastically, wondering what was next in my wicked, dirty mind. Well, he'd soon find out, and he'd be delighted, just delighted, I was sure.

He returned with the condoms, a game look on his face, ready for whatever was going to happen next. I let him relax for a minute or two because he would need his strength for the final part of my plan. And what a grand finale it would be! I giggled aloud at the thought of it and aroused the curiosity of both Renee and Kevin. Even Renee didn't know exactly what was going to happen, although she had agreed to the general game plan. Now it was time to begin the finale.

Since all of us were somewhat gooey from our previous pleasures, I commanded Kevin to wash himself and then return with the two bowls filled with nice warm water, soap, many more towels, and two plastic garbage bags. I directed him to lay the plastic bags out on the carpet right next to each other and cover them with towels. Taking Renee by the hand, we got up from the sofa and lay on our backs on the towels, our bodies and thighs pressed closely together and our arms entwined. Then I ordered Kevin to wash both of us. Kevin was dexterous as well as a great pole dancer and he used one hand to wash Renee at the same time he used the other hand to wash me. He was doing a thorough but very erotic job of it, and in no time at all, Renee and I turned partially onto our sides and began kissing each other and fondling each other's breasts. Kevin's cock began to grow again, excited at touching us and seeing us kiss and touch each other at the same time.

As our kisses grew more passionate, I allowed Kevin the liberty of slipping his fingers into our pussies as he bathed us. As our passion increased, Renee and I practically rolled over completely onto our sides to face each other and drew our outermost legs up to give Kevin access to our soapy and gooey pussies.

"More, Kevin, more," I panted out. "Find our hot spots and make us come."

Renee echoed these words, accompanied by the begging and pleading one would expect of a good slave. Kevin drove his fingers deeper into us and sought out each of our inside buttons. Being the excellent lover that he was, Kevin made both of us come at the same time. Our simultaneous screams and moans made him all the harder, which was exactly what I wanted.

"Take your fingers out of us, Kevin, and rinse us off," I said, still breathless.

Renee and I disentangled ourselves from each other and lay flat on our backs as Kevin rinsed the soap off us. Then, without being told, he carefully and teasingly dried each of us. The wet towels beneath Renee and me had become a cold and unwanted distraction, so by rolling from one side to the other, Kevin was able to remove them and take them away. Renee and I lay on the floor in each other's arms and kissed until he returned. When he saw us, he stood there for a minute taking in the eroticism of two women kissing in each other's arms. Out of the corner of my eye I could see his gorgeous cock standing at full attention. I said nothing, and Renee and I continued to kiss and once again began to fondle each other. We could hear Kevin's gasping breaths as he beheld us; the sound of them further excited us. But the final step of the grand finale was yet to come.

Renee and I broke our kiss, and I leaned up one elbow as she continued to loll around on the floor. "Lie down, Kevin, on your back, in the middle of the floor," I told him seductively but giving him no clue as to what was going to happen next.

He hurried to obey, his cock at full attention, sticking out from his body like a tent pole. I ripped open one of the condoms, and placing it in my mouth, I worked it down over his cock. This was obviously new to him, and a trick he was sure to remember. He groaned in pleasure as I worked the condom down to the base of his cock as if I was giving him head. I applied a generous amount of lube and then I straddled his hips. As I situated myself over his beautiful and hard cock, I commanded Renee to straddle his face. She hurried over and with one knee on either side of his head, positioned her pussy right over his mouth. Reaching down I spread my lips, which had soaked themselves at the mere thought of what was to come and began to lower myself onto his cock. At the same time, I silently motioned to Renee to place her lips on his and ordered him in a kitty-cat voice to eat her out. Then I added that she liked it a little rough. I knew that he would know exactly what I meant by *a little rough* and that he would obey me with great enthusiasm.

I was very tight, even though Kevin has been allowed to finger me while he washed me, and I had to work my way down his cock slowly. Heavenly, just heavenly. Renee was going wild as Kevin ate her out, grinding her denuded pussy into his face, bouncing up and down, and moaning mindlessly, "Yes, yes, bite me, bite my lips, stick your tongue in me, yes, do it, do it, eat me," and other endearing little encouragements. As this was happening, I had gotten as far down onto Kevin's cock as I could. I leaned forward to brace myself with my arms so that I could begin my own pole dance. As Renee could well take care of herself as she sat on his face, Kevin reached down and grabbed my buttocks, and in no time at all, his hips began to meet my thrusts, greatly increasing my pleasure. Soon I collapsed against his chest, my face close to Renee's pussy, and let him thrust into me as he pleased. Knowing quite well where it was, he hit my hot spot every third stroke. My juices drenched both of us, and as he pumped me, my pussy made wet juicy noises with each stroke.

But for all of his thrusting into me, Kevin had not forgotten Renee; by her continuous groans and moans, I knew she was being attended to as well. I decided I wanted all three of us to come together. Somehow I managed to gasp the words out in between Kevin's thrusts, and everyone made a noise of agreement. No countdown was needed; we were all ready and very in tune with each other. I felt Kevin go into his come stroke, and he began to groan with exertion. I was moaning and whimpering uncontrollably while Renee ground her pussy into Kevin's face. I knew by the little shrieks she was making that he was biting her clitoris. As I screamed out, "Yes, yes, oh yeeessss," I had the most smashing orgasm. I felt Kevin's cock jerk inside of me as he came and heard Renee's sweet, familiar come moan at the same time.

The three of us stayed where we were for a few minutes, too overcome to move. Then I slowly moved off Kevin's cock, relishing the feel of it as it vacated me. Renee sat back on her heels, still panting heavily. Kevin just lay there, his eyes closed, his chest heaving from his exertions. I lay down on one side of him and Renee on the other. He wrapped an arm around each of us as we curled up alongside him, our heads on his chest, one of our legs wrapped around one of his.

Although we had started out as The Mistress and her male and female slaves, now we were just three cuddling people who had shared a transcendental experience. I just love it when things go according to plan.

The Mistress's Men

It is the deepest desire of all slaves to worship The Mistress between her thighs but few are willing to perform the strict and necessary actions, sacrifices, and humiliations to earn this honor. The Mistress knew this well and very few slaves had ever passed her test. Tonight two well-trained and experienced slaves were at her disposal, Kyle and Jake, so that there was a small chance they would actually succeed. But only time would tell, wouldn't it? And a perfect performance from the slaves was no guarantee that their deepest desire would be granted them. The Mistress had dressed for the occasion. She wore a tightly laced red latex corset, red latex opera gloves, and red low platform shoes that accessorized her white latex ball gown. Her normally straight hair was curled and fluffed out; her eye makeup was smolderingly dark, making her light, reddish-hazelnut eyes piercing. The Mistress felt that her wardrobe should fit the occasion and establish her authority immediately. She never failed at this.

When Jake arrived, he, of course, had no idea that another slave, Kyle, was there before him. Neither Jake nor Kyle knew what The Mistress had in store for them; although Kyle did know that another slave would be arriving, he did not know that the other slave was also a male. Before Jake had arrived, The Mistress had taken Kyle into her bedroom. Kyle was an experienced and beautiful hunk of well toned muscular male meat and one of The Mistress's favorite toys. He was totally naked, very aroused, and had a bright red ball gag in his mouth. In one hand, Kyle held a red bandana, which he was to drop as his safe signal. The Mistress had restrained Kyle with leather wrist cuffs that were attached by clip hooks to eye rings at shoulder level and securely bolted into the wall across from the bed. Leather ankle cuffs, attached to a spreader bar, allowed him to keep his feet flat on the floor, but not to close his legs or kick. Then she left him there, completely vulnerable and unable to speak, while she awaited Jake's arrival.

When Jake arrived, The Mistress led him into the parlor to perform the ritual strip and visual and physical inspection. Jake was also quite handsome, but his body was different from Kyle's muscular gym-toned form. Jake was slender with more of a swimmer's or dancer's lean physique. A good contrast, especially for what The Mistress had in her wicked, creative mind.

After Jake had stripped, passed inspection, and given The Mistress the proper homage, she commanded him to stay on his knees and crawl after her to the bedroom. She set a brisk pace down the hallway, and Jake had to work hard to keep up on the bare wooden floor, which hurt his knees. The Mistress opened the bedroom door and gestured Jake to follow her into the room. When he saw Kyle gagged and restrained to the wall, Jake's surprise and apprehension was clearly visible on his face, but The Mistress was unconcerned. Both Kyle and Jake had long ago confessed to her that they would like to be with another man, but she had pretended that she had forgotten all about it until a great amount of time had passed. Now it was time to see if either Kyle or Jake or both would have the courage of their confessions.

"You didn't think you were my only slave, did you?" The Mistress asked Jake mockingly, a smile on her face. "I require much devotion, attention, and diversion, much more than one mere male creature can provide. And isn't he just the most gorgeous hunk of male meat you have very seen?"

The Mistress gave Jake a moment to take in not only Kyle but the impact of the scenario in front of him before she continued. "Both of you have expressed to me your most secret desire to be with another man. Kyle, you have confessed that you wanted to be the receiver of the male's attention, and Jake, you have confessed that you wished to be the giver of such attention. So, in my great kindness and for my entertainment and pleasure, I have arranged for each of you to fulfill your desires."

Both Jake and Kyle expressed their gratitude and devotion to The Mistress for the care she had taken to realize their desires. The Mistress sat down on the bed and graciously accepted their thanks.

"Jake, come to me. You are about to demonstrate by your actions your great devotion to me. You will do anything for me, won't you, Jake? Of course you will! And this is just one of the things you will do for me. Remain on your knees and put your head and shoulders on the floor. I want your hips held high and your knees wide apart."

Jake did as she instructed, filled with fear, anticipation, and excitement. From his position on the floor, he could see Kyle watching him with enormous interest.

"I have gotten you a very special toy just for this evening, Jake. Reach back and spread your cheeks," The Mistress commanded him politely.

Jake obeyed and shortly felt something cold and wet being swiped on his puckered opening. He realized it was lubricating gel and that he was about to be penetrated.

"What I have here for you, Jake, is a cigar-shaped metal tube that I am going to insert deeply into your anus," The Mistress said, as if it was nothing at all.

He felt two of her gloved fingers penetrate him two or three times to ready him for the cigar-shaped metal tube. Then he felt the cold metal of the tube itself being inserted into his anus until all of it was imbedded inside of him. But still he felt something thin hanging out of his opening.

"Jake, you have noticed that there is something that feels like a string hanging out from between your cheeks. It is a very thin electrical wire that is attached to the unit I have in my hand. The electrical unit has a variable current. I am going to give you a small taste of the current so that you will know what will happen to you if you do not please me. You will incur my displeasure if you do not perform as ordered with the naked and very erect Kyle. It seems that Kyle has gotten very aroused by watching me insert my new toy into you," The Mistress said.

Having said that, The Mistress turned a knob on the unit and sent a small jolt into Jake. Kyle looked on in fascination as he grew harder and harder witnessing Jake's response. "I see that even that little bit of a buzz made you clench your cheeks together very tightly, didn't it? You better do what you are told because the current can get much, much stronger and last much, much longer than that little buzz!" The Mistress said with asperity.

"Now, get the nipple clamps out of the toy box and put them on Kyle quickly! Tighten them until you see the little teeth bite slightly into Kyle's skin, but don't you dare draw any blood! Just ignore his tortured whining, he does that all the time. The gag keeps him from speaking, but I rather enjoy those charming little noises he makes deep down in his throat," said The Mistress, obviously enjoying herself.

"Jake, now I want you to get down on your knees in front of Kyle. You know what I want to see, don't you? Nuzzle your face right up to his groin! Rub your face on his cock! Smash your face into his sack! Now use your hands to play with him, make his erection so hard that it throbs and pulses. I want to see you cup and fondle him," The Mistress said.

She watched both Kyle and Jake carefully from her position on the end of the bed, her full attention focused on them while Jake did her bidding. After a couple of minutes, she said to Jake, "I don't think you are putting as much of your heart and soul into this as I would like! So here is some motivation!" The Mistress turned the knob on the unit she still had in her hand and gave Jake a healthy *zap!* of current between his cheeks. Jake's cheeks clenched at the attack on his anus and he gave a cry of pain. This pleased The Mistress greatly, and a look of glee entered Kyle's eyes.

"That did motivate you, didn't it?"

"Yes, Mistress," Jake said humbly.

"Good! Now get those hands busy! I want you to stroke and pump Kyle's member into a long hard pole of flesh so that you can demonstrate your oral skills for me!"

Both Jake and Kyle groaned at The Mistress's decree, but The Mistress heard the note of pleasure in their groans. Jake applied himself to the task at hand, stroking and pumping Kyle's member as The Mistress directed.

"That's better," The Mistress said, giving Jake another *zap!* of current from her little unit just for good measure. "You are doing so much better now that you understand exactly who is in control here! And my hunk of a male play toy is very hard now."

The Mistress watched Jake play with Kyle's engorged member for a few more minutes before issuing her next command. "Jake, open your mouth. Don't look at me like that! Do it!" A large quick jolt of electric current zinged up Jake's anus. "Do I have to keep giving you shocking displays of my control to make you obey me?" Again, The Mistress turned the knob on the unit and poured a steady stinging and tingling charge of current up Jake's anus. She kept the current up until Jake begged for mercy and promised to obey her every command with great enthusiasm. Then she turned the current down but not off, allowing a smaller current to keep invading Jake's anus. Kyle's eyes were wide with excitement at witnessing Jake's punishment and humiliation, and his rock-hard member bobbed around as if it had a mind of its own.

"Jake, now suck him as I commanded you! Put Kyle's whole swollen head into your mouth and flick it with your tongue! I want to see lots of lip action; I want to see your mouth encompassing more and more of Kyle's cock! Keep those hands moving too. Use one at the bottom of his cock and the other to massage his balls! Look at you! You are a real little sucking slut for your Mistress now, aren't you? And you love to give me a good show, don't you, Jake?"

Jake put his all into following The Mistress's commands and imagined himself to be the sucking machine The Mistress had called him. The Mistress lounged on the bed, the nasty little unit still in her hand, the low steady electrical current still running up Jake's anus, urging him on to greater efforts to please her. Although Jake couldn't see the look on her face, Kyle could, and what he saw there was wicked glee at the control she was exerting over both of them. As for Kyle, he couldn't believe how much he was enjoying the very intimate attention he was receiving from Jake. Not even in his wildest dreams did he imagine that getting head from another man would be so enjoyable, so exciting. It was almost better than getting a blow job from a woman! Jake's mouth was bigger, he sucked harder, and under the watchful eye of The Mistress in her gorgeous outfit, combined with the constant threat of that nasty little electrical tube up Jake's anus, Kyle had never dreamed that a male-on-male encounter could be, would be so exhilarating.

After several minutes of watching Jake perform on Kyle, The Mistress spoke. "Jake, I want you to jerk Kyle off into your mouth."

Jake gave The Mistress a pleading look but did not take Kyle's member out of his mouth. "Bad boy! What is that look for? You know you want this, you want it as much as Kyle does, and as much as I do! Do you think I went through all of this trouble just to have you chicken out?" Her tone was coolly angry, and Jake knew she was deadly serious. He was reminded of this by another quick high jolt of electricity up his anus. "I want to hear you beg to swallow Kyle's hot, white juices! Beg me to allow it!"

Jake began to beg, by alternating between begging and pleading and by showing great attention to Kyle's hard member. Finally, The Mistress relented and gave Jake her permission to swallow Kyle's come. But she kept speaking to urge them both on.

"I just hate it when you beg. I expect immediate obedience from you! You don't see Kyle struggling, and he has not dropped his bandana to signal his distress!" She turned up her little electrical device a notch or two more and kept it that way, even though Jake was doing a great job of working over Kyle's member. As Jake's head went up and down on Kyle's cock, The Mistress gave Jake little power surges in time to his cock-sucking rhythm. In spite of himself, Jake had become almost as aroused as Kyle. But still The Mistress urged him on.

"You love having your mouth full of thick throbbing meat, don't you? You love having your body penetrated and invaded by me! And my little jolts make you harder each time I give you one. So why don't I give you one now?" The Mistress did just as she said she would, and another surge of current shot up Jake's anus.

A whimper from Kyle told The Mistress that he was ready to gush into Jake's mouth. She got up from the bed and took Jake's head in both her hands, held Jake's head down on Kyle's cock, and urged Kyle to empty himself into Jake's mouth.

"Take it! Gulp it up! Swallow every drop he spurts down your throat!" The Mistress exhorted Jake.

Jake felt Kyle's member start to jerk, and he knew that Kyle would soon come, and Kyle's white, hot, sticky stream would shoot down the back of Jake's throat. He almost choked, but afraid of further punishment from the device The Mistress had inserted into his anus, he prepared himself to swallow all of Kyle's come.

Just as Kyle started to spurt, from far away Jake heard The Mistress say, "As Kyle empties himself into your mouth, I give you permission to use one hand to release yourself. That is your reward for your show of devotion to your Mistress."

Jake needed no further encouragement to obey her. In just a few strokes, Jake had spurted his own pearly white stream onto Kyle's feet. This greatly amused The Mistress.

"Jake, lick Kyle's feet clean. Then take off Kyle's gag and his nipple clamps, release his arms, and free his legs from the spreader bar. Remove the tube from your anus, giving Kyle a good view of what you are doing. Then you may both rest for ten minutes. After that you are to get dressed and go."

"Yes, Mistress," replied Jake, a little disappointed. This disappointment was reflected in Kyle's face as well.

The Mistress knew what this look of disappointment meant: they had expected to be rewarded by worshiping The Mistress between her thighs for their service. They should have known from her choice of wardrobe that this was not a possibility.

As if reading their minds, The Mistress said, "I don't recall promising you that . . ." as she retreated down the hallway, laughing. It had been a most amusing evening.

On His Toes

Her place was an old and spacious apartment with high ceilings and steam heat cranking out of cast iron radiators. The apartment faced south and west. Suburbia was off in the distance when looking out to the south; when looking west, in the foreground was a Buddhist temple with a deep blue tiled pagoda roof, and in the distance, the Manhattan skyline. The favorite granddaughter, she had inherited the lease on the place from her grandmother when the dear old woman had passed on. There were five large rooms in the apartment: the living room/dining room, the bedroom, the kitchen, the library/office, and the room he was waiting in. He sometimes called this room "the chamber," and at other times "the dungeon." It was the chamber when she was tender and affectionate to him, and the dungeon when he was to be corrected. Which one it would be now he did not know, as she had only told him to wait for her in "the room."

He waited for her, dressed as she had ordered: tight black jeans, black T-shirt, and black snakeskin boots. He had, he knew, a beautiful physique, which was what had first caught her eye when they met at the nightclub, Pagan Angels. That moment, now three years past, was the most vivid memory of his life—he, a different person then, flippant and unfocused, a child in a man's body, noticed her from across the room. She was looking at his torso. Maybe feeling his eyes on her, she looked up at his face suddenly, as if she were surprised to find it there, as if she thought there was nothing else to him, and as if his whole person existed only to support that gorgeous torso. Their eyes locked.

Though he did not know it at the time, he was seeing his new world—*her*. She had great presence, which she called "the glamour," and told him it was an ancient trick of the Wiccans. She could be commanding and stern and always expected to receive the obedience due her. She was quite capable of harshly correcting any errors or misbehavior with paddle, cane, flogger, or hand. Yet many times she was playful, with a mischievous streak, and could be very tender and nurturing. He loved that most of all, her unpredictability; he never knew what he was in for when she summoned him, and he lived in a continual state of longing and trepidation. This was why she owned him.

As he sat waiting for her in *the room*, he relived last night's session. When they came back from dinner, they kissed in the doorway; then she inclined her head to indicate that they were going directly to *the room*. When the door was closed and the rest of the world had vanished, he kissed her again. He kissed her neck, her breasts, and her belly and then knelt and slowly, with a mixture of homage and desire, repeatedly kissed her crotch through her skirt. After a long time, she gently pulled his head away and sat down in the straight-backed chair. Sometimes it seemed as if they could read each other's minds. He, understanding, rose and stood in front of her. They looked into each other's eyes for a moment. She stared at his black jeans, looked down at the floor, and made a small gesture. He unbuckled his pants, pulled them and his underwear down to his knees, and slowly, deliberately, lay across her lap. He braced himself by placing his hands on the floor and locking his elbows. She spanked him, gently at first, then more and more firmly, but lovingly all along, stopping every so often to trail her long, square nails up and down his back. They made love afterwards right there on the floor of *the room*, and then she held him tightly to her for a long time, his head resting on her breast.

Not a word had been exchanged since they entered the apartment. He sat alone in *the room*, lost in his memories and reveling in them.

"Miles!" she called out from the library. Her voice was stern and carried an order to come to her.

Had he done something wrong? Had he displeased her? He rushed into the library. She spoke quietly, looking directly at him. "I need you to run an errand for me. Go to the office at this address. A 'Ms. A. Grant' there has a package for me. I need to have the work completed and faxed out by 5:45, so you have a half hour to get there and back. There's too much traffic for a cab, it'll be faster if you run. Now go."

She handed him a slip of paper with an address on it. He was about to leave; then he thought about how he was dressed. It was hardly very "corporate," and the boots weren't exactly designed for running either. He asked her if he might change his clothes first, and she refused, saying there wasn't enough time. Obediently he left.

As he rode down in the elevator, he looked at the address she had given him. It was eleven blocks away. He had just enough time to get there and back again. He knew that every eye on the street would be focused on him, dressed as he was. He would have to put up with a lot because of that, but it didn't matter. They were just a blur of faces, and he would ignore their stares. What did they matter to him anyway? He would endure whatever he had to, with one thought in his mind—*her*. He was her property, and she had given him orders.

Miles reached the lobby and headed out. The first person he saw was the doorman. Though the doorman noticed how he was dressed, he was far too professional for it to register on his face as he opened the door for him. Then he passed two well-dressed women in their fifties whose conversation suddenly stopped as he hurried by. He noticed this and knew exactly what they were thinking and what sort of typical catty nonsense was going through their minds. To him, they were among the generally "unenlightened," the vanilla people, and, given the opportunity, either or both of them would trade places with his Mistress in a heartbeat. He ran faster and held himself more proudly. He eventually arrived at the address, a small office building on a cross street. Miles rode up the elevator and found the office; then he entered and approached the desk.

"I'm here to pick up a package from Ms. A. Grant, for Miss Varrin." The bright-looking young woman behind the desk took a moment to find her voice. "Yes, I . . . well, there's nothing here . . . I'll take you to Ms. Grant's office." She led him down a hall to a door marked "A. Grant," opened it for him, and left. Looking out of the window of the office was a gorgeous woman, a blond with a voluptuous figure. She wore a black miniskirt business suit with a crisp white blouse, black hosiery, and black high-heeled pumps. She was on the telephone. She turned and looked Miles up and down intently without interrupting her conversation for an instant. "Yes, we're shipping on the twenty-fourth. Mae approved the prototype yesterday." She had deep blue eyes, a model's cheekbones, and legs as shapely as his Mistress's. There was an enigmatic smile on her face as she gestured for Miles to sit down. Miles did so, hesitantly; he had to get that package and to get moving if he was not to fail his Mistress.

After several more minutes on the telephone, the woman, leaning against the front of her desk and staring at Miles all the while, put the call on hold and addressed him. "What can I do for you?" her voice had a Southern accent that could melt him, if given enough time.

"I'm here to pick up a package for Miss Varrin."

"I see. This won't take much longer," she said, pressing a button on the phone set. The young woman from the outer office appeared instantaneously.

"Tamara, this young man must be extremely uncomfortable from walking all the way here in those boots. Massage his feet."

Before Miles could say anything about being in a hurry, the woman turned to the window again and was back on the phone. He wondered how the woman knew of him walking here while the young woman knelt in front of him, removed his boots, and began massaging his socked feet. This *was* pleasant—Ms. Grant was right, those boots could certainly be uncomfortable, especially to have run so far in—but he could not take his eyes off the clock on the wall. It was 5:40. Miles was already behind schedule. He had to get that package and leave immediately.

He started to speak. "Excuse me, Ms. Grant, but—"

The woman turned to him, gestured to him to remain quiet, smiled, and turned back to the window. The young woman, meanwhile, never once raised her eyes from Miles's feet. She was very gifted at what she was doing, Miles thought; she must have had a lot of practice. But he could no longer relax and enjoy it. He kept looking at the clock. Finally, Ms. Grant hung up the phone.

"That will be all, Tamara," Ms. Grant said pleasantly.

Tamara put Miles's boots back on, gently but quickly, and left.

"Now what is it you're here for?" Ms. Grant inquired—again.

"A package for Miss Varrin," he said, as calmly as he could.

"Oh, of course, here you are," Ms. A. Grant said in that killer Southern accent.

She handed him a manila envelope that had been on top of her desk, three feet from where Miles was sitting all along. Miles took it, said "thank you" as he turned away, and bolted from the office. With neither the time nor the patience to wait for the elevator, he ran down the stairs, ran out into the street, and ran for home. He was letting his Mistress down, and he was heartbroken.

Two blocks before home he tripped and fell. He didn't rip his jeans, but he did skin his knees and they hurt badly. Hardly caring about anything other than getting back to his Mistress as soon as he could, he picked himself up instantly and ran on. On entering the building, he practically knocked over the doorman but didn't even notice. He ran up the five flights of stairs, entered the apartment, and went directly to the library. The clock read 6:10, and his Mistress was not there. He knew where she was.

He entered *the room* and knelt. Not able to face her, his chin was on his chest as he fought back tears. The Mistress stood before him holding her heaviest cat-o'-nine tails. She lifted his chin and led him to a standing position at the end of the spanking bench, where she roughly pulled his jeans down to his ankles. She used a knife to cut off his underwear. She laid him down on the bench lengthwise and cuffed his wrists and ankles to its legs. She put soft, formable earplugs into his ears. Then she blindfolded him with a flexible, wide black band that she used when she wished to deprive him of his sight; she slid the band over his eyes and his ears. She picked up the whip, walked behind him, and let it fly. It was the hardest she had ever hit him.

She continued beating him. His tears flowed freely, half from his punishment and half from remorse at having disappointed her. He tried to keep his sobs quiet. He knew he deserved this punishment, and was even, in a way, grateful for it. Though he could not undo his failure, at least he could accept his Mistress's justice and hope to be forgiven afterward.

After a solid half hour of this, his bottom now bright red and extremely painful, The Mistress uncuffed him, removed the earplugs but not the blindfold, and stood him on his feet. He put his whole heart into thanking her for what he had received at her hands. She touched his lips to silence him.

"We are not nearly through yet," she said in a soft voice.

She returned him to the spanking bench, this time laying him on his back. The Mistress removed his boots and socks, pulled his black T-shirt off over his head, and then pulled off his jeans completely. She locked his wrists in the cuffs below him and his ankles in a set of cuffs, which she lowered from the ceiling. She then raised the ankle cuffs so that his bottom was eight inches off the bench, extremely accessible and unprotected.

She said, "I have a surprise for you," and pulled off the blindfold.

Standing next to the bench was the gorgeous Southern belle, Ms. A. Grant.

Now Miles knew the reason for the earplugs: it was to prevent him from hearing Ms. A. Grant's arrival during his whipping. Smiling enigmatically as she had when Miles entered her office, the woman looked into Miles's eyes and to his surprise, she giggled. She was the last person he expected to see or hear. The last thing Miles saw as Ms. Grant straddled him and lowered herself onto Miles's mouth was The Mistress taking a cane down from the wall.

Once Ms. Grant was solidly in position, The Mistress began to cane Miles. The blows were swift, hard, and well landed. His Mistress never missed. He tried to count them but lost track at about fifty-five. The pain was too great. He shrieked, yelped, and cried directly into Ms.

Grant's thong, while she amused herself by pinching his nipples and grinding her sturdy thong on his face. Ms. "A." Grant was a very effective and interesting form of bondage.

As The Mistress continued to cane him, she said, "Make her come. Use your tongue on Ms. Grant's thong to give her an orgasm."

Spurred on by the pain of the cane as well as the beauty of Ms. Grant and his current predicament, if one could call it that, Miles used his tongue as best as he knew how. Ms. Grant rode his face, aiding him in his efforts to some degree. When he located her button through her thong and grasped it in his lips, he flicked his tongue back and forth across her little penis. Ms. Grant began to moan and cry out, "Yes, there, there, harder, more pressure, . . ." Miles did as he was told and in just a few more seconds, he felt her juices soak her thong. Then he sucked as much of her nectar out of the thong as he could. As soon as Ms. Grant came, his Mistress stopped caning him.

Many hours later, after Ms. "A." Grant had gone, Miles lay in bed next to the sleeping Claudia, thinking over the day's events. Had he really let Claudia down, or had she "set him up"? He never knew what to expect from her, which kept him on his toes, eager and anxious, all the time; that was how she exerted such control over him. It absently crossed his mind that he never found out what the "A" in Ms. A. Grant stood for.

He rolled over, put his head on Claudia's breast, and fell asleep.

A Perfect Example of an Imperfect Slave

As the domina, I want my slave to use his reasoning—as in "think"—and exhibit some independent thought on occasion, as long as it is not whiny and demanding or contrary to my wishes. Most dominants would agree with me when I say that no one wants a brainless "submissive" who wants his domina to do all the thinking for him. This type of submissive or "slave" is not a helpful and happy addition to your life; this type is an albatross around your neck, a child who never grows up, the old ball and chain. In one of my overnight sessions with Mistress Elizabeth, we sessioned with a just-past-young, just-past-boyish-charm submissive foot worshipper whom I shall call

Wayne. Unfortunately, Wayne did not realize that he had passed the age of "young" a few years back, nor did he realize that as he aged, his boyish charm had aged as well, and now fell short of the mark. He could no longer charm his way into or out of anything. He was with two very experienced mistresses, and he lied about the extent of his previous training and experiences. And, of course, he thought he was the most wonderful slave in the world. I guess he had come from a very, very small world that was very, very far away.

Let me tell you, sister, he was so untrained that perhaps if Elizabeth and I had a week to train him intensively each and every day, separately and together, at the end of that week, he might have gotten some idea of what it was really about. He was harmless when he wasn't driving a car but extremely dense. We told him the rules, gave him his word and signal, and confirmed everything. Thinking someone had already *trained* him, we thought he got it. We thought incorrectly. We rolled our eyes in our heads so many times, we gave ourselves headaches. At some point, it became amusing, and I must say, speaking for myself only, I did begin to enjoy playing a nonromantic sadist. I wanted to hurt him—badly.

His scene was to be caged, allowed to worship my feet and lower legs and, under the protection of Mistress Elizabeth and myself, to go to a BDSM party in a local nightclub. Then he added that he be forced to eat bugs. Mistress Elizabeth has three beautiful cages: a jail cell, a birdcage, and a cage that used to be my dining-table base. The cages really turned him on, especially the jail cell and birdcage. We instructed him to remove the birdcage from its hook in the living room and bring it into the dungeon where he then secured it to the ceiling and floor. He executed this task to our satisfaction (the cage was quite heavy), so we stripped him. Then Mistress Elizabeth and I put him into the cage and blindfolded him. We secured his hands at waist level to the bars of the cage with leather wrist restraints and made him spread his legs as far as the bars would allow so that we could secure his ankles in the same manner. Spacey music was playing softly in the background; we shut off all the lights and left him there for two hours before letting him out.

On his release we expected him to be a bit unstable and disoriented, so we let him sit down, gave him water, and rubbed his wrists and ankles where the restraints had been. But after that he turned into a complete unthinking selfish boob. We told him to serve us tea at the dining table, and we might as well have gotten up and prepared it ourselves. One would expect that someone who had never been in your home before wouldn't know where the tea makings were, but he didn't even ask where the spoons, napkins, milk, sugar, and artificial sweetener were kept, he just brought out the cups of tea. We pointed out only one deficiency at a time so that he had to make separate trips for each item, walking back and forth to the kitchen five times before the tea was ready. But did he learn anything? No!

After finally completing the "tea serving ceremony," he did not return to his prearranged place at my feet, but rather stood around lurking over the table as Elizabeth and I tried to hold a conversation. I ordered him to kneel on the floor, his buttocks on his heels and his forehead on the floor. Then I told him to make himself as small and unobtrusive as possible, to be still, and to be silent. Well, *that* lasted about four minutes before he began to squirm around. On looking down at him, my first impression was that his knees or something else had started to bother him, and he was readjusting himself. More interested in talking with Elizabeth, I let it go, but I put my foot on the back of his neck, thinking that would quiet him down.

It didn't. Instead it spurred him on to greater efforts, and soon he'd squirmed and wiggled until he was flat on his belly on the floor. I let it go this far because I wanted to see how far it would go. Just when I thought it had gone far enough, it hadn't. And I was somewhat astonished. My bare feet were resting on the lowest rung of the chair, and there was just enough room for Wayne to get his head under them. He wiggled himself into position and launched an outright and premeditated attack on my feet, which earned him several good slaps across his face, using my feet instead of my hands, and a severe scolding, which reiterated the rules.

Then we made him curl up into the cage that was the dining-table base. I had specifically made this cage high and narrow and very difficult to get into. One had to fold oneself into it head first, then shoulders, and so on, to fit inside. At each of his fumbled attempts to get in, Mistress Elizabeth and I verbally and physically humiliated him. Finally, he managed to squeeze himself into the cage. We got a big heavy lock and bolted him in. Then Mistress Elizabeth got us each a pair of wickedly pointy toed shoes, and as we continued drinking our tea, we used them to poke at him through the bars of the cage. Since he was quite large and the cage quite tall and narrow, anywhere we poked our shoe through the bars landed on his flesh. He looked utterly mystified by our displeasure; perhaps his other mistress allowed such behavior, but we did not—so we made him repeat the rules back to us. It seems he then forgot them instantly. He had one idea in his head, and that idea was that he was a "good submissive," and no one was going to tell him differently. Perhaps he thought that being "in the way" and "under foot" were synonymous phrases for good submissive.

That night, Mistress Elizabeth and I took him to the Fetish Box party in Miami. Since he was from the other side of the country, the chances of him being seen by someone he knew were almost nonexistent. He had, at least, rented a Cadillac and we rode there in style. The party was not a heavy play party to us but rather a mild mix, a good first party for a newcomer—lots of eye candy as well as some action. The club had a stage for those who wished to play, a dance floor with an adjoining bar, and a lounge area, which had comfortable sofas and was somewhat quieter. I will say one thing for him: he was so unjaded that the club party, which to Elizabeth and I was a fun dance and play party, completely blew his mind. He had never seen so many people in fetish dress dancing and playing in the same place at the same time. I used him as a footstool, an ottoman, and a table, and in his innocence, he thought everyone in the club was looking at him. I did not disillusion him, although hardly anyone cast a glance his way.

A friend came and sat for a chat while Wayne was giving me a massage through the killer boots I was wearing. As I conversed with my friend, I noticed that Wayne's touch had gotten softer and softer until I could hardly feel it through the thick patent leather of the boots. So I told him, "Harder." His touch remained the same—inadequate. So I said it again, louder this time, "Harder!" Again nothing. So I kicked him with my other foot, which he took to mean I wanted him to rub that one now. I turned to my friend, who was a submissive himself at one time, and said, "Can you believe this?" He, having the voice of Stentor, called out to him, "Hey you, dummy, your Mistress requires your attention." Only then did Wayne turn his attention to me and my desires, so intent was he on fulfilling his own desires. But did

Wayne learn anything? No! When I told him he could kiss my boots, paying special attention to the platforms, it was as if I'd never even spoken! He was so absorbed in what he was doing that he didn't even have half an ear open for me.

But this was the worst: Before we even set out for the club, I told Wayne that he was only allowed to have two drinks; I felt that more than that would impair his driving, and Elizabeth and I were in the car too. The police in that state are particularly aggressive but not particularly honest, a bad combination, and they make a commission for each arrest, which is a very bad system. But Wayne was sneaky as well as a dolt—also a bad combination. Each time Elizabeth or I needed a drink from the bar, he cheerfully went at our command. And while he was there, he later admitted to downing at least two drinks while he waited for ours to be made. Waited for our drinks to be made? We had ordered bottles of water! So he had ordered his own drinks first, exceeding his drinking limit by several vodka cock-tails and then ordered our water. How utterly brainless!

His drunkenness didn't become apparent until the harrowing ride home. I hate drunken men. I have three words for them: slow, sloppy, and stupid, which I think makes an accurate description of your aver-age drunken male. Although Elizabeth and I each offered to drive and then commanded him to pull over so that one of us could take the wheel, he just wouldn't stop the car. Fortunately, we didn't get pulled over, and we made it back to Elizabeth's in one piece.

Shaken, we had him make us tea, which was served in a marginally more proficient manner this time, and I allowed the drunken Wayne to lie under my feet and caress them. While he was down there, I posed these questions to him: If I, your mistress, commanded you to be silent and the draperies caught on fire, what would you do? Would you keep your mouth shut and let the house burn down because I commanded you to silence, or would you disobey and rush to tell me of the disaster? Which do you think would displease me more: your disobedience or my house burning down? He looked at me in all seri-ousness and said that he "would keep his vow of silence." I can't say I was surprised by his answer, but come on! What kind of boob would sit there and let the house burn down around us because he was "commanded" to keep silent? Obviously, when real life bursts in, you deal with it rationally.

But this was not the end of it. Mistress Elizabeth and I gave him his supplies for spending the night in the red light of the jail cell: bottle of water, small bucket, bell, slave's pillow, and blanket. Then we "locked" him in, although we did leave the key to the antique-style padlock within easy reach of the cell. We left him there and relaxed in the living room without his disruptive presence and obtrusive personality. We let him out at ten in the morning and gave him thirteen minutes to perform the five "esses," shower, shampoo, shave, shit and shine up, before presenting himself to us. We were in street clothes. He came out all clean and shiny, and we ordered him to make us tea and serve it to us at the counter, not at the table. His tea service had improved a bit more, but after tea was served, he sat down at the counter with us! Elizabeth and I were astonished. His day had started off with a series of commands. Why would he now think that he could sit with us as equals? Then we remembered he wrote he wanted to eat bugs, and it was breakfast time!

Elizabeth, the considerate dear, had obligingly gone to the bait-and-tackle shop down the road and purchased a small wonton-soup-size Styrofoam container full of fat, juicy, wiggling worms in dirt, just for Wayne. I got the container of worms, which was in a brown paper bag, and handed it to Wayne. He thought we were giving him a "present" (of all things!), and he opened it eagerly. When he saw the container, he was puzzled but still game. Placing it on the counter, he opened the lid. We all let out a little shout, even though Elizabeth and I obviously knew what was in there, because there was a rather fat, long, pink worm frantically wiggling around right on top. Then, the worm jumped, which made all of us exclaim in surprise. Wayne looked at me, and I mean really looked at me, possibly for the first time since he had been here, and his confusion was plain.

I smiled and said in a very normal tone of voice, "You did write that you wanted to eat bugs, didn't you? You should be careful what you wish for because you just might get your wish." His look of confusion turned to horror when he realized we meant it.

I got a plastic fork, and finding myself none too comfortable with the thought of trying to twirl the big fat juicy guy from the top, I dug through the dirt and found a worm that was about as round as a strand of spaghetti and about three inches long. Perfect for twirling!

So I twirled the little sucker up, presented it to Wayne, and smilingly said, "Breakfast! And I want you to listen to every word I say if you don't want to find yourself chewing on that worm." He took the fork from me hesitantly, and I fully expected him not to listen to my instructions. If he refused to eat it at all, Elizabeth and I threatened to force-feed it to him. I told him to take half a mouthful of water and then open his mouth just enough to get the worm inside. He was not to chew, no matter how strong the urge, then he was to take another gulp of water. As he was opening his lips to take the second gulp, I told him to swallow the worm that was floating in the first mouthful and then to wash it down in short order with the second gulp. Much to my surprise, he finally listened to me and swallowed that worm exactly the way I told him to.

What could possibly happen next? Well, he had just eaten a worm and was looking a little green around the gills. What do you think happened? As Elizabeth and I were talking and drinking our tea, I heard Wayne going into little heaves—little heaves that were soon to become big ones. And was he heading for the bathroom? Of course not! Seemingly, he was just going to sit there heaving, vomit on me and then on Elizabeth's rug. Angrily, I ordered him into the en suite bathroom in the chamber and told him to stay there until he was finished. And I told him that if he threw up on Elizabeth's rug, he was going to lick it clean first and then scrub it clean. He ran off, and presently we heard quite a few volcanic eruptions. When he returned several minutes later, he told us that he had tossed up everything he had ever eaten or drunk in his life, except for that worm!

Being me, I lost no time in teasing him about his new little friend. "In some cultures, worms are considered delicacies." "A little protein never hurt anybody." "Don't worry, your stomach acids will dissolve it." "At least it wasn't the big fat juicy pink one from the top." With that, he made one final run for the bathroom; I guess he hadn't lost quite everything on his previous trip.

To his credit, he did take Mistress Elizabeth and me shopping that afternoon as he had promised and was very generous in his gifts. Since he had never had a real session, the plan was that when we returned to Elizabeth's after shopping, we would bring him into the dungeon for a proper erotic introduction. But Wayne was still Wayne, and although I told him to leave extra time for spontaneous eruptions of playing, he did not. He had done as men do, scheduling dinner with a male friend at six instead of eight, and so he lost out on his introductory session.

Men will be men and maybe someday, just maybe, they will learn just how much they are missing when they do not listen to their betters.

The Tall People

Amanda and Tim are an attractive young couple from Illinois. I call them the Tall People because Amanda is five feet ten and Tim is six feet five. Not knowing that Tim had an undisclosed interest in BDSM, Amanda took a chance and bought *The Art of Sensual Female Dominance* because she liked the cover and was intrigued and excited by what she read. When she approached Tim about it, he was just as interested, and she began to train herself and him, using my book as her guiding light. Then they made plans to see me. Tim made the initial contact, but since I require that I speak to the woman, Amanda wrote back to me. Then we spoke on the phone, discussed the plan, and set up the interlude.

During our first interlude Amanda and I had a great time, but Tim was a little disappointed because his expectations were different. First, he didn't account for the "pack animal" instinct that surfaces when two or more of the same sex are present. This would include even the most elegant of dominas. We weren't all that interested in what he wanted—we were only interested in doing what appealed to us (as long as it was on his yes list). Second, he didn't realize that there were specific techniques his wife had asked me to help her with or teach her. Since he was outnumbered two to one, we reduced him to an object, a demonstration toy, just there for the use of the dominas to learn this technique or that. And last, he thought that he was going to have two beautifully dressed dominas, one his dear wife and the other, me, cooing and clucking over him as if we were his own two little hens, there to cater to his every need. *Ha!*

Amanda and I really enjoyed this, and Tim got his first lesson in objectification. At Amanda's request we did origami-style bondage and the hog-tie on him. We practiced different flogging techniques and drilled him in how to pay us homage. Then I didn't see them again for almost two years.

I was delighted to hear from Amanda again. They were going to be in town and wanted another playtime. She said that Tim had come a long way since our last meeting and that I would be delighted at his progress. Because of my special status we were going to meet at a BDSM club that was not open to the public that night and have our jollies there. I noticed that they had brought along a dozen long-stemmed red roses, as well as their gear. I played the heavy, wearing a latex sergeant's uniform, red platform boots with lots of buckles, and the sheriff's hat I had brought home from Prague. Amanda wore black, a combination of leather and lace, and very feminine shoes, a much softer look than mine and a good contrast. After we sat, Tim paid us each the proper homage, and his execution was perfect; I could see she had been drilling him. As I looked on, Amanda collared and gagged him as part of his acceptance ceremony, and he automatically assumed position four.

Obviously, this was a part of their at-home opening ceremony, and I was happy they had shared it with me. She and I decided to lounge comfortably in our chairs and chat about Tim and his progress while he waited for us on his knees. Amanda told me that after his first session and disappointment at being nothing more than an object, she trained him to become an object, and in two years, he had become a very good one. Now he liked being used as an object, as well as providing excellent service and being something of a masochist, the joy of every mistress.

Being who I am, I had to put this claim to the test, and Amanda was more than happy to show off her training skills. She asked me if I had any new whip techniques, and a wicked gleam came into my eyes. Lady Sadist had made her appearance. It just so happened that while in Prague, along with the sheriff's hat, I also bought a single-tail whip, about five feet long. I had practiced with it in my friend's dungeon in London on equipment such as the spanking horse, the back of the throne, and, finally, a small padded area on the cross;

these were all places where I could add an invisible (to all but me) body and aim for that area. I was good for a first timer, so good that the people upstairs, a master, his live-in female slave, and his live-in male slave, came down to watch me. On the cross, the smallest target, I hit the mark thirty-seven out of forty times. If someone had been standing there, I wouldn't have missed at all. The target was about four inches wide and six inches long. A human back is a bit bigger. In any case, the single tail was/is really nasty.

Back to Amanda and Tim. I said to Amanda coyly, "Well, I *do* have one thing but it is really mean." She immediately ordered him into position four, "attention," and then wanted to see it. I had the whip wrapped about my waist like a belt, but I guess she hadn't seen it in the dark. The quickness with which I produced it and where I kept it made Amanda smile. Then we looked at Tim, kneeling motionless in position four, and saw fear in his eyes. I wanted to giggle, but I suppressed that urge and fed the giggle energy into the wicked gleam in my eyes. I looked at Amanda, and she had the gleam too. Let me say that we both knew we weren't going to hit him with it—we just wanted to scare him with it. So I showed her how to use it on the spanking bench, in an overhead X motion on the top of it and then how to flick it at the end of the bench, where his ass would be, had he been bent over it. As we took turns beating the bejeezus out of the furniture, Tim looked on in terror. Amanda and I were getting so excited, I guess he really thought he was next! He was shaking from head to toe as he knelt at attention.

Amanda ordered him to his feet and to the X-frame (where, I am sure, he thought he was going to get the beating of his life), and the two of us fastened the leather cuffs to his wrists. I snapped the single tail around a few more times for effect while she got out her favorite flogger; then we switched so that I could get mine. Not knowing anything about the whip exchange, Tim was all aquiver, the only leaf shaking on the whole tree on a windless day. He began to moan from behind his bright red ball gag. From her reaction, Amanda liked to hear moaning as much as I do. When she first brought the flogger down on Tim, he overreacted in anticipation of the single tail and jumped so high that he, with his height, almost touched the ceiling! Amanda and I found this hilarious and began laughing; Tim found our laughing at him to be wonderfully humiliating, especially since he had done something so deserving of it.

We took turns flogging him; we flogged him in unison, she hitting his back and I his bottom; we flogged him alternately, a smack to his back and then a smack to his bottom; we both flogged his back; we both flogged his ass; we switched sides. We flogged Tim every which way but loose and then flogged him some more. We worked up a "nice perspiration" flogging him, released him into position three, and sat down to take a breather. I was about to find out what the dozen long-stemmed roses were for.

The Rose Game was to be the closing ceremony of our evening. I sat on the spanking bench while Amanda took off Tim's gag and, after letting him have some water and get a good look at the room, she blindfolded him. She ran to place a chair across the staircase so that Tim, in his quest, would not accidentally tumble down the stairs. His mission, if Tim chose to accept it, was to crawl around and gather up, one at a time, all "twelve" roses and bring them to me in his mouth while on his hands and knees, and blindfolded, keeping count of how many roses he had bought to me. Tim chose to accept his mission so Amanda scattered eleven of the roses around the room, keeping the twelfth in her hand. Amanda and I decided, from the generosity of our hearts, that we could call out "cold, colder, warm, warmer, hot, hotter" as appropriate so that Tim wouldn't bump his head into the furniture. But when he approached the large but understuffed beanbag, Amanda and I exchanged just one glance and psychically decided not to say anything, just to wait and see what happened. It was pretty amusing. Not expecting to land on a soft surface, his arms somewhat collapsed underneath him and he went face down into the beanbag chair, his ass sticking up sporting the lash marks from his flogging. His struggles to disengage himself made his situation worse. Amanda and I had tears rolling down our faces.

At last, we took pity on him and rescued him by dragging him out by his legs and setting him off in the right direction. He had only a few roses to go, and he made quick work of bringing the rest to me, right up until the eleventh rose. He crawled around in endless circles looking for that twelfth rose, clearly mystified as to its location. The room wasn't all that large; where could it be? Finally, Amanda told

Tim to remove the blindfold. She was standing in front of him when he took it off so that the first thing he saw was that twelfth rose, which she was twirling in her hand. Suddenly, she tossed it into the farthest corner of the room, and Tim was off after it in a shot. He brought the twelfth rose to me with a very happy puppy look on his face. I, of course, accepted it graciously and ruffled his hair in affection. Then, being more considerate than I may appear at times, I left the room.

I have seen Amanda and Tim many times since then.

About the Author

Diva Claudia Varrin has been active in the BDSM scene since 1991. Through her writings, public appearances, speaking engagements, magazine interviews, and television and movie appearances, Varrin has become a well-known advocate of the BDSM love-style as well as a world-renowned author. Diva Claudia lives life among the incurable curious, which often confuses some people as to whether she is "truly dominant," or not. Diva Claudia believes that no one is truly dominant 24/7 and thinks that people who say that they are always, and only, dominant are deceiving themselves. (Occasionally, everyone, dominant or not, needs a shoulder to cry on.) Diva Claudia thinks of herself as an author and artist first whose gift for writing about her understanding of dominance and submission has led her to share her experiences as a domina and diva with you. She loves to experiment and to know what her slaves and submissives are feeling. To do this, Claudia will experiment on herself as much as possible. She finds self-bondage extremely interesting and loves to invent new ways of torture, humiliation, and edge play.

Varrin's interest in the BDSM community and promotion of the love-style is genuine, not a put-on for curiosity seekers. Diva Claudia is a genuine Fetish Diva and Domina and a great supporter of the global BDSM community. Diva Claudia is a latex fetishist who loves to travel to international events, with a special preference for the Rubber Ball, Club Rub, and Torture Garden in London, England; Nuit Demonia in Paris, France; Euro-Perve in Amsterdam, The Netherlands; the Texas Latex Party in Houston, Texas; the Alter Ego Parties in Fort Lauderdale, Florida; and the anniversary celebrations at the Other World Kingdom, Czech Republic. (The Diva thinks Prague is one of the most beautiful cities in the world.) She appears at these worldwide events and functions to promote international acceptance of the alternate BDSM love-style, gives generously of her time, and donates books and BDSM-related items as often as possible to worthy causes.

Her passion for shoes and latex remains unabated. Here are Diva Claudia Varrin's credentials:

Published Works

1997   *The Anne Rice Reader* edited by Katherine Ramsland, Ph.D., fully accredited chapter entitled "How Do They Rate? Eliot Slater and Lasher as Love Slaves."

1998   *The Art of Sensual Female Dominance: A Guide for Women,** Kensington Books, New York, hardcover (out of print).

2000   *The Art of Sensual Female Dominance*, Kensington Books, New York, in seventh paperback printing.

2001   *Erotic Surrender: The Sensual Joys of Female Submission,** Kensington Books, New York, hardcover.

2002   *NYFU: New York Fetish Underground Guide*, Kensington Books, New York, paperback.

2003   *Erotic Surrender: The Sensual Joys of Female Submission*, Kensington Books, New York, paperback.

2004   *Female Dominance: Rituals and Practices,** Kensington Books, New York, hardcover.

2005   *The Female Dominant: Games She Plays*, Kensington Books, New York, paperback.

Television Appearances and Movie Cameos

Maury, 1994

Geraldo, 1994

The Joan Rivers Show, 1995

Real Personal with Bob Berkowitz, 1994, 1994, 1995, 1996 (four-time guest panelist)

Playboy Channel's *Sextetera*, 18 airings in January 2002

No Body Is Perfect, an independent film by Raphael Sybilla, 2004

*Available in German.

SPEAKING ENGAGEMENTS

Aural Sex, Rubber Ball, London, 1998
Dom/Sub Friends, New York, 2001, 2002, 2004, 2005
Kink in the Caribbean, Jamaica, 2001
The Nutcracker Suite, New York, 2002

PUBLIC APPEARANCES AS A SPECIAL GUEST

Rubber Ball, London, 1996, 1997, 1998, 1999, 2000, 2002, 2003, 2004
Euro-Perve, Amsterdam, 2000, 2001, 2002, 2005
Libertine Ball, Philadelphia, 1999
Alter Ego, Fort Lauderdale, 1997, 1998, 1999, 2000, 2001, 2002, 2003, 2004, 2005
Miss Fetish NYC Pageant, honored guest, 2000; contest judge, 2001
Kink in the Caribbean, Jamaica, 2001
Dressing for Pleasure, Edison, New Jersey, 1992
Black and Blue Ball, New York, 1995, 1996, 2000, 2001, 2002, 2003, 2004, 2005
Leather Pride Night, New York, 1996, 2000, 2001, 2002, 2004
Fetish in Paradise, Man-Ray Club, Boston, 2002
Boston Fetish Flea Market, Boston, 2002
Nuit Demonia, Paris, 2002, 2003, 2004
The Playground, Fort Lauderdale, 2002, 2003, 2004
The Other World Kingdom, Czech Republic, Anniversary Celebration in May 2003, special visit in March 2004; awarded Citizenship in June 2004
The Baroness's Black and Blue Ball Fetish Retinue, New York, May 2003
The Gomorrah Black and Blue Pre-Ball Gala, New York, May 2003, 2004, 2005
The Texas Latex Party, Houston, 2004
Club Rub Christmas Party, London, 2004

MAGAZINE AND BOOK INTERVIEWS

Dresseuse magazine, Paris, 2003

"Mistresses of the Night," by Mistress Rene, *Extreme Ink*, Madison, Wisconsin, 2002

Demonia magazine, Paris, 2003

Desire magazine, London, 2004

CONTRIBUTING AUTHOR

American Dommes Magazine

Fetish Magazine

Mistress Mine